Physical Language Learning Spaces in the Digital Age

Also available from Bloomsbury

Language Learning Strategies and Individual Learner Characteristics,
edited by Rebecca L. Oxford and Carmen M. Amerstorfer
Language Education in the School Curriculum, Ken Cruickshank, Stephen
Black, Honglin Chen, Linda Tsung, and Jan Wright

Physical Language Learning Spaces in the Digital Age

Felix A. Kronenberg

BLOOMSBURY ACADEMIC
LONDON • NEW YORK • OXFORD • NEW DELHI • SYDNEY

BLOOMSBURY ACADEMIC
Bloomsbury Publishing Plc, 50 Bedford Square, London, WC1B 3DP, UK
Bloomsbury Publishing Inc, 1359 Broadway, New York, NY 10018, USA
Bloomsbury Publishing Ireland, 29 Earlsfort Terrace, Dublin 2, D02 AY28, Ireland

BLOOMSBURY, BLOOMSBURY ACADEMIC and the Diana logo are
trademarks of Bloomsbury Publishing Plc

First published in Great Britain 2024
This paperback edition published in 2025

Copyright © Felix A. Kronenberg, 2024

Felix A. Kronenberg has asserted his right under the Copyright, Designs and
Patents Act, 1988, to be identified as Author of this work.

Cover design: Grace Ridge
Cover image © recep-bg / Getty Images

All rights reserved. No part of this publication may be: i) reproduced or transmitted
in any form, electronic or mechanical, including photocopying, recording or by means
of any information storage or retrieval system without prior permission in writing from
the publishers; or ii) used or reproduced in any way for the training, development or
operation of artificial intelligence (AI) technologies, including generative AI technologies.
The rights holders expressly reserve this publication from the text and data mining
exception as per Article 4(3) of the Digital Single Market Directive (EU) 2019/790.

Bloomsbury Publishing Plc does not have any control over, or responsibility for, any
third-party websites referred to or in this book. All internet addresses given in this
book were correct at the time of going to press. The author and publisher regret
any inconvenience caused if addresses have changed or sites have ceased
to exist, but can accept no responsibility for any such changes.

A catalogue record for this book is available from the British Library.

A catalogue record for this book is available from the Library of Congress.

ISBN: HB: 978-1-3502-8715-0
PB: 978-1-3502-8741-9
ePDF: 978-1-3502-8716-7
eBook: 978-1-3502-8743-3

Typeset by Integra Software Services Pvt. Ltd.

For product safety related questions contact productsafety@bloomsbury.com.

To find out more about our authors and books visit www.bloomsbury.com
and sign up for our newsletters.

Contents

List of Figures   vi
Preface   vii

Introduction: Why a Book about Physical Language Learning Spaces in This Digital Age?   1

1   From Theory to Practice: What Are Language Learning Spaces?   7
2   From Generic to Discipline-Specific: Properties of Language Learning Spaces   41
3   Physical Language Learning Spaces beyond the Classroom   65
4   Design and Administration of Language Learning Spaces   99
5   The Physicality of Hybrid Language Learning Spaces   155

Conclusion: The Future of Physical Language Learning Spaces   169

References   174
Index   191

Figures

1	Stairs with different languages signifying threshold and boundary	83
2	Hallway with student sitting on the floor with laptop	85
3	Video viewing room at a US language center	106
4	Language classroom door with notes posted by maintenance staff	107
5	Round, experimental 360 classroom	163

Preface

"Design a new language center from the ground up": That was the main task of my first job at Pomona College in Claremont, CA, right after finishing my dissertation manuscript. I was hired in 2005 to not merely build a modernized version of a language lab but to reinvent it. As a junior language educator and researcher, I did not know much at the time about architecture, emerging learning spaces research, or differences between space and place. Neither could I anticipate cloud, mobile, and ubiquitous computing, Web 2.0, and how much new technologies would change and challenge old paradigms. I didn't yet know that my research and my professional work would center around physical, virtual, and hybrid language-learning spaces, that I would help other institutions and programs design or redesign learning spaces, or that I would give a Ted X talk about this topic. I could not have imagined that one-and-a-half decades later a pandemic would put many of the lessons I had learned into question and force the world to "catch up" on virtual spaces for learning and reexamine the necessity, but also the affordances, of our physical spaces.

I found back then that relatively little research had been published on the topic. I was fortunate to attend a workshop called "Language Center Design" a few weeks after I started that first position. It was offered by the International Association for Language Learning and Technology (IALLT), which was originally an organization for language laboratory professionals. That workshop allowed me to see language centers, and learning spaces in general, in a new light. In 2009, IALLT asked me to organize the workshop and since then I've offered it at every IALLT conference until today. IALLT and its regional affiliates (for me SWALLT, MAALLT, and now MWALLT) gave my growing interest in learning-space design a home, an audience, and wonderful colleagues from whom I have learned so much.

When we talk about innovations in the field of language learning and teaching, we usually think about digital spaces: communicative technologies, learning management systems, apps, collaborative tools, and creative software. Digital has become the new frontier. Individual language professionals have a hard time keeping up with the never-ending onslaught of new, improved, and ever move sophisticated and slick possibilities. As an advocate of technology-driven language-learning innovations, I have been—and continue to be—a big supporter. If you don't follow blindly, if you are digitally resilient and are conscious of good practice, there's an ever-growing treasure trove out there.

But physical spaces do have an important role to play in this digital age. I often get asked what the future of the classroom and learning spaces will be like. Will it be physical? Will it be digital? The answer is "both."

Introduction: Why a Book about Physical Language Learning Spaces in This Digital Age?

It seems anachronistic to publish a book about physical spaces for language learning in 2023. But this book is not written as an alternative to digital spaces. Rather, it is about being intentional in learning-space choices and design, about being mindful about the affordances of each, and to recognize that these two distinct types of spaces are not an *either/or* proposition, but a *both/and* one. There is a new hybridity that defies simple polar opposites and asks us to consider them as a spectrum.

During the Covid-19 pandemic, interest in digital-only educational spaces grew rapidly. But the pandemic also triggered a new appreciation of physical learning spaces. We know that there are real benefits to human-to-human interaction in physical spaces. The cognitive, affective, social, and psychomotor domains all play an important role in today's higher education landscape. This book addresses several urgent questions: How can we build spaces that are inclusive, accessible, and equitable? How can they be safe and impart a sense of belonging? How can they set the right conditions to make learning more effective, more efficient, more flexible, and more motivating? And how can these spaces aid language learning (and teaching) in particular?

Language learning can take place in planned and unplanned spaces, in the classroom, in specialty spaces such as language centers or language houses, in social spaces, and "in the wild." It also takes place in spaces we wouldn't immediately consider learning spaces, but that nonetheless plays an important role: in corridors and hallways, offices, thresholds, outdoors, food spaces, residential spaces, etc. Due to increasingly mobile and ubiquitous technology, physical language learning spaces have changed. No longer do we need rooms full of tape players, computers, loanable equipment, physical media, and other resources. In most physical locations, on and off campus, learners can access digital spaces.

Physical spaces matter. Learners are human beings, and cognition is not isolated in the brain. Extended cognition research shows us how our physicality, our place, and proximity to people shape how we think, interact, and learn: "Thinking outside the brain means skillfully engaging entities external to our heads—the feelings and movements of our bodies, the physical spaces in which we learn and work, and the minds of other people around us—drawing them into our own mental processes" (Paul 2021: 1). While the pandemic did force many educators and learners into remote emergency teaching, it also showed us how we have taken many physical aspects of our lives for granted: "Our uses of space have been regulated as never before, by lockdowns, curfews, international border controls, and domestic travel bans. Meanwhile, there is a new awakening, awareness and appreciation of local and immediate physical environments … For all of us, it has been a sharp reminder how much space matters" (Benson 2021: 140). As learners have more choices than ever in regard to modalities and learning formats, it is important to consider that our physical spaces need to make optimal use of their affordances. This requires an understanding of the attributes of physical learning spaces.

While educators and professionals cannot design noninstitutional learning spaces, they can create spaces on our campuses and in our schools. We need to better understand why our current learning spaces are the way they are, how many of them have become normalized, and how they reflect and influence our teaching. Physical language learning spaces are an active agent in the learning process, they set directions and prestructure expectations. All stakeholders need to pay attention to careful, sustainable, flexible, and resilient design of such spaces.

This book is neither a text on a second language acquisition, nor is it one on architecture. It is also not a blueprint for specific spaces or a manual. But it weaves together all of these into a book that is aimed to be a foundation for being more mindful and more intentional about our physical spaces for language learning.

Why Now?

Research and scholarship on physical language learning spaces is relatively rare. Aronin (2018: 21) argues that "Physical and material settings in which language learning and use take place is a fairly recent dimension of scholarly interest." Guerrettaz (2021: 47) similarly posits that "Classrooms' physical-spatial dynamics are especially overlooked in research and most transcription conventions." Murray and Lamb (2018c: 257) call for more scholarship in this area:

> While in this volume "construction" has been used as a metaphor for the development of places for language learning, we propose that future research will also have to focus on the construction of actual physical spaces. In pursuing this line of enquiry, it may be helpful to view physical spaces as entities ... Universities around the world are currently investing huge sums of money into not only the creation of various types of formal learning centres but also informal spaces in which learners come together in order to learn with and from each other.

Much of the language education research that deals with physical spaces has not necessarily been interested in *institutional* spaces, but rather those outside of them, in the community, out "in the wild." There is a plurality of spaces that can be used for language education, and they deserve further attention, as Benson (2021: 134) writes:

> Much out-of-class language learning research is conducted in schools and universities and involves custom-designed facilities such as self-access centres, computer laboratories and other kinds of learning spaces. Although the design of these spaces deserves more attention, there is also a need for SLA research to spread out into a much wider variety of settings. Within educational institutions, these might include libraries, extracurricular clubs, open spaces and "schoolscapes."

Much of the learning spaces' literature does not focus on languages-specific learning spaces but rather on libraries, STEM (science, technology, engineering, and math) learning spaces, generic classrooms, or campuses and schools as a whole. This book draws on many of such studies, ideas, and concepts from those publications, even though they do not focus on language learning specifically. The 2017 Horizon Report sees "Redesigning Learning Spaces" as a driving trend in education for the coming years. Boys (2015: 96) argues that what is needed "is both a better understanding of what matters about space for learning and the development of a more diverse range of actual spaces in higher education, which produce an efficient and flexible match across formal, informal, social and specialist requirements." Language learning spaces cannot only learn from other disciplines' spaces or more generic spaces, they can also contribute to a healthy ecosystem of innovative and effective learning spaces and drive transformation in this arena.

In a way, this book is a *Bestandsaufnahme*, the taking of inventory or stock, and provides a starting point for further investigations and research in physical language leaning spaces. The book also tries to provide theoretical and practical advice for those fortunate to be in a position to more intentionally design new learning spaces or redesign existing ones. During a time of decreasing enrollments in world language classes in the United States (Looney and Lusin, 2019; Heidrich Uebel, Kronenberg, and Sterling, 2023), it is the goal of this book to support this additional tool in our discipline's toolbox that can make language learning more effective and efficient, but also more attractive and motivating.

Limitations of the Book

It should be noted that this book focuses on higher education, but it provides examples and advice from and for other types of institutions and levels as well. Furthermore, while many examples and much of the research come from several parts of the world, the space discussions focus more on the United States than on other countries or regions of the world.

The book is not about nonphysical, noninstitutional, or conceptual language learning spaces, such as community-based learning, learning outside of the classroom, learning in the wild, using video games, e-mail tandems, project-based work, bilingual learning spaces, autonomous learning spaces, etc. Those spaces are important, and currently there is excellent research being conducted about such learning spaces. For this book, the focus is narrower, on physical, institutional spaces.

Theoretical and Practical Approach

This book combines theory and praxis to provide a framework for a diverse audience, including teacher trainers; language program and curriculum designers; architects and facilities planners; language faculty; teachers, researchers, and graduate students; university and school administrators; and instructional technologists. It weaves different disciplinary perspectives and leverages interdisciplinary intersections to provide a framework for understanding physical language learning spaces and discussing and approaching their design. While it does not support any particular language teaching approach or methodology, it is mindful of more current trends, including communicative approaches to language teaching, a more student-centered focus, and more open, active, and less rigid ways of viewing language education. Physical language learning spaces fit well with some more recent views of language education that do not ignore physical realities, including pedagogical ergonomics, "which uniquely integrates research, theory, and practice, with potential to advance the much-needed area of materials-use inquiry in particular. As with other areas of ergonomics study, language teaching is simultaneously art, craft, and engineering of the cognitive, social, and material dynamics of classrooms" (Guerrettaz 2021: 62). Furthermore, sociomaterialism is a related concept in that it:

> encourages us to closely examine sociomaterial assemblages, and to query in schooling sites how human bodies, the physical setup of classrooms, classroom materials (furniture, books, paper, computers, and so on), discourses about teaching and learning, what is considered to be knowledge, school district policies, the curriculum, and so on are entangled with one another, and how they may be moving and changing together.
> (Toohey et al. 2015: 465)

Whenever I have the privilege to visit a campus as a consultant for a language learning space design project, the hosts usually assume that I will tell them what technologies to buy, how to choose new furniture, and how to spatially best arrange everything. But what usually happens, and must happen, is that the program and the faculty have to come around an understanding of what language learning is. That seems simple, but many departments and programs only have vague consensus of what it is that they are teaching. The physical space is, in many ways, the representation of their educational philosophies, or built pedagogy (see Chapter 1). Space design is not and cannot be isolated from the program's mission, vision, values, and goals. Furthermore, it is not a product but a process, and the initial design is only one part of this process.

The book attempts to introduce and explain relevant concepts to readers without any prior knowledge of design or architecture. It discusses different kinds of language learning spaces, from residential learning spaces to active classrooms, from social and experiential spaces to language centers and the many alternatives to normalized classrooms. It provides advice on how to conceptualize and create supportive, resilient, flexible, inclusive, accessible, affordable, sustainable, intentional, and safe physical learning spaces. Instead of looking back, this book is about the future. It is about how we can set up physical spaces so that they do not become divided, obsolete, uninspired, and underutilized. It is about how learning spaces can be vibrant, feasible, useful, adaptable, flexible, accessible, transformative, exciting, and inviting. It is not written in opposition to digital or virtual learning spaces, but rather in a complimentary fashion to provide a foundation so we can focus on a more intentional use of physical spaces for language learning in addition to other possible learning spaces. And lastly, it is meant to provide a framework for all those who plan to design new spaces or redesign existing ones.

1

From Theory to Practice: What Are Language Learning Spaces?

This chapter sets out to explain and define what we mean by *spaces*. Physical language learning spaces are spaces with three modifiers. *Learning* spaces are particular types of spaces that share characteristics, but also differ from other kinds of spaces. *Language* learning spaces introduce the disciplinary aspect of learning spaces, in that they need to take different characteristics, goals, and affordances into account. *Physical* language learning spaces take into consideration that there are other kinds of spaces that are more conceptual in nature. The term *space* is often used interchangeably with other concepts, such as place, and learning spaces are often equated with classrooms. The chapter explains these differences and similarities in order to develop a shared and more concise vocabulary when dealing with physical language learning spaces. The classroom, in particular, is further analyzed within the framework of technology and normalization. And finally, the concept of built pedagogy, which describes how physical spaces embody educational philosophies (Monahan 2002), provides a theoretical foundation for this book.

Learning Spaces, Learning Places

Space

Speaking with a geographer, a philosopher, or an architect will likely yield three rather different interpretations of this complex term. Written with interdisciplinarity in mind, this book will not try to give an extensive overview of the concept's history and various theoretical interpretations (see Benson [2021] for a more in-depth discussion of the term). But it is important to give a basic overview at this point. We can understand "space" as continually created, as its production is an ongoing process (Milgrom 2008). Spaces are not merely empty, geographical, or architectural containers or areas (Lefebvre 1991) but are created through our interactions (McGregor 2003) and are complex (Lefebvre 1991). Spaces do not simply exist, but rather are, as Löw (2016: xiv) posits, "created in action and as spatial structures are embodied in institutions that pre-structure action." Thus, we cannot regard them in isolation but must understand them within their various contexts. Spaces can also be regarded as "one of our means of thinking about the world and of embodying thought into action" (Boys 2011: 6). Space and time are linked in complex ways (or what Massey (2001) calls space-time) and influence each other. For example, the times set for classes to begin and end will determine when a classroom is used and how it is used, and the beginning, breaks, and end of each semester set a rhythm for its usage. "Spatiality (or space-time) is more than physical or social space. It is the recursive interplay between the spatial and the social, the product of complex ongoing relations" (McGregor 2003: 363). Kern (2020: 11) posits that a space, such as a city, "resides in the imagination as well as in its material form." This is certainly also true for learning spaces.

Indeed, different definitions of space are often in tension with each other. One useful approach is to distinguish between smooth and striated space (Bayne 2004: 303): "Where smooth space is informal and amorphous, striated space is formal and structured. Striated space is associated with arboreal, hierarchical thought, which Deleuze & Guattari oppose to rhizomatic thought—non-hierarchical, underground, multiply-connected." These are not opposed to each other but have a "tendency to *pervade* each other—for striation to appropriate the smooth, and for the smooth to emerge from the striated." This is important for the purposes of this book's argument: striated spaces, such as formal language classrooms, cannot be seen in isolation from smooth language learning spaces, such as more informal, conceptual, transitional, or transnational spaces.

It is worth noting that the term *space* has different meanings and connotations when translated into other languages, as Forty (2000: 256) notes: "The development of space as an architectural category took place in Germany, and it is to German writers that one must turn for its origins, and purposes. This immediately presents a problem for an English-language discussion of the subject, for the German word for space, *Raum*, at once signifies both a material enclosure, a 'room,' and a philosophical concept." Even the English term *space* elicits different responses and associations from different disciplines which have adopted and changed the term. Fenwick et al. (2011: 130) note that "[T]here are different trajectories that have resulted in the increased interest in questions of space, so that it is no longer the concern only of geographers, architects and urban planners."

For the purposes of this book, it is important to acknowledge that the term *space* is often used by second language educators and researchers in contexts that do not necessarily have the built environment as its prime focus. Therefore, the modifier *physical* is generally used in this book, and often implies *intentionally designed* spaces. Nevertheless, spaces overlap and cannot be neatly separated.

Place

Space and place are often used interchangeably, including in applied linguistics research (Higgins 2017: 103). Even though "place" shares a number of characteristics with "space," they are different. Places generally have names and are more than mere locations or generic spaces (Cresswell 2019), but there is also an emphasis on the "localized features of place" (Brooks, Fuller and Waters 2012: 262), on the locality compared to spaces (Hutchison and Orr 2004: 11):

> The term "place" conjures up visions of locality, spatial representations of those places with which we are familiar, and those places the unfamiliarity of which intrigues us. We reside in places, go to work and recreate in places, travel daily through places that are sometimes meaningful to us and other times ignored or taken for granted. We identify with those places that played some formative (if still elusive) role in our childhood years, those places that are associated with good times or bad. The term "place" is imbued with emotion, defined by the boundaries it imposes on space, and informed by the utility to which space is put in our lives. Place can be understood as an individually constructed reality—a reality informed by the unique experiences, histories, motives, and goals that each of us brings to the spaces with which we identify. Yet place can also be understood as a socially constructed reality.

Gulson and Symes (2007: 2) argue that:

> [T]here is an element of fixity pertaining to them ... Space is more generic, more quotidian—not subject of parenthesizing and naming in quite the same way place is. The fact that it is usual to refer to spatial practices is also revealing: places do not have practices in quite the same way. Space in this sense is more of a verb than a noun.

Counter to spaces, Löw (2016: xvii) argues, "places are always markable, nameable, and unique." But despite the name, despite the label, Massey (1997: 323) reminds us that places "do not have single, unique 'identities'" but that "they are full of internal conflicts." These identities are important differentiator that are important to consider when it comes to learning space design. There is an emotional quality to places (Hutchison and Orr 2004) that seems to evade more generic spaces. Places have a sense of materiality to them, even when they are imagined (Cresswell 2014). They are full of things, items, and bodies that are constantly changing, shifting, appearing, and dissolving frequently. All places are constituted of material and immaterial presence, and are thus assemblages (Dovey 2010). What is remarkable is that they are never static but processes (Massey 1997), "never complete, finished, or bounded but are always becoming" (Cresswell 2014: 68). Löw (2016: xvii) argues that "it is characteristic of places (whatever spaces are connected with them) that they endure in time either as individual realms or, with more sociological relevance, as collective realms of meaning." While much of this book is about spaces, it will be argued that in order to fully comprehend language learning spaces, we must look at specific, situated language learning *places* and more intentionally support placemaking (Middleton 2018). To sum it up, when examining *spaces* we will look for more generalizable features, and when examining *places*, we will view the situated, localized, individual, unique, and concrete features.

Learning Spaces

Learning space design as a topic of intentional inquiry has garnered considerable attention in recent years, resulting in a growing body of research. What we mean by the term *learning spaces* seems, at first sight, to be too simple or obvious to explain. But depending on the disciplinary lens, a definition is not easy to come by. In fact, most articles assume that we know what learning spaces are. Some researchers equate the term with *physical* learning spaces (e.g., Oblinger's 2006 seminal publication "Learning Spaces"), while others focus on conceptual or nonphysical learning spaces. The term is often used interchangeably with terms such as *(learning) place, environment,* and *classroom*. Yet these are not all the same. Boys (2011: 1) posited more than a decade ago: "key basic questions about what we mean by 'space' and what matters about it in relation to learning, remain unanswered. What kinds of space are we talking about—conceptual, physical, virtual, social and/or personal? What are the relationships between the nature of these various spaces and how they actually impact on learning activities?" Brooks et al. (2012: 262) list various elements that "together are constitutive of learning space," which include "the localized features of place and situation and the more extended and amorphous spatial dimensions in which they are embedded."

Learning spaces are deeply embedded in educational, social, political, organizational, and economic policies, practices, and norms. The concept of time-space is useful here (Massey 2001), as educational and institutional practices, such as course schedules, academic calendars, school bells, instructional unit length, etc., all pre-structure action in conjunction with space, and at the same time also structure space. Even those learning spaces outside of institutional practices are structured by social expectations, economic realities, and cultural norms. In general, we can distinguish different types of learning spaces, such as specialized, generic, and informal learning spaces (Harrison and Hutton 2014: 48). These can be physical and material in nature, but the same applies to conceptual, virtual, or personal ones as well.

The term *learning* in *learning spaces*, which has become the generally accepted and widely used term, can be misleading as it lumps together spaces for teaching; institutional spaces for learning; personal and collective spaces for learning; formal, informal, transitory, and categorizable learning spaces; as well as abstract conceptualizations. It seems that at times we refer to all educational spaces as learning spaces. The *Journal of Learning Spaces* provides this definition: "*Learning spaces* are designed to support, facilitate, stimulate, or enhance learning and teaching. *Learning spaces* encompass formal, informal, and virtual environments." While this definition does not specifically mention conceptual, individual, and private learning spaces, I would argue that they are included in this broad view of learning spaces. McGregor (2003: 354) argues that "[s]pace is literally made through our interactions." The complicated social and organizational human relationships and interactions—whether they be in-person, virtual, mediated, or abstract—continuously shape, create, and re-create learning spaces. Rajaee Pitehnoee, Arabmofrad, and Modaberi (2020) discuss the term "classroomscape" as a space where people and the material world come together and intra-act, which Guerrettaz (2021) defines as being similar to *space* but narrower in scope.

Thornburg (1996) uses the primordial metaphors of the "campfire," the "cave," the "watering hole," and "life" to describe the different aspects of learning spaces that are still crucial components even in the twenty-first century and the digital age. These metaphors help translate the multitude of spaces and ever-changing possibilities into a few basic needs that share learners across time and cultures. There is a need to learn collectively with peers and more informally (watering hole), through more official and formal means (campfire), individually (cave), and through experience and application beyond specified and dedicated learning spaces (life). Diverse and effective learning spaces matter because they are central to a healthy learning ecosystem. Savin-Baden (2008: 2) goes one step further in arguing that the "creation and re-creation of learning spaces is vital for the survival of the academic community." The Covid-19 pandemic has brought developments in education, including internationalization, digitization, and new ways of looking at education, to the fore, and it is more important than ever to more intentionally view and design spaces for learning. Chapter 5 expands on this point further.

While Thornburg's four metaphors provide an important foundation and wider view of learning, the now widely adopted term *learning spaces* is often more constricted and narrow within institutional and educational contexts. Fenwick et al. (2011: vii) provide a useful argument for not equating education with learning:

> Let us begin by acknowledging that, by education, we mean intentional activity to promote learning for particular purposes in any situation: classrooms, worksites, virtual spaces, mentoring meetings, community projects, social movements, and so forth. Education in all of these enactments is centrally material—its energies, processes, motives and outcomes are fully entangled with material practice, nature, time, space, technologies and objects of all kinds. These material entanglements are often not acknowledged in the conventional educational preoccupations with understanding human cognition, human activity and intentions, human meaning-making and human relationships.

It is the intentionality and a certain degree of formality that sets *designed* learning spaces apart from others: "The problem lies in the very fact that education is *institutional* whereas learning can be, and increasingly is, located outside of formal institutions of education" (Edwards and Usher 2008: 127).

Physical Learning Spaces

Learning spaces include a variety of possible spaces, including physical as well as conceptual and virtual spaces. Depending on the context, the term *learning spaces* is sometimes equated with *physical learning spaces*. Here, I will use the attribute *physical* intentionally to situate these spaces among the larger group of *learning spaces*. One defining criterion of physical spaces (and places) is that our body can only be in one location at a time. While we can be in many virtual, abstract, or conceptual spaces at once—in "the chaos of simultaneity and multiplicity" (Massey 1994: 1)—our embodied selves cannot be divided up. If we regard spaces and places vertically rather than horizontally, we are technically in different locations at once: on earth, in the United States, in East Lansing, at Michigan State University, in Wells Hall, in room A108, on a chair in the corner of the room. Places can have different scales but align vertically in terms of location.

The phenomenon of "one body—one location" seems trivial and obvious. In this increasingly digital, connected world, possible virtual spaces have proliferated in education, in addition to the many other nonphysical learning spaces. But the physical space matters for all of these. Even if a student is in an online language class, the student's body is somewhere, whether at home, at the library, on a train, or in a cafe. And each influences the learning situation. The choice of where the body is, and in what kind of physical space, matters. Benson (2021: 23) writes that "social, ideational or metaphorical spaces only exist in the context of physical space. The social distances of politeness and intimacy, the distances between social classes, the divisions among genres of art, music and literature, the virtual spaces of the internet, the disciplinary fields of knowledge and so on are all grounded in physical space." Throughout this book I will argue that the lines between physical learning spaces on one side and virtual—conceptual, theoretical, etc.—learning spaces on the other side are blurred lines at best. They are all layered, interconnected, and woven together. And physical spaces cannot be seen as purely objective, independent entities. Higgins (2017: 102) reminds us that Henri Lefebvre:

> theorized space as a triad of physical, social, and imagined spaces, and argued that since imagined space is where we conceive and analyze social events and the physical environment, all three spaces are ultimately inseparable. An important consequence of this triadic view is that a physical space is never really an objective space since it is always conceived by and for people. Hence, all spaces are ultimately political realms, and power is constantly embedded in their representation and in how people experience them.

One distinction that is often made in the field learning space design is between formal and informal learning spaces. Formal spaces tend to be those designated for more structured, guided, or planned learning activities. They include spaces such as classrooms, labs, lecture halls, etc. Informal learning spaces, which have increasingly garnered attention, are often a catch-all category for unguided, less-planned, or unplanned learning activities. These include both individual as well as more social spaces. This binary view is often increased by viewing formal spaces as mandatory, serious, and attached to for-credit learning, and thus seeing informal spaces as more optional, more autonomous, perhaps more engaging, but also less institutionalized and less important. Overcoming this dichotomy is difficult. This book tries to look at both ends of the paradigm to overcome this division.

One further distinction is important at this point: are the physical learning spaces built or not? There is often the assumption that physical learning spaces have been created by humans. While this is the case in most circumstances, there are instances when natural spaces are available, possible, and even desirable. These are, however, rare, but they will be included in this book. Most examples that will be dealt with in the following chapters refer to *built* physical learning spaces. This book focuses on physical learning spaces in higher education, but it should be acknowledged that age is an important variable to be considered. Rajaee Pitehnoee, Arabmofrad, and Modaberi (2020) summarize that adult learners are less affected than younger ones by physical spaces. Furthermore, we must acknowledge the different scales of physical learning spaces, such as the campus scale, the building scale, the room scale, etc. For example, within the building scale, one might focus on a certain area or floor with multiple rooms. So, when discussing learning spaces, we should not only focus on the room scale, which is most common, but also be able to zoom out and take a more holistic ecosystem approach.

Physical Language Learning Spaces

So far, our discussions have been about physical learning spaces in general. In this section, we will take a closer look at such spaces through a disciplinary lens: learning spaces for language learning (and teaching). Learning a language shares many characteristics with the study of other subjects, such as physics, history, or supply chain management. Generic learning spaces and classrooms do have the advantage of scheduling flexibility, but they do have the tendency to disassociate space from place: "generic space lacks third place qualities such as homeliness … and this potentially impacts adversely on a student's sense of belonging" (Middleton 2018: 44). As the following chapters further discuss, place matters when it comes to spaces for specific disciplinary areas, such as languages.

There are criteria that make learning a language unique. For example, the focus on communication often requires certain kinds of interlocutor communication set-ups, from pair work to group work, and learning a language requires different kinds of scaffolding as not all directions and advice are necessarily understood by the learners. Furthermore, language education is guided through different sets of standards, learning goals, and assessment practices. All of these are discussed in detail in Chapter 2. The disciplinary lens does require us to look at learning spaces anew in order to design the best possible spaces specifically for language learning. And this goes beyond choosing tables, chairs, or posters on the wall. All these are undoubtedly important, but in order to gain a deeper understanding, it is useful to reframe the concept of physical language learning spaces as sociomaterial assemblages.

Physical Language Learning Spaces as Sociomaterial Assemblages

Benson (2021: 91) distinguishes between two views of language learning environments: "an 'areal' perspective in which the environment is viewed as a geographical area (e.g., a campus, a city or a region) and an 'individual' perspective in which the environment is viewed as a configuration of settings assembled by an individual learner." Both are undoubtedly important and not separate from each other. This section will examine the complex sociomateriality of our spaces. Learning spaces are more than merely physical environments; rather, they encompass often "unseen" elements, "not obviously tangible phenomena" (Aronin and Ó Laoire 2013: 10), that constitute such spaces. Some are intangible or not easily and immediately visible: the culture of its place, the norms of the department and the institution, smells and sound waves, the learning goals aspired to, and the values held by individuals and groups. Others are physical and tangible, such as posters and signs, pens and pencils, whiteboards and blackboards, projectors and smart boards, the time of the day or year, the learners in it, handbooks, and manuals. All of these seemingly trivial or mundane but "important material dynamics" are usually not given much attention in educational settings and research (Fenwick et al. 2011: xi). Increasingly, however, there is a developing body of research and theory that "discusses the importance of the nonhuman in human action and sees both the human and the non-human as coparticipants in shifting flows of activity" (Toohey et al. 2015: 465). In other words, the "material is entangled in meaning, not assumed to be separate from it" (Fenwick et al. 2011: vi). We will first take a look at these new approaches and theories often grouped under the term "[s]ociomaterialism." Recently, Guerrettaz (2021: 59) explicitly connected this wide field to the language classroom, seeking to "understand how classroom 'happenings' happen." She posits that "[C]lassroom activity and interaction can arguably be distilled down to the two foundational dynamics at the heart of this study: materials and action." In her research project, she looks at how materialities—nonhuman entities—play a role in the language classroom. It follows the sociomaterial tradition of looking at small, often overlooked or not consciously perceived material aspects and their enactments in formal language learning settings. Fenwick et al. (2011: vii) conceptualize this sociomaterial research approach:

> Sociomaterial studies try to reveal the minute dynamics and connections that are continuously enacting taken-for-granted in educational events: the clothing, timetables, passwords, pencils, windows, stories, plans, buzzers, bubblegum, desks, electricity and lights—not as separate objects, but as continually changing patterns of materiality. These patterns comprise human and non-human energies, each with historical trajectories, continually combining with (and dissolving away from) other assemblages. Humans, and what they take to be their learning and social processes, do not float, distinct, in container-like contexts of education, such as classrooms and community sites, that can be conceptualized and dismissed simply a wash of material stuff and spaces.

These materials can be of great importance to practitioners in an actual language classroom. Is there a board to write on? Are whiteboards markers or chalk provided in the room? Can the door be closed, and should it be? Do outside noises enter the classroom, or are there sounds that the room's technologies emit? Are there speakers and a digital projector? Is their quality high? Such questions may seem trivial and are often absent in discussions around language education methodologies, research, and theories. The reason we don't usually talk about these in academic and research discourses is because these all appear to be simple things: "everyday stuff" (Fenwick 2015: 86).

In discussions about physical learning spaces, these materialities only play a partial role. Certainly, some of these elements are planned and designed, often in a replicable way: the chairs and tables, the writing surfaces, the computer, and projection set-up, etc. But then there are also elements in these spaces that are centrally unplanned and included, used, or added in spaces by their users. These add a sense of control and agency and thus meaning. These unplanned, personalized, localized, lived-in materialities are often not recognized in formal discourses about learning spaces, and yet they are important to their users, and influence the processes that take place in the learning spaces.

It is important for us to define what these materialities are, how they relate to space, and how they constitute it. For Lawn (1999: 82) "[T]ools and aids, furniture and walls, space and form, rules and meaning all create teaching and are inseparable from it." For language learning and teaching in particular, materials are "any or all of the very wide range of resources capable of aiding language learning" (Waters 2009: 311), such as "entities, signs, texts, technologies, environments" (Guerrettaz 2021: 40). Engman and Hermes (2021: 86) argue that traditionally "the term 'classroom materials' has long functioned as shorthand for text-based instruction inside walled classrooms." And yet, many practitioners would argue that what can be seen as materials has a much broader range and matters in the praxis of language teaching. "Educators working from sociomaterial approaches are encouraging learners to attend to these quotidian material details that stitch together their practice, knowledge and environments—not just to *attune* very closely to the connections, but also to *tinker* and improvise, to interrupt, and to seize emerging possibilities" (Fenwick 2015: 84). Van Lier (2004: 82) defines "emergence" as "a reorganization of simple elements into a more complex system."

The organization and reorganization into what we may refer to as "assemblages" is an important element in what constitutes our physical language learning spaces. Assemblages are made up of individual parts and their interactions with each other. They "*intra*-act" (Fenwick 2015: 87). They are not static, and the "ways in which these parts are combined are not necessary or preordained but contingent. Individual parts can be removed and become parts of other assemblages. Places are good examples of assemblages" (Cresswell 2019: 172). Furthermore, Fenwick (2015: 87) asserts that "all sociomaterial objects, are in fact *heterogeneous assemblages*. They are gatherings of *heterogeneous* natural, technical and cognitive elements. All objects and material settings embed a history of these gatherings in the negotiation of their design and accumulated uses, whether lecture halls, presentation software, testing instruments, essays, pedagogical protocols, etc."

The concept of assemblages is useful also specifically in language learning contexts. Benson (2021: 6) argues that:

> [L]anguage interacts with various physical objects to form what I call "language-bearing assemblages." These are, at a basic level, thought, speech and writing, and, at more complex levels, they include assemblages such as conversation and meetings, letters and notes, and technologically enhanced assemblages such as printed documents, audio and video recordings, and broadcast audio and speech. From this point of view, language is a non-physical object that can *only* be present in the space of the world as a component of physical language-bearing assemblages.

Physical language learning spaces as sociomaterial assemblages then are a unique whole created of various, heterogeneous, and individual parts, which may or may not be physical. A physical language classroom, for example, is made up of its walls, vertical writing surfaces, desks, chairs, pens, posters, signs, etc. But it also includes various aspects and interactions not immediately apparent. For example, institutional decision-making processes led to the choice of its components, its organizing processes, its structures, and interrelatedness, and they continue to have an ongoing impact. When looking at various physical learning spaces in this book and beyond, we must incorporate the complex parts of these contingent and never static assemblages. Cowley (2012: 24) proposes that to understand language learning, we must move away from linguistics-centric perspectives and instead examine actions in "rich learning environments."

Whether one wants to make sense of existing spaces, be more mindful in their practical application, or design new spaces or redesign old spaces, I propose to take a holistic, intentionally material assemblage-focused view. Aronin (2018: 24) argues that "[M]aterial culture is of utmost importance for the language teaching classroom, and for motivation, for minority language groups, and maintaining lesser-used languages, for keeping a language for future generations, as well as for understanding emotions, and behaviour, and resolving many issues in multilingual settings." In this view, people are not the only sources of action but rather embedded in sociomaterial inter- and intradependencies in a complex way. The following sections of this chapter outline how these dependencies take shape.

The Normalization of the Language Classroom

A very common kind of learning space is the classroom. It is both a particular type of room as well as a symbolic space that stands for instructed, formalized education. Many classrooms are generic and not discipline-specific. They are an efficient way of organizing space. The number of primary and secondary school classrooms grew rapidly due to pressures to provide physical learning spaces during industrialization and the rapid population growth that followed, especially in urban areas (Grosvenor and Burke 2008). This relative efficiency, replicability, and scalability served these purposes at the expense of more effective space because it minimized student movements. Higher education classrooms differ from their K-12 counterparts in the level of control that instructors have over them. In the United States, K-12 teachers often stay in their classrooms, giving them a higher level of control and autonomy over space decisions. It is common that K-12 rooms are personalized, and that different settings and arrangements can stay in place over longer periods of time.

In higher education, the focus of this book, faculty usually do not stay in classrooms. Rather, they are commonly assigned a room by the registrar's office before the semester starts, and they do not have control over the room's design, furniture, or other individualizations. It is also likely that they will have different rooms for different courses they teach, and that different rooms are assigned each semester. Specialized language classrooms, often provided by language centers, provide an exception to this common practice.

Lawn (1999: 66) calls the classroom a "known but invisible part of teaching." The classroom is ubiquitous, common, and normalized: "Most of us spent a considerable part of our lives in classrooms, and some of us still do. And yet the classroom is a neglected space" (Baggerman 2012: 159). This section is about how we define the classroom and understand its blueprint in order to not only consider alternatives, but also to think how its properties might be better adapted to suit language education in particular. Hutchison and Orr (2004: 52) assert that "[W]ith few exceptions, this basic plan for the design of self-contained classrooms, each opening up into a common corridor, continues to be the most prominent design philosophy at work in schools today." Koutamanis and Majewski-Steijns (2012: 204) similarly describe the blueprint that is common in the United States and many other countries:

> Following a relatively short period of experimentation with different arrangements of desks and openings, as well as class sizes, the current stereotype of the classroom became firmly established: rectangular space housing around 30 pupils, with fenestration on the one side and one or more entrances on the opposite side. The other two sides are usually blank walls that separate classrooms. The fenestration side is normally part of the external envelope of the building, while the entrance side invariably goes into the corridor that links classrooms to each other and to other circulation spaces.

There are alternative concepts, such as active learning spaces, which emphasize mobile furniture, flexibility, interactivity, deeper technology integration, and deemphasize the front of the room. But they have not fully replaced existing classrooms and are rather the exception than the norm (Whiteside 2014). Most classrooms have seen incremental upgrades and additions. Most drastically, the introduction of electrical lighting allowed them to be used during all phases of the day, and allowed for more directional flexibility as windows did not have to be to the right side of the students—at the time, writing with their left hand was not allowed in most schools. Other technologies that were introduced were Wi-Fi nodes, new writing surfaces, overhead projectors and later digital projectors, smart boards, TVs, speakers, and documents cameras. But changes have been incremental and did not alter the design in a fundamental way. In other countries, variations might be found. For example, in Germany rooms with a U-shape or horseshoe configuration are quite common; but they, too, have a central focus on the instructor (Stang 2016).

Language Classrooms

Specialist rooms, which differ from generic classrooms (Grosvenor and Burke 2008), such as specific language classrooms, are uncommon, perhaps except for language laboratories or centers. The classroom, both conceptually and physically, is the "prototypical context" for instructed second language acquisition (Loewen and Sato 2017: 2), even though there are increasingly other spaces available for language instruction. Van Lier (1996: 139) argues that "the classroom can be a laboratory, a window on the language world, an arena for action, a planning center, and many things besides. But in being any or all those things, the classroom should never have to deny being a classroom." The classroom context sets certain expectations for all stakeholders, first and foremost instructors and students, it guides, channels, and approves activities; and provides a widely accepted framework. The physical space has different properties depending on the setting, Benson (2021: 103) reminds us:

> A classroom is a setting for language learning when language students, language teachers, and other language resources are present and interacting with each other. At other times, it may be a setting for other kinds of learning, and when the classroom is locked up and empty at the end of the day it is no longer a setting for anything at all. A bus stop can be a setting for language learning, if a language learner strikes up a conversation in the target language with a fellow passenger. Under other circumstances it is simply a setting for waiting. This suggests that settings have both a spatial aspect and temporal or durational aspects.

When we discuss physical learning space design, we must acknowledge that the physical attributes are only one aspect in a complex web of characteristics and dependencies with sociomaterial assemblages. It is through the deconstruction not only of the physical but also other materialities that we can better understand individual properties, processes, and cultures of the classroom.

Classrooms as Normalized Technologies

Usually, we see classrooms through an architectural lens or as a concept. It is also a technology—not merely housing technology in it, but being a technology itself. Lawn (1999: 67–8) argues that:

> [T]echnology can be defined as a tool, and the thinking the tool represents: actually it is both. In a simple way, the classroom is a technology; it is a design solution, or series of solutions, to a problem. It is, at the same time, a simple machine, a process of systematic solutions and a particular way or thread of thinking about using technology.

We often equate other educational spaces as technologies. For example, a course management system would be regarded as an educational technology as well as a virtual space. In this technological view, the physical classroom solves several problems, such as providing a sheltered space that creates certain conditions that support its supposed purpose. The physical classroom protects its users from the elements, outside noises, and other distractions. It also houses other technologies, such as books, writing boards, technical equipment, and materials. It also intentionally separates users from others, segments, imposes norms and expectations, and suggests specific ways of doing things. Bijker (1987: 4) distinguishes between three ways of defining technologies:

> First, there is the level of *physical objects* or *artifacts*. For example bicycles, lamps, and Bakelite. Second "technology" may refer to *activities* and *processes*, such as steel making or molding. Third "technology" can refer to what people *know* as well as what they do; an example is the "know-how" that goes into designing a bicycle or operating an ultrasound device in the obstetrics clinic.

If we follow Lawn and see the classroom as technology, we can apply concepts of technology in general, and educational technology in particular, to be more intentional in its use. Faculty and students generally receive support and training for educational technologies. Faculty usually consider the affordances and limitations of particular educational technologies and can make critical choices. Will the technology provide an added benefit that an existing mechanism cannot provide? Is it faster, more efficient, more effective, or more appealing? Furthermore, educational technologies rarely exist in isolation but are rather part of a larger system of other technologies, values, and processes. Intentional design and support for ongoing improvement and development are common characteristics of educational technologies. Technology is often divided into hardware and software; structure and procedures; and tangible, rather fixed aspects and operating systems. These two need to support each other, take each other's affordances into account. One would not work without the other. Mathews and Soistmann (2016: 64) discuss how web design can be responsive and ask if this might be transferable: "Can we apply this concept to our physical spaces as well? What if our environments could adapt based upon the time of the day or the point in the semester?"

I propose that we view classrooms and other physical learning spaces as educational technologies that we are not fully leveraging for language learning. Training to use and utilize classrooms and physical learning spaces is minimal at best. Most language teacher programs do not discuss physical space or conceptualize its intentional use. It is expected that an instructor can use it like other invisible and normalized technologies. There is little inquiry into the particular affordances and limitations for the language learning process, and instructors often do not have the agency to choose a particular learning space—it is assigned to them by the registrar's office or other administrative unit.

There is little pedagogical support for classrooms, most support mechanisms are limited to technology troubleshooting and mechanical or cleaning assistance. Classrooms are regarded as isolated, individual, distinct, and siloed units. The corridors that connect them are often purely transitory spaces. Processes for intentional design of classrooms are anemic, and usually undertaken by those who are not regular users of these spaces. Architects, designers, campus planners, media specialists, and administrators are those most involved in the design process, not students and instructors. Skill and Young (2002: 23) argue that most educators "have remained almost complacent about the conditions of the physical learning environments where they ply their craft on a near-daily basis and where the vast majority of learners gather."

Furthermore, physical spaces in the post-occupancy phase remain largely static, with only minor additions and maintenance if something is broken. New developments usually come from technological breakthroughs. If we see physical learning spaces as social technologies, we can more intentionally design for optimal learning outcomes.

> It will be necessary to see the classroom as a hardware and a software; it is the material structure (spaces, walls, furniture, tools) and the working procedures, series of ideas and knowledge systems, operating within it. The classroom is the integration of artefacts and rules and teachers. Within the sociology of technology the artefact is not seen as inactive: it may be an actor in a network of which it is part.
>
> (Lawn 1999: 77–8)

Changes and improvements in physical learning spaces are rare. Partly this is due to the cost of physical spaces and their longevity. A technology such as a laser disc player has a shelf life, which expires when a new and improved technology pushes it aside and makes it obsolete. Physical learning spaces that have been designed long ago continue to make an impact in present language instruction. Cresswell (2019: 109) argues that "[T]he past continues to exert its influence on the present through this material presence and the inertia it represents."

Despite the plethora of new approaches and methods, despite new technologies, despite new interdisciplinary insights into better ways to support learning, the classroom has not changed much in more than a century. With the exception of a few new technologies, such as chalkboards, whiteboards, or digital projectors, which have brought some change, the basic concept has changed very little. Language teaching methodologies have undergone several paradigm shifts over the last century (e.g., grammar and translation method, the audio-lingual method, and the communicative approach), but physical spaces have not followed and meaningfully adapted to those developments.

Normalization

There are good arguments for a view that describes classrooms as normalized. Bax (2011: 1) defines normalization as "the state when a pedagogical technology such as a textbook or pen has become in effect invisible, so seamlessly is it employed in our everyday practice in the service of language learning." Most formal physical language learning spaces, in particular classrooms, are technologies that once were innovative. They have simply become an uncontested background to educational activities and their actors. This is not a new development. Lawn (1999: 72) asserts that "historians of education have privileged the actor over the wider technology so that a focus on the teacher or the curriculum (or, more often, on regulation and site narratives) has treated the classroom as invisible." The classroom has become the default that is widely accepted as a workable, proven design solution. Non-normalized technologies are usually discussed in polarized ways, with "excessive 'awe' and exaggerated 'fear'" (Bax 2011: 3), and we sometimes see this in a few experimental physical learning spaces, such as technology-heavy active learning classrooms or experimental setups.

Normalization has advantages and disadvantages. When technologies or processes are normalized, they lose their divisiveness and free up resources and mental bandwidth. "Language teachers are very much working within a complex system of opportunity and constraint. Normalization then becomes a process of understanding the infrastructure, the support networks, and the materials, and working effectively with them" (Levy and Stockwell 2006: 234). Normalization also allows technologies and processes to be standardized and scaled up. The flip side is that when classrooms and learning spaces are designed, past designs continue to be the default for new spaces. This can hinder innovation or a complete rethinking of what is possible. Innovation, and lack thereof, in the design of classrooms and other learning spaces is not restricted to the room scale. It also happens to sub-room, building, and institutional scales and, as complex assemblages, is reinforced through long-time practices:

> Take the place of the university as another example. Universities clearly have a number of more of less established meanings as centers of learning, culture, objectivity, humanistic endeavor, and reflection. These have been produced through a long history of learning and institution-building going back to the Middle Ages. Over time these places developed separate faculties of arts, sciences, law, medicine, business, and others. A way of establishing the authority of "professors" was devised and built into the structure of lecture halls (with seated students facing a standing professor on a heightened platform). The university you have inherited is, in other words, the product of hundreds of years of the practice of education in particular ways.
>
> (Cresswell 2014: 67–8)

Popular Cultural Reinforcements

As discussed above, the physical classroom is not often deliberately addressed in language education and second language acquisition discussions and research. There are many assumptions that often are not the subject of deep reflections. For example, why are there chairs in classrooms? While chairs will be discussed in detail in Chapter 4, it should suffice here to say that they are a normalized and usually unquestioned part of classrooms in some parts of the world: "sitting in chairs is now deeply ingrained in Western culture, and even prized as a symbol of modernization around the world" (Cranz 1998: 19). Such powerful external common practice and validation is not easy to dislodge. The classroom has always been more than merely a physical, neutral brick-and-mortar container, as Grosvenor, Lawn, and Rousmaniere (1999: 7–8) posit: "it is also a work of imagination, regulation and mythology. It is a designed solution to mass schooling and it is a social space that generations have in common."

Before children reach school age, they have already learned and internalized what a classroom is, what it looks like, and what is expected. Cartoons, toys, video games, and children's books introduce the concept along with visuals and descriptions, providing a basis in cultural productions that reinforce the classroom's normalized image. Examples abound, from novels such as *Harry Potter*, *Ready Player One*, and *Stoner* to TV series and movies. Even in science fiction texts, we usually find a reproduction of the classroom that differs relatively little from our current stereotype, including those displayed in popular science fiction TV series, such as in *Star Trek*, *The Mandalorian*, and *The Lower Decks*. Fisher, Harris, and Jarvis (2008: 14) discuss how these representations over time have led to a normalization of classrooms not only in educational circles but in all of society:

> At the level of the human body, as opposed to the mind, a basic requirement for control was physical enclosure and the subsequent management of time. Educational establishments took on some characteristics of industrial environments whereby designs reinforced hierarchy, facilitated supervision and prescribed behaviour. Popular culture's focus on the conventional classroom and the traditional lecture theatre is indicative of the impact this has had on the collective imagination.

It is difficult to even imagine that there are possible learning space options for learning in general and language learning in particular. For innovation and innovators to "un-normalize" the classroom, a complex web of attributes and associations must be untangled, researched, iteratively tested, and shared widely.

Innovation

Most classrooms are designed by those who usually do not teach, such as architects, interior designers, administrators, and media specialists. Design processes are controlled by those who are usually outside of the classroom. Thus, the system is set up in a way that it is slow to adapt to new educational practices and innovations: it leads to a perpetuation of the normalized traditional classroom and prevents other forms of built educational environments from becoming normalized.

There are examples of physical language learning space innovations, but they have not become widely adopted. Innovation diffusion theory (IDT) (Rogers 2003) can help us understand why they have not superseded or replaced the normalized classroom. The five attributes of relative advantage, compatibility, complexity, trialability, and observability provide a basis not only for explaining why innovations succeed or fail, but also for envisioning ways of being able to intentionally alter the status quo. Regarding language learning, the language laboratory (see also Chapter 3) is an example of a widely adopted innovation during the Cold War era. Its decline and replacement by other innovations can also be illuminated by looking at the five attributes in relation to the Cold War Era language lab more closely.

Relative Advantage

New, innovative learning spaces must provide a relative advantage over normalized ones. If they are not truly better, an institution or a department would likely not risk making changes. At the time, traditional language laboratories did have the clear advantage in that they provided affordances that other rooms did not: the ability to listen to pre-recorded L2 voices, and later to record one's own voice and listen to that recording as well. They also freed up faculty time by automating or even outsourcing some parts of language classes that were traditionally done in class by the faculty member. Now, a graduate assistant or staff member could supervise a class session. A big advantage also came in the form of government subsidies. The listening and recording advantages have disappeared in the twenty-first century as more mobile, flexible, cheaper, and more ubiquitous digital alternatives have gained the relative advantage (and have also been increasingly adopted).

Compatibility

The language laboratory was compatible with the methodology at the time, the audio-lingual method. The two worked in tandem, and the adoption of one supported the other. As new methods and approaches became more common, such as communicative approaches, task-based language teaching, or project-based language learning, to name only a few, the lab was no longer compatible.

Complexity

While the language lab was something that many educators could understand, it did provide significant hurdles, such as initial set-up, cost, maintenance, troubleshooting, and support. Faculty had to be trained in the new methodology and often in the technology. Usually, a dedicated staff member, such as a lab manager, was hired. The complexity of the lab eventually led to alternatives that were less complex and easier to use and maintain.

Trialability

Being able to test an innovation before adopting it leads to higher adoption probability. For the language lab, trying the innovation was only possible at institutions that had already built one. This limited adoption initially, but as they became more ubiquitous, they were easier to be tested. Usually, labs could not be tried out on one's own campus, and thus not by the majority of potential users. There may have also been a tendency to self-select, as lab enthusiasts were more likely to seek out opportunities to visit and test the installations. Adoption of digital audio capabilities that replaced lab capabilities was easier to be tested without travel. Especially after laptops and smartphones were ubiquitous, this could be done easily from anywhere, without the need for specialized staff or setups.

Observability

To be adopted, users and stakeholders have to be able to observe the innovation. For our example, the language lab, this means something similar to trialability. There were ways of observing without visiting an existing lab, such as through video recordings, photos, or written accounts. Being able to visit and see the spaces in action means that observers can develop their own opinions, but also judge how useful the space might be. This point is a particularly important for other learning spaces as well: if they have not been built, how can they be observed? Because building spaces is expensive, there might not be a prototype available in the real world.

Key elements of diffusion are important to consider when observing or fostering innovation diffusion. Adopters are people who try out an innovation and adopt it. Rogers (2003) lists five types in the order of how early and how likely they will choose to embrace the new over the old: innovators, early adopters, early majority, late majority, and laggards. Furthermore, communication channels provide avenues of disseminating information about innovations. For language learning spaces, these can range from books, journal articles, blog posts, podcasts, social media posts to conference presentations, workshops, and conversations between colleagues. Time is an important attribute as it helps normalize innovations, making them less drastic and immediate. Lastly, one must consider the social system, which includes external influences. For the language lab example, it benefited from the government massively subsidizing labs and promoting language education as something important to national prosperity and security, along with colleagues trying new ways of teaching in them. Prominent researchers and academic leaders can be part of the social system that fosters new spaces and technologies.

The classroom, compared to the lab, has not been superseded by innovations because newer alternatives did not sufficiently meet all or most of the five attributes of IDT. It is difficult to unthink the current classroom stereotype because it works well enough, even though it is not optimal. Educators and space designers can use IDT attributes and key elements to consider ways of promoting new language learning space innovations: identifying innovators and early adopters, finding and using appropriate communication channels, allowing time to help spread the innovation, and being intentional about identifying and utilizing social systems.

Without representative examples, prototypes, imaginaries of learning spaces, and ways to share their advantages, an innovative alternative is unlikely to be widely adopted. It is important to ask some difficult questions: Do the newly imagined language learning spaces actually provide advantages over existing spaces and concepts? Would they work in other institutions? Are they easy to understand, maintain, implement, and operate? Are there ways for others to observe and test them before committing time, energy, money, and resources? The cost factor should not be underestimated: often, innovations cost more resources and money than established, normalized practices. Lawn (1999: 70) asks regarding the normalized classroom: "While the invention of the standard rule related to new pedagogical flexibilities, did the cheapness of its production affect its spread?" In times of rising tuition costs and new virtual and hybrid options in education, the financial aspect is significant and must be included in design deliberations. Reducing costs would be an innovation advantage for a language learning paradigm shift.

Language education is a field in which many innovations, such as the use of media, games, project-based learning, or flipped classroom approaches, were implemented before other disciplines adopted them. Physical learning spaces are another area in which language education can not only be active, but one that it can lead by creating models and visions of improving on normalized spaces. Such spaces can be an embodied vision of how language education has changed and adapted.

Built Pedagogy, Control, and the Extended Mind

All spaces, including educational spaces, influence, shape, and direct often unconscious (Kroll 1984) and unnoticed ways. "Space is neither innocent nor neutral: it is an instrument of the political; it has a performative aspect for whoever inhabits it; it works on its occupants. At the micro level, space prohibits, decides what may occur, lays down the law, implies a certain order, commands and locates bodies" (Patrick Pouler 1994: 175). Famously, Winston Churchill spoke in favor of the Commons Chamber's rectangular design when its rebuilding was debated after it had been destroyed during the Second World War: "we shape our buildings and afterwards our buildings shape us" (UK Parliament). There is a directive authority in the built form that has a physical, immediate, and personally felt power in stark and subtle ways. Physical spaces, including physical learning spaces, appear to be neutral, objective, concrete, and something that can be measured and described in different ways. But they are also representations of values, processes, structures, cultures, and trends, and they are highly contextual. "[T]he organization of schooling as an educational form is predicated on claims that knowledge can be decontextualized, and yet schools themselves as social institutions and as places of learning constitute very specific contexts" (Lave and Wenger 1991: 40). The design of educational institutions is the embodiment of ideas, values, attitudes, and beliefs: "the design of school buildings, both the exterior shell and the interior ordering of spaces and furnishings, is in a symbiotic relationship with ideas about childhood, education, and community" (Grosvenor and Burke 2008: 12). Higher education spaces as well represent more than merely functional containers for education—they serve as built expressions of a value system, implicitly or explicitly, consciously or unconsciously, sometimes intentionally, but often unintentionally. Bringing intentionality into their design, just as Churchill proclaimed, can lead to spaces more attuned to an institution's values and goals.

Built Pedagogy

The design of the classroom or any other learning space embodies educational ideologies and philosophies (Monahan 2002). Monahan argues that a "classroom with neat rows of desks embodies pedagogies or 'tacit curricula' of discipline and conformity, whereas spaces personifying the flexible properties discussed thus far can be said to embody pedagogies of freedom and self-discovery." Later, Monahan (2005: 34) further refines his definition of built pedagogy: it "describes how spaces teach individuals proper comportment through affordances that privilege certain movements, activities, or states of being over others ... Built pedagogy further signifies the ideologies and values embodied in material structures, in tangent with the social practices that constitute space and saturate it with meaning." Oblinger (2006) defines built pedagogy in her seminal edited volume simply as "the ability of space to define how one teaches." Lawn (1999: 75) asserts that "the classroom was designed and built to represent and shape a particular form of teaching behaviour." Different classrooms designs and setups can create different affordances, and thus make some activities more or less likely to occur. Michelson (1970: 25) calls this concept "intersystems congruence." For example, rows of permanently installed benches will not permit the teacher or students to easily change the classroom configuration, making activities such as group work less likely. The design of the classroom can change how students and teachers feel and act:

> Properties are spatial characteristics that can be used to transform behavior and mood. Each of these characteristics is adjustable and can be calibrated—on a scale, as in from "open" to "closed"—to radically alter the mood in a situation. These are simple tweaks, and even a small change to a single property can fundamentally alter the nature of an interaction (Doorley and Witthoft 2012: 43). Strange and Banning (2001: 21) illustrate how the arrangement of furniture (see also chapter 4) and its distance and arrangement influence the mood and expectations: "If a student walks into a classroom and the teaching podium is 20 feet away from the first row of chairs, then a distinct message regarding the formal nature of the upcoming classroom experience is communicated very clearly."

Guerrettaz (2021) analyzes how a language classroom, or "classroomscape," and its traditional layout and its conventions changed a language teacher's pedagogical authority. The text of the classroom prompts its users to follow invisible yet socially and conventionally agreed-upon expectations and roles.

Controlling Bodies, Controlling Minds

As discussed earlier, physical learning spaces are not merely empty containers but contain all kinds of materials: "objects, bodies, technologies and settings," which "permit some actions, and prevent others" (Fenwick 2015: 85). These all work in a connected way, sometimes subtly, sometimes overtly. At a basic level, space orders, commands, and locates bodies. Foucault (1977: 143) famously described spaces of enclosure within a disciplinary machinery, such as prison cells and monastic cells. This also can extend to traditional classrooms:

> This machinery works in space in a much more flexible and detailed way. It does this first of all on the principle of elementary location or *partitioning*. Each individual has his own place; and each place its individual. Avoid distributions in groups; break up collective dispositions; analyze confused, massive or transient pluralities. Disciplinary space tends to be divided into as many sections as there are bodies or elements to be distributed.

Hamilton (2013: 5) describes the design and management of schools and factories as machineries of control: "the social philosophies that inform their respective management practices are just as important as the technological developments that govern their choice of material resources. Indeed, educational production, like its industrial counterpart, entails a fusion of both technical and social considerations." Educational institutions' functions are set apart from the rest of society, from other spaces. Many US institutions of higher learning were built in remote areas during previous centuries, away from population centers to promote a cloistered and undistracted learning environment. Likewise, boundaries for primary and secondary schools were not permeable:

> Elements of the population seen as impurities are by the nineteenth century confined in a range of institutions with common architectural languages: the asylum, the workhouse, the infirmary, the prison and the school, whilst the productive poor are incarcerated in factories. Not only the deviant, vagrant and insane but also the dead, who deflate the notion of perfection in their putrefaction, and the mess of the living, are, from the eighteenth century, excluded from the visible and sensible city.
>
> (Miles 1997: 33)

There are subtler ways of increased surveillance and discipline, such as the direction and arrangement of desks, as Hutchison and Orr (2004: 78) point out: "the arrangement of desks into cells makes both for clearer pathways in and around each student's desk and metaphorically supports the notion of the individual as a discrete learning unit." Reform-minded educators and scholars, such as the American pragmatist John Dewey (1991), have long ago connected the physical space with the educational mission and philosophies, including the issue of control:

> If we put before the mind's eye the ordinary schoolroom, with its rows of ugly desks placed in geometrical order, crowded together so that there shall be as little moving room as possible, desks almost all of the same size, with just space

enough to hold books, pencils, and paper, and add a table, some chairs, the bare walls, and possibly a few pictures, we can reconstruct the only educational activity that can possibly go on in such a place. It is all made "for listening"—because simply studying lessons out of a book is only another kind of listening; it marks the dependency of one mind upon another.

The furniture itself, further discussed in Chapter 4, imparts levels of control. Grosvenor and Burke (2008: 10) write that "[D]esign features that permit observation and surveillance—controlling, ordering and disciplining children within the school walls—have always been crucial, and continue to be part of modern schooling, and they have always exploited technological developments, for example chairs designed to control posture." Furniture controls sitting positions, which include "social significance," sets of conventions, and "orthopedic constraints" (Fiell and Fiell 2000: 7). For example, students are made to face in a certain direction, or prevented from wiggling or changing positions (Bendele 1984): "By having students face the same direction and sit apart from one another, the challenges of surveillance and discipline are managed more easily" (Hutchison and Orr 2004: 78). Control of students is also achieved through segmentation according to age or aptitude, beginning in the eighteenth century:

> "[R]ank" begins to define the great form of distribution of individuals in the educational order: rows or ranks of pupils in the class, corridors, courtyards; rank attributed to each pupil at the end of each task and each examination; the rank he obtains from week to week, month to month, year to year; an alignment of age groups, one after another; a succession of subjects taught and questions treated, according to an order of increasing difficulty (Foucault 1977: 146–7). The hierarchical system was directly tied to the physical space, as students moved up from one row to the next, and could still be found in some schools in Germany in the beginning of the 20th century (Bendele 1984). The term "sitzen bleiben" (literally "to stay seated") is still used today in German for students who have not successfully completed a school year and must repeat the whole year. The system of control is achieved through symbolic, spatial, technological, and procedural attributes, which will be dealt in further detail in chapter 4.3; their conscious choice can be used to align values and missions that differ from those of control, surveillance, and strict hierarchies.

Foucault (1977: 148) deconstructs the complex system put in place:

> In organizing "cells," "places" and "ranks," the disciplines create complex spaces that are at once architectural, functional and hierarchical. It is spaces that provide fixed positions and permit circulation; they carve out individual segments and establish operational links; they mark places and indicate values;

they guarantee the obedience of individuals, but also a better economy of time and gesture. They are mixed spaces: real because they govern the disposition of buildings, rooms, furniture, but also ideal, because they are projected over this arrangement of characterizations, assessments, hierarchies.

Panopticism refers to surveillance and the "homogenous effects of power" (Foucault 1977: 202) and control it produces. It can be achieved through technologies, but also through systems, regulations, and "through the disciplines, those tiny, everyday, physical mechanisms, those systems of micropower that are essentially non-egalitarian and asymmetrical. The disciplines characterise, classify, specialise; they distribute along a scale, around a norm, hierarchise, individuals in relation to one another and, if necessary, disqualify and invalidate" (Sarup 1982: 20). Classrooms, supported by their architectural design and choice and arrangements of furniture, are spaces of enclosure in multiple ways. Their design is not unimportant. They keep knowledge production confined to an agreed-upon space, they keep certain actors in and out, they restrict movement and flow, and they reinforce social expectations and hierarchies. "In today's schools no less than earlier ones, the abiding concern is with accounting for the location of bodies and not the development of minds. Scholastic progress is checked sporadically but the location of the bodies is accounted for several times daily" (Oldenburg 1999: 278). As very personal spaces for students and teachers—highly regulated through rules, timetables, degree and age requirements, appointments—classrooms are nearly invisible to all those outside of them, both physically and figuratively.

Curriculum

The design of curricula is a central part in guiding the design of learning spaces and is in return influenced by their design. How curricula are designed, and by whom, influences teacher autonomy and thus the use of space. Ferster (2014: 1) describes the concept of teacher proofing as the "practice of limiting the autonomy of individual teachers to produce a more uniform and controlled experience. Various techniques include strict curricular content control and rigid pacing guidelines, high-stakes testing, standardized textbooks, and practices such as direct instruction." Hamilton (2013: 153–4) critiques these trends as standardization alienates schooling from society:

> At root, technocratic thinking is driven by a vision of control and standardization. It succeeds, therefore, to the degree that it is able to create teacher-proof and learner-proof curricula, and to the degree that it can ignore the differences

among schools and schoolrooms. But, in its denial of the goal-setting capacities of teachers and learners, and in its denial of variations among school settings, technocratic thinking is ultimately self-defeating. Schooling designed to its specifications is alienated from the social, economic and political anchor-points that, hitherto, have held it in place. It remains "of" society but ceases to be "in" society.

Often, control works best, Löw (2016: xix) argues, when such institutionalized arrangements and spaces are not perceived consciously: "Accordingly, the synthesizing of social goods to yield spaces, the drawing boundaries, and the constitution of places take place effectively when they can rely on existing knowledge that is already established in conventions and routines." We find such arrangements in curricula, policies, and the structuring, standardizing, and normalizing of conventions and their material embodiments: class schedules, bells, meeting protocols, voting procedures, timetables, etc. Stakeholders, including students and instructors, adapt to the physical settings and their materialities in which their educational activities take place. Each one of these materialities seems to not matter very much individually. But it is their combined assemblage that influences learning and teaching: they "*act*, together with other types of things and forces, to exclude, invite, and regulate activity" (Fenwick 2015: 87). Physical learning spaces and the materials they contain collect, reinforce, and influence educational practices.

Extended Cognition

Learning spaces are an extension of cognition. Recently, there has been increased interest and research in how our brains are not isolated from the outside world. *Situated cognition* explores the role place plays in cognition. We can be in a variety of spaces at the same time and "learning can plausibly be said to take place in a multiplicity and diversity of sites" (Edwards and Usher 2008: 90). For example, I can be in my office while on a zoom call with my students spread across the state. I can also be in a learning management system and our shared cloud storage spaces simultaneously. But our bodies can only be in one physical place at a time, and this influences how we think and learn. One such process is *priming*: "Because simply thinking of an action prepares the mind to perform it, priming guides us through our daily routines without our having to exert mental effort in thinking what we should do next" (Goleman 2007: 47). Cox (2018: 1078) argues that "physical characteristics of the places where learning happens may influence learning as a process." For example, a language student walking into a language classroom, an L2 language-only dining hall, or a language self-access center, will already have primed their mind to engage with the L2, creating an immersive effect. Through intentional design, that effect can be intensified and focused.

Embodied cognition examines our bodies and their role in thinking and learning. The body-mind link is well established. Just thinking about a difficult exam, for example, can trigger a number of physical responses and sensations, such as sweating, shaking, tingling, or a quickened heartbeat. In return, physical responses and states can influence how well we are able to learn, concentrate, communicate, or participate. If our body is too hot or cold, we might not be able to perform as well as when we are in a comfortable temperature setting. Such physical influences can include visual stimuli, auditory signals, or olfactory influences. Furthermore, gestures may help with thinking and learning, which is particularly important when it comes to language learning as they can substitute for vocabulary items and concepts that the learner cannot otherwise express. Instructors can use the body to scaffold difficult or new concepts. Movements and body positions are another aspect of embodied cognition: "The thoughts we have when walking are different from those we have when sitting … How we read text on a tablet differs from how we read a traditional book, partly because of the physical differences … The experiences of the senses are culturally shaped" (Cox 2018: 1078). The situatedness of physical learning spaces in different cultural contexts is important to consider in the design process. Learners and instructors are used to settings and materialities based on their location and culture. One other aspect of embodied cognition is thinking with objects. This has been widely studied with children, especially younger ones, but is also influential in different fields, such as museum pedagogy and languages. "[L]anguage pedagogy," Guerrettaz (2021: 41) posits, "is also a purposeful human activity involving human–object engagements and praxis." An instructor holding up a physical representation of a vocabulary item and passing it to a student allows not only for creating a mental connection between the two but also a shared classroom experience.

Distributed cognition is a third important type of extended cognition. It involves thinking and learning with other people. As many newer approaches to language learning emphasize communication and practice with partners and within small groups, this type of cognition is an important factor when considering physical language learning spaces. The connection made when communicating with other humans is important in the learning process and creates an *interbrain circuit*: "When two entities loop together, their brains send and receive an ongoing stream of signals that allow them to create tacit harmony—and, if the flow goes the right way, amplify their resonance. Looping lets feelings, thoughts, and actions synchronize. We send and receive internal states for better or for worse—whether laughter and tenderness, or tension and rancor" (Goleman 2007: 40). Such "physical synchronies" through gestures and expressions and the resulting "shared rhythm of movement" (Mathews and Soistmann 2016: 105) make certain behaviors more likely, more common, more expected, and even more enjoyable. A shared connection can be supported through physical learning spaces in both formal and informal settings and influence desired behaviors.

Another useful approach to situate materialities more intentionally in educational processes is *pedagogical ergonomics*, which "integrates the three branches of traditional ergonomics—cognitive, social, and physical—to eschew artificial boundaries between human thought, social activity, and the material world …" (Guerrettaz 2021: 41). The proposed framework integrates theory and praxis, and is based in the reality of much of what language instruction is. Ergonomics help us understand human behavior in interacting systems that are purposeful and allow us to apply that to design interactions in concrete, real settings (Wilson 2000). It is an interdisciplinary and multi-disciplinary approach to include disparate components into a seamless whole. By mindful design and choice of spatial properties, we change behaviors and moods: "Each of these characteristics is adjustable and can be calibrated—on a scale, as in from 'open' to 'closed'—to radically alter the mood in a situation. These are simple tweaks, and even a small change to a single property can fundamentally alter the nature of an interaction" (Doorley and Witthoft 2012: 43). They discuss six different categories: posture (physical positioning of the human body), orientation (positioning of people and assets relative to each other), surface (orientation of work surfaces and planes), ambiance (atmospheric quality of an environment), density, and storage. Chapter 4 discusses design processes that allow us to intentionally align properties with values and educational goals.

Ideologies—Toward Learning Spaces That Support a More Open Pedagogy

Hutchison and Orr (2004: 27) argue that "when it comes to teaching and learning, educational institutions are as much ideological constructions of place as they are physical buildings." Physical learning spaces are not separate from ideologies, methods, approaches, schools of thought, and beliefs. As discussed above, often they can be their physical embodiments and representations. Some approaches and methods do not specifically address the physical and focus more on other aspects; for others, physical space as an agentive entity is emphasized. For example, whole-body learning, Total Physical Response (TPR), Montessori, and Waldorf all include the physical environment, natural or built or both. In the Reggio Emilia approach, the environment is often referred to as the *Third Teacher* (the first and second being the teacher and the parent(s)). Physical learning spaces are influenced by ideologies and often externalize and reinforce them. Edwards and Usher (2008: 128) argue that "education's 'spaces of enclosure' of the book, the classroom and the curriculum have always worked to enclose meaning and experience such that learning becomes the extraction of a singular canonical understanding and teaching the exercise of authority in terms of correct interpretation and accuracy." Moreno Martínez (2005: 82) describes Dewey's complaints:

> Furniture provides evidence, a palpable, material witness of what happens in the heart of the school, a means at the service of a certain style of teaching. The geometric layout of the furniture, very close so that there is as little movement in the room as possible, with only the space indispensable for placing books, paper and pencil, clearly indicates an intellectualist school where learning is conceived of as listening, passivity.

Chapter 4 will elaborate on how design decisions should be based on values, goals, and educational missions. *How* we design spaces for language learning (and teaching) depends on educators', programs', and institutions' beliefs about learning. Lawn (1999: 75) argues that "the classroom was designed and built to represent and shape a particular form of teaching behaviour." The same goes for all learning spaces, not just classrooms. Indeed, what *kinds* of spaces we build matters as much as their individual properties and attributes.

Mathews and Soistmann (2016: 122) link our understanding of learning to our learning spaces: "Learning is not linear. So shouldn't our spaces operate in this manner as well?" In order to even begin to think about transforming learning spaces for language learning, we must agree on fundamental principles, which can form the basis of design processes. "It seems obvious but is often forgotten: Teaching and learning should shape the building, not vice versa" (OWP/P Architects, VS Furniture and Bruce Mau Design 2010: 69). Chapter 2 will look more closely at learning and teaching in general and language learning and teaching in particular. Understanding the research, methods, beliefs, principles, standards, and goals will help us not only define them better. It may also lead us to uncover discrepancies between the physical spaces and the education that they embody.

Conclusion

Physical language learning spaces are sociomaterial assemblages that overlap and are intertwined and woven with other types of non-physical spaces, including conceptual, experiential, virtual, and symbolic learning spaces. The metaphor of weaving is a useful one, as we cannot separate physical and non-physical learning spaces from each other. Physical spaces are influenced by less tangible spaces, by conventions, ideologies, beliefs, methodologies, and procedures. They are mental extensions and agentive frameworks consisting of materials, humans, and their intra-actions.

The basic blueprint of the physical language classroom has not changed all that much in over a century, even as new language teaching methods and approaches, new technologies, and new interdisciplinary insights into better ways to support learning have greatly advanced during that same timeframe. Usually, we regard the physical classroom as a container for technologies, but we can also understand it as a technology itself: "[I]t is a design solution, or series of solutions, to a problem. It is, at the same time, a simple machine, a process of systematic solutions and a particular way or thread of thinking about using technology" (Lawn 1999: 68). If we regard physical spaces as technologies, we can apply Stephen Bax' (2011) insights into the normalization of technologies. They have become generally accepted as the norm of a formal learning space, and the more active learning spaces that have been developed more recently have not yet become normalized. Skill and Young (2002: 31) argued two decades ago that "[T]he classroom is no longer the center of the learning universe. Traditional 'teaching boxes' must be redesigned to support collaborative and self-directed learning." It can be a challenge to conceive of other ways to design and build them to be more flexible and supportive of new approaches to language teaching, such as hybrid, student-centered, project-based, or mobile language learning.

This chapter tried to lay the foundation for an analysis and potential design of physical language learning spaces. Such spaces have a long history of conventions that are rooted in values and goals not necessarily still prioritized today. Learning space types and designs, such as the classroom, have become normalized and thus almost invisible. But today's spaces should better reflect and support our values and goals in the area of language learning. They could and should embody them in their intentional design and construction. Just as we pay close attention to other materialities, such as handouts, PowerPoint slides, or the structure of our course management systems and sites, so too should we be more deliberate in framing our physical environments. Through built pedagogy, our physical learning spaces create a hidden curriculum and subtly exert power over what students learn and how faculty teach.

So how can we unthink how we design physical language learning spaces and envision better spaces? How can we "un-normalize" our current space concepts? There are certainly no quick fixes. Simply replacing one type of chair for another or buying newer computers does not necessarily address the fundamental paradigm. But we can start by being more intentional, by supporting and training faculty in physical space use, and talking more openly about the physical aspects of language learning and teaching. The technology analogy can provide some possible ways forward. Bax (2003) refers to the "sole agent fallacy" as "the common assumption that the key or only factor in successful implementation of the technology is the technology itself" (p. 26): it is "clear that normalisation depends on far more than the attributes of the technology itself or any other sole agent, and that it involves a host of social and cultural elements operating together in complex ways" (Bax 2011: 13). Bijker (1997: 6) argues that "one should never take the meaning of a technical artifact or technological system as residing in the technology itself. Instead, one must study how technologies are shaped and acquire their meanings in the heterogeneity of social interactions." Discussions and visions of learning spaces should center on the intricate concept of learning itself, how it distinguishes from teaching, its frequent conflation with, yet distinction from, credentialing, the beliefs held by stakeholders, the disparity between theory and praxis, the influence of systems on its conception, and our aspirations for its implementation. Fenwick et al. (2011: 167–8) support this framework view:

> [S]ociomaterial arenas accept the fundamental uncertainty of practices and activity, such as those involved in educational processes. They suggest practical approaches for both understanding and experimenting productively with and inside education's radical contingency, without resorting simply to either complicated mechanisms of control, or to passive surrender to impossible undecidability. This does not mean that these arenas fail to generate a political project, educative purpose, or practical strategies for more democratic, more just and imaginative education. What their proponents argue, in fact, is that to actually reconfigure, even transform, the complexities of systems holding

current practices firmly in place, we need educational analyses and alternatives that take account of all the materialities in play. These are often difficult to discern and understand as they engage with more than the human social, cultural, and psychological elements that are so central in much educational research.

If we regard physical languages learning spaces as sociomaterial assemblages, we must deconstruct the complex elements that are attached to them. The following chapter takes a closer look at what makes language learning different from that of other disciplines and subject areas.

2

From Generic to Discipline-Specific: Properties of Language Learning Spaces

Physical language learning spaces share many characteristics with generic learning spaces. But they are also marked by several characteristics that are specific to the field of language learning. Learning a language has unique properties, goals, and practices that differ from those of other disciplines. Most physical learning spaces are generic to allow for flexibility. For example, most classrooms can be used not only for languages but many other subject areas and disciplines as well. Languages are usually not considered to be among disciplines and subjects that necessarily need dedicated learning spaces, such as art, theater, many of the natural sciences, physical education, etc. They are generally included in a group of subjects that includes most of the humanities in most cases and that are usually housed in generic physical spaces, most often classrooms. But this is a simplified, superficial categorization that does not take into account the many ways that language learning differs from other disciplines. In fact, much of the learning spaces research either focuses on generic spaces, more STEM-oriented spaces, or generic communal and social spaces, such as libraries. With some exceptions, there is very little published on matching physical spaces to language education.

This chapter seeks to highlight the unique properties of language education in relation to physical learning space design. What makes language learning different from other types of learning? Much of this depends on the goals and philosophies of how we view language education. "[T]he *how* and the *where* of language learning" Benson (2021: 91) argues, "are inseparable from an environmental point of view." If we follow more recent approaches, language education tends to be highly communicative; is dependent on scaffolding; is prone to utilize a variety media and modes; incorporates different interactional forms, such dyads, triads, groups, or individual work; pays particular attention to motivation and affect; and seeks to use the target language as the instructional discourse language. There has also been a long trend of moving from teacher-centric models to student-centric models: "Foreign language education has made great efforts to decenter the language teaching enterprise away from the authority of the teacher, the textbook, the literary canon, the academic ivory tower, and focus it on the actual needs of actual language learners, the *vox populi* of the language learning enterprise" (Kramsch 1993: 236).

As discussed in the previous chapter, built pedagogy is the matching of educational philosophies to the built environment. This chapter discusses properties of recent language teaching methods and approaches and second language acquisition research with the goal of conceptualizing design implications, which are then developed in the following chapters.

Matching Learning Spaces' Properties to Language Learning Goals and Standards

As a discipline, language education is guided by well-established guidelines, standards, and goals. In the United States, the American Council on the Teaching of Foreign Languages (ACTFL) World-Readiness Standards for Language Learning are a good starting point for our discussion as they provide a reliable common denominator for creating criteria for physical language learning spaces. The "World-Readiness Standards for Learning Language" by ACTFL, often also known in the field as "the 5 C's," provide an integrated framework that focuses on five key goal areas: Communication, Cultures, Connections, Comparisons, and Communities. Each of these contains two or three specific standards. Due to the focus of this book, I will discuss only those that interface with physical language learning spaces in particular.

Communication

The goal of Communication, which includes interpersonal, interpretive, and presentational communication, is certainly influenced by the modality and space of instruction. For interpretive communication, the role of acoustics for listening and light for reading is of particular importance. Sound in physical spaces matters because L2 learners have to direct considerable cognitive resources toward receiving, decoding, and interpreting sound input. If not all parts of a sentence or utterance are received, it is particularly difficult to compensate for the lost information to be filled in. There is also an equity and accessibility argument to be made, which we will discuss later in Chapter 4, as not all learners might receive the same amount and quality of audio input. Furthermore, noise and sounds external to a course or learning situation can lead to distraction, higher cognitive load, and even promote anxiety or stress. Sound can be managed in different ways, through the initial design of a physical space, through postoccupancy changes and additions, and through course processes and rules. Different flooring materials have different levels of sound absorption. Carpet, for example, in contrast to smooth surfaces like linoleum or concrete, reduces echoes. Sound is influenced by wall materials, number and type of items on the walls, amount of furniture and objects, ceiling height and materials, etc. All of the materials have other characteristics unrelated to sound and must be balanced and chosen according to what priorities and goals exist for any given space. For example, the ability to clean floors and furniture might be in tension with the wish to have more soft-touch, sound-absorbing materials. Once a space is built, other materials can be added retroactively, such as wall, ceiling, and floor treatments, or sound-absorbing furniture. Rugs may be added but can make a space less accessible and might be a tripping hazard. Policies, rules, and expectations can also provide soundscapes, and an intentional approach can yield beneficial results: Will doors or windows be opened? Who moves furniture around, when, and how often? What devices are acceptable to be used?

Light is crucial for many language interpretive communication classroom activities. Typically, students will read handouts, consult their notes, scan their textbooks, or look at a screen, TV, blackboard, or smartboard. Since electrical lighting has become common in many language classrooms throughout the world, we do not pay particular attention to light, but it is a crucial component in physical environments. Optimal lighting is context dependent. When students view a video clip on a screen they need dimmed lights, whereas reading a text on a handout requires brighter lights. Ideally the space enables the instructor and its learners to change the lightscapes throughout a class session, depending on the activity. Innovations in recent years, such as LED lighting and smart lighting, have led to new possibilities in learning space design. Inspiration can be taken from the airline industry, which now has constantly but subtly changing colors and brightness on its newest planes. This creates different effects and moods for different activities, such as when entering the plane, during meal service, before a sleep period, after waking up, or before landing. The research from this industry can help customize lightscapes to support different activities in the classroom, promote alertness, or reduce anxiety. Lighting when it is dark outside should be different from lighting during a bright, sunny day. Incorporating natural lighting is also of importance. Later in the book, the concept of biophilia is discussed further. But for this section, it should be noted that natural light can be included in the initial design phase but can also be used post occupancy by using different kinds of window shades. Presentational communication likewise would benefit from these considerations. Interpersonal communication is even more complex and will be discussed further below.

Connections

The standard "Making connections" in the goal area "Connections" highlights the need to connect to other disciplines, perspectives, and practices. In physical spaces, this goal can be reinforced and intentionally designed, through interdisciplinary spaces, makerspaces, transitory spaces, social spaces, and experiential spaces. These connections can be bidirectional. Students studying languages can be guided toward other disciplines, and students not focusing on languages can be brought into proximity and awareness of languages through physical space design. One example is an active hallway with information and inspiration regarding languages through which nonlanguage students pass and which allows for students from different disciplines and backgrounds to meet and mingle. Interdisciplinary spaces can combine different disciplinary areas and foster synergies among them. Chapter 3 provides more concrete examples.

Communities

The standard "School and Global Communities" in the goal area "Communities" emphasizes that "Learners use the language both within and beyond the classroom to interact and collaborate in their community and the globalized world." This underscores the need to understand language spaces as more than formal learning spaces, such as classrooms and language labs or centers. It calls for a more expansive view that includes experiential spaces, informal spaces, and social spaces. For example, study abroad or international support spaces can be integrated with language learning spaces, providing a rich social environment that makes community building more likely. Again, this could and should be supported by robust processes and programming.

Another goal area is lifelong learning. Positive spaces and associations created therein create lasting, positive associations and memories. Spaces that students experience not only as comfortable, but those in which they feel they belong, which are meaningful, and which promote wellbeing to the body and the mind, can make a positive impact. It is important to note that the standards discussed thus far pertain to the United States. In other parts of the world, other standards apply, such as the European Framework for Languages in Europe. Standards are localized, as is how we need to conceive learning spaces. "Affirmations of standards may mask an imperative for homogeneity. Education based in Perth *should* be different from that offered in New York, Brighton or Osaka" (Brabazon 2007: 208).

Language Teaching Methods and Approaches

The standards discussed above are a useful guide to match language learning space properties to spatial properties because they are mostly agreed-upon. Language teaching methodologies, approaches, ideologies, and beliefs, on the other hand, are often hotly debated, often contested, and constantly evolving. But they matter in how they influence and inform the design and usage of physical learning spaces. Favoring project-based education, community-based learning, or focus on form will result in three different sets of design parameters and learning spaces characteristics. Chapter 3 further details how some methodologies resulted in specific examples of built pedagogy. While methodologies and approaches in language education tend to be well defined, it is less clear when we add in the myriad individual beliefs as well as new trends. There is no shortage of new pedagogical ideas and postulates, as can be seen in Cerbin and Chew's (2017) cynical "buzzword wasteland" list:

> If we were to synthesize current trends in pedagogy, we would conclude that the best teaching practice is: high impact, student centered, engaging, hands-on, just-in-time, technology enhanced, flipped, blended, hybrid, transformational, cooperative, collaborative, reflective, authentic, situated, guided, integrative, supplemental, reciprocal, gamified, experiential, adaptive, disruptive and active. It is also brain based, peer based, inquiry based, group based, team based, project based, case based, community based, discovery based, competency based, evidence based, mastery based, research based, service based, problem based and data driven, not to mention massive, open and online.

For physical spaces such new trends can be a challenge, as the built environment is much slower (and costlier) to adapt to new trends and ideas. Physical spaces must be flexible enough to be able to adapt to trends not yet foreseeable.

How we view learning and our beliefs matter in space design. Many of our learning space assemblages include processes and structures, which suggest linearity and a certain type of logical path: there is a segmentation to daily and semesterly schedules, we have successive units or modules in our courses, you go from middle to high school, from junior college to college, from French 101 to French 102, from high school diploma to a BA to an MA to a Ph.D., etc. Some newer physical space designs tend to deemphasize such linearity and segmentation and highlight the complex and often not well understood nature of learning.

At this point it is worth noting that the educational terms of *teaching*, *learning*, and *credentialing* are related yet distinct. When we speak about *learning*, we emphasize learners and their development. This *can* happen without formal instructors, structures, courses, grades, tests, etc. *Teaching* involves a person who structures, guides, assists, mentors, and or assesses learners, usually but not necessarily in an institutional or otherwise structured environment. *Credentialing* involves some kind of course credit and formal assessment mechanisms that create tokens, such as grades, related to certain performance measures. How a language is learned matters in regard to what properties physical spaces should embody. There are also secondary or additional learning goals that may not be directly related to language learning. Good citizenship, active listening to each other and the teacher, respect, resilience, critical thinking, and empathy are all examples of learning goals that may not be stated explicitly as outcomes in language education, and yet they can be secondary goals.

Conclusion

Physical spaces can support and emphasize certain learning ideologies, beliefs, methods, or approaches. Through built pedagogy, they can reinforce existing structures and concepts, but they can also be agents of change (Oblinger 2006; Murray and Lamb 2018a). When designing new spaces or redesigning or reconceptualizing existing ones, a fundamental discussion about what language learning is is crucial. This process will be discussed in more detail in Chapter 4.

Context is crucially important in conceptualizing physical language learning spaces. Younger learners have other needs than older students. A residential campus differs from a commuter school. Smaller seminars are different from larger classes. Courses in commonly taught languages have different needs than less commonly taught languages or Indigenous languages. General language courses differ from "languages for specific purposes" (LSP) courses. Space considerations must be situated and context dependent. It should be noted that the above-mentioned goals and standards target instructed language learning. If we look at learning more holistically, other factors need to be included as well.

Physicality, Materials, and Scaffolding

Physicality, Movement, and Language Learning

In recent years there has been an increased interest in the physicality of the learner. The body, with all its needs, attributes, and characteristics, matters in the learning process. "Our scientific journals mostly proceed from the premise that the mental organ is a disembodied, placeless, asocial entity, a 'brain in a vat'" (Paul 2021: ix). Cox (2018: 1078) supports this by arguing that learning "is experienced as an embodied, not just a cognitive (and emotional), process." Language learning is an embodied activity, and language education and communication are not purely cognitive but also physical acts. Zheng, Newgarden, and Young (2012: 339–40) argue that language education is about "doing" and involves "whole physical bodies and the world we experience and act on."

Many language courses are highly physical in praxis, something not necessarily reflected in past and current research: "Language education research must adapt to better reflect the 'general project' of language teaching practice, which is tangible action in the sociomaterial world" (Guerrettaz 2021: 62). The pandemic and the move to emergency remote instruction highlighted for many just how much the body matters. This was embodied in the masks, hand-sanitizing stations, plexiglass shields, social distancing signage and floor treatments, ever-evolving rules, forbidden gestures such as handshakes, and cohort schedules. We understood the body to be a major agent in the learning process in a much more direct way during the pandemic, and not just regarded it as a given. Chapter 5 explores the implications of this further, in addition to other learning modalities, and envisions a future that takes these lessons into account.

Benson (2021: 102) argues that language learners require a certain infrastructure, both language resources as well as nonlinguistic resources:

> They also require what might be called a certain "furniture," consisting of places to meet and study, comfortable chairs and tables to sit at, snacks and cups of tea or coffee, things to look at and talk about and so on. These are not necessarily language-bearing resources (although they often are); rather, they represent the infrastructure of the settings in which learners interact with language resources.

These very tangible, often seemingly mundane things are important to individuals and learning processes: "The importance of the sensory aspect of this learning landscape, reminds us that the body is central to learning. It does not seem convincing to see learning as simply about quieting the body so that the mind can think, in some Cartesian dualism" (Cox 2018: 1087). Even more so, we must recognize that people and their bodies create spaces. "The variety of spatial phenomena cannot simply be derived from the building form; rather, it forces us to recognize that the emergence of space is not only bound to the materiality of the objects built, but also to the movement of bodies" (Löw 2016: xii).

Any practitioner knows that the physical plays a role in many language classes and other learning situations: the room is too cold or hot, there's a storm outside that is distracting, a student is late and interrupts an activity, someone brings food to the class and its smells, the loudspeaker crackles and the sound it emits is difficult to listen to, someone has to go to the bathroom, etc. These are all scenarios that have an impact. The question of whether restricting or encouraging physical movement in learning spaces is an old one. Some research explores how learners with certain learning disabilities can benefit from allowing movement or fidgeting (more on that in Chapter 4).

For language learning in particular, the body plays an important role. Engman and Hermes (2021: 102) assert that "[L]anguage is a multimodal range of sense making and relating that includes embodiment, gestures, senses, gaze, memory, and verbal production." Receiving and sending information is a physical act, whether listening through one's ears, reading with one's eyes, writing with one's fingers, and speaking with one's mouth. Several language learning methods and approaches have paid attention to physicality and movement, such as total physical response (TPR), Silent Way, or Suggestopedia. Regardless of the approach, physicality is included in many activities directly or indirectly, through pairing students or building groups, through handouts and other materials, or through encouraging gestures or movements. Such physical dynamics often happen unconsciously and in unplanned ways, and have been underrepresented until recently in training and research (Guerrettaz 2021). The link of physical activity and learning outcomes has received more attention in recent years as well. Sedentary learning is less effective and even small movements, breaks, or simply standing up for a short moment can promote learning. Liu et al. (2017) report that physical activity can aid language learning both generally as well as at the specific level of training; for example, the lexical level. Paul (2021: 54) writes that "[W]hen we connect movement with information, we activate both types of memory, and our recall is more accurate as a result." This "enactment effect" shows that physical acts can support memorization and cognition (The Enactment Effect 2022). For our purposes that mean that it is important to be more mindful of how physical movement can be more consciously included in language learning situations.

Simply making students aware that movement in the classroom is encouraged can be a first step. As will be discussed later in the book, furniture and other physical design elements can encourage a more intentional approach to acknowledging movement and physicality in the language learning process. Furniture can also support (or hinder) movements and physical activities. Deskless language teaching (Rankin 2018), for example, can be used to create more usable space and more fluidity (see Chapter 4) to encourage movement.

Extended Mind

Chapter 1 argued that cognition is not a process limited to just the mind and the brain. Extralinguistic elements of communication are important for all interlocutors, particularly for language learners during the beginner and intermediate stages. Extralinguistic elements of communication provide scaffolding through gestures, facial expressions, body language, use of objects, use of three-dimensional spaces, etc. Many language learners know that an L2 phone conversation is more difficult than a conversation in person. Many language educators know that using one's body and various objects in a beginning language class that is conducted mostly in the L2 is a useful teaching technique. Gestures, for example, can support spoken language through visual cues, and lower mental load (Paul 2021).

Affordances are important both in formal and informal learning contexts. Within the field of language education, Benson (2021: 95) defines affordances as "objects in the environment that are perceived as resources for learning. Affordances are the resources the environment offers and what learners do with them." Resources can of course also be virtual, but the immediacy and tangible nature of the physical environment makes them particularly useful and at times intuitive. The processes of materializing and externalizing allow users to make the abstract become tangible or visible. There is a performative aspect in the material world that is particularly effective. Fenwick (2015: 85) summarizes Waltz' illustrative example of a school playground, "where equipment combines with children's behaviours to produce particular activities, speech, social groupings and exclusions, injuries, even gender identities. The point is here that material things are performative. They act, together with other types of things and forces, to exclude, invite and regulate particular forms of participation." This also happens with older learners, and in language classes. Learners think in place and with others: their shared activities are situated and distributed. Objects in space, for example images or words on the wall or sounds in a room, can provide opportunities for targeted or incidental exposure (Bisson et al. 2013). In more formal settings, actions tend to be more targeted, planned, and intentional than in more informal contexts. Guerrettaz (2021: 40) conceptualizes classroom interaction as "polysemiotic 'action formation,'" which can be described as "patterns of everyday activities composed of entangled 'action streams.'" These action streams include physical acts and movement, communicative gestures, and linguistic actions.

Materials and Scaffolding

Using materials is not unique to language learning. "Tools, media, and cultural artefacts are the tangible forms, through which we make sense of our world and negotiate meaning with others" (Ackermann 2004: 17). Negotiating meaning, of course, is a tenet and goal of language education. There are particular kinds of materials and pedagogies for language learning and teaching in contrast to other disciplines. Language educators employ a number of such resources: worksheets, handouts, textbooks, posters, realia, games, media, projected PowerPoint slides, etc. Guerrettaz and Johnston (2013: 779) provide a wide definition "of materials as any artifacts that prompt the learning and use of language in the language Classroom." This then includes the physical space itself and anything in it, seen or unseen. Language education makes use of materials as they provide scaffolds for language learning, potentially lowering frustration and cognitive load. They can also provide rich contexts that allow learners to immerse themselves with language and culture that otherwise wouldn't be in their immediate environment. Benson (2021: 97) reminds us that "[I]n second language learning, the target language is a *scarce* resource. It must either find its way into the learner's immediate environment, or the learner must go out and construct an environment in which it is present." Educators can provide access to language-bearing assemblages in a number of ways, including through the physical environment. With the abundance of resources we have access to today in the digital realm, materials in the physical realm can limit and direct in a way that is not overwhelming.

Physical spaces themselves can be scaffolds. Learners spend a lot of time looking at their surroundings, as this personal narrative from a middle schooler's narrative illustrates:

> The walls, funny how we never notice them. The paint, carefully chosen, is always a calm color. Whipped blue, creamy green, warm milk, lemon pudding. Too quiet.

The teachers make it louder. Construction paper, the brightest you can buy, spells out something on the wall. Bulletin boards, some simple with a message, others educational; the best are personal. Posters with cute sayings live on the walls; you get to know them. When you're bored, these walls become your friends.

(Goodall 1997: 86)

In many dedicated language classrooms, especially at the K-12 level, you can find inspirational posters, verb charts, maps, flags, infographics, cartoons, student work, etc. According to Cheryan, Ziegler, Plaut, and Meltzoff (2014), physical features in classrooms can be either symbolic or structural. They can also be both. In general, this distinction can be applied to all materialities used in learning environments. Symbolic and ambient attributes and materials are often individually chosen, and can be enriching, supporting, and inspiring (Rajaee Pitehnoee, Arabmofrad, and Modaberi 2020), but can also have negative effects if their quantity is too high or if they do not fit the space conceptually. In either case, through their choice and placement they send a message to learners about what is important and what should be paid attention to. A grammar chart might be helpful, but it also suggests that grammatical accuracy is valued. Flags can signal an international dimension but also promote a national view of languages and can be exclusionary (see Chapter 4).

Materials are also used for placemaking, which can support the learning process: "When a place embodies an idea, it brings a person's body and whole being into the experience, not only their minds" (Parker 2018: 55). Placing language materials in learning spaces can create an ambiance that implies what activities are expected and supported. If using the target language and not the L1 is a goal in the space, whether it's formal or informal, in class or out of class, symbolic features and materials reinforce what language users should use. Realia are a form of materialities that are particularly appropriate for language learning. There is relatively little research or guidance on using realia within a physical learning spaces' framework:

There are a few guidelines for helping students analyze artifacts, including digital footprints and physical spaces, as a springboard for multimodality in their literacy. Educators can choose to focus on the five senses, which is more approachable for younger children, or go deeper by asking about function, modes of expression, or even what an object says about power relations. Modeling how to critically engage with artifacts through interrogating and examining is key so that objects don't simply become props in the classroom, regardless of the guidelines you choose.

(McFadden 2021)

Guerrettaz and Johnston (2013: 792) argue that "materials offer emergent language learning affordances as the processes and activities of the classroom unfold." Many language centers in the United States, after they transitioned out of their language lab roles, became language *resource* centers, providing materials and artifacts for studying, learning, and teaching of languages. Such materials can provide objects that can be experienced through different senses, that are direct and immediate, that can add authenticity and concreteness. Materials are a scaffold as they can support, structure, and aid language learning. They fill in gaps, prompt communication, and allow learners and educators to use the whole body and learning space as a resource. They provide a space with agency, making it a part of the learning process rather than merely a container.

Conclusion

The physical domain is an important component of communication and language learning processes. The physical bodies of learners and instructors can support communication. Physical spaces can provide additional information, scaffolding, rich environments, and additional materials. If intentionally designed, physical spaces and their materialities can support language learning.

Affect, Motivation, and Wellbeing

Language learning is not merely a cognitive act. It is a complex interplay of cognitive, affective, and psychomotor domains. As previously discussed, physical discomfort can interfere with learning, while advantageous surroundings can support learning. Negative affective variables can also hinder or impede language learning. The affective filter, which can include various feelings, such as lack of motivation or anxieties, can make learning languages less effective. While these feelings are certainly often unrelated to physical space, careful design can help decrease or minimize compounding external negative factors and mitigate their effects. As L2 learning itself can be a cause for anxiety and influence the learning process, well-designed spaces can provide engaging, supportive, restorative, inclusive, and focused environments. Careful space design can help individuals not only learn better but also provide more positive connections and associations with language education. During times of decreasing language enrollments, creating additional factors to support students in choosing language education is critical (Heidrich Uebel, Kronenberg, and Sterling, 2023).

Boys (2011: 34) argues that "affective emotions may be implicit, vague and often unacknowledged but are in fact high-level cognitive abilities, which monitor, interpret and guide us through our encounters with ideas, objects and spaces as well as others." Emotions can be directly tied to not only cognitive processes but also the physical, including "visual, auditory, and tactile sensations" and subjective experiences (Lundström et al. 2016: 419). Emotions are not only experienced through the whole body but also expressed by it (Tversky 2019). "Interpreting others' spoken words and facial expressions may yield only a coolly abstract sense of the emotions that churn within. The body acts as a critical conduit, supplying the brain with the visceral information it lacks" (Paul 2021: 40). Using the body for communication is an often subconscious way of exchanging important information. Without a word, an interlocutor can show joy, fear, disgust, anxiety, etc. For language learning, this cannot be underestimated, as complicated concepts and nuances are difficult to express verbally for even advanced L2 learners. Communicating emotions is more effective when whole bodies are present rather than just parts, whether in person or virtually:

> Bodies, too, express emotion. Bodies have large advantages over faces: they are larger. Bodies can make bigger expressions and they can be seen from a greater distance. Normally, bodies and faces work together, as integrated units. Conveniently, experiments can separate and realign face and body. When face and body are congruent, expressing the same emotion, appraisals are more accurate. If face and body are incongruent, expressing different emotions, the body carries more weight than the face in judging emotions.
>
> (Tversky 2019: 47)

Language learners are often in a "position of subordination," as Kramsch (1993: 238) argues: "Constrained by the linguistic rules of the foreign language and its rules of use, constrained also by their own socialization patterns in their own culture, language learners are indeed in a position of subordination and powerlessness." She argues that even for more advanced learners, such a position, while improving, never goes away: "For acquisition of knowledge and competence in a foreign language is not an additive process, but a dialectic one." This position dynamic is also reflected in the large teacher-student knowledge and skill discrepancy. Teachers not only possess more knowledge of information but also control the class processes when the L2 is the mode of communication in the classroom. Spaces can exacerbate or level these power dynamics. In a classroom without a front, for example, the teacher is less sage on the stage (early classrooms often had a raised teacher desk, and many lecture halls still do) but more a guide on the side. Open and transparent support spaces and offices are more likely to be visited for students who seek help. Some normalized and unconscious classroom design choices support the student-teacher position binary: in most classrooms, the teacher has a different chair and desk than the students do. The students usually all have the same chair, even though their bodies are all different. Chapter 4 provides a more detailed discussion of such choices and their effects.

Stress and anxiety can add to cognitive load, leading to lower learning outcomes. Our minds can only process so much. Choi, van Merriënboer, and Paas (2014) find that the physical environment is indeed a distinct factor in cognitive load considerations. The learning environment can mitigate effects of instruction on cognitive load, and being more intentional in implementing design choices can have a positive effect on not only reducing stress and anxiety but also mental load. The following chapters provide more details and concrete examples. The choices are not only in the design process, but also in classroom policies, which in turn can be supported by space design. For example, allowing for low intensity body movements (rather than sitting still), fidgeting, using mental extensions, and engaging in embodied self-regulation has been shown to be beneficial for learning. Prohibiting such movements and asking students to sit quietly, for example in a classroom setting, increases cognitive load (Paul 2021). Testing is another area of potential stress and anxiety. Rajaee Pitehnoee, Arabmofrad, and Modaberi (2020) report that environmental and spatial factors influence test taking performance. Conacher and Kelly-Holmes (2007: 21) argue that "[D]iversity of learning demands diversity of assessment." It is important to consider designing physical testing environments to match different types of assessment. Chapter 4 further explains ways of designing environments that reduce stress and anxiety.

Motivation

Tohidi and Jabbari (2012: 823) argue that "[B]ecause students are not always internally motivated, they sometimes need situated motivation, which is found in environmental conditions that the teacher creates." Motivation is an individual learner characteristic tied to agency and affect. Physical spaces (and places) are an important factor of people's feelings and sense of wellbeing. Murray and Lamb (2018c: 255) argue that the "relationship between autonomy and our emotional, psychological and physical well-being must not be underestimated." Physically providing autonomy can be functional or symbolic and can be done on a small scale. Providing the ability to choose—for example, between different seating locations or furniture options—to move and rearrange furniture, to decorate a space, or to personalize are simple ways of providing learners and teachers with some autonomy. Paul (2021: 126) posits that "when people occupy spaces that they consider their own, they experience themselves as more confident and capable. They are more efficient and productive. They are more focused and less distractible." Alzubaidi et al. (2016) found that there is a correlation between the perception of the learning environment and learner motivation and self-regulation. Built pedagogy extends to autonomy and motivation as well. When students are given choices and agency in their environment, they receive a signal that they are there not only to react but become active participants. And as we will discuss further in different sections of Chapter 4, ideally stakeholders are included in the design processes to maximize a sense of ownership and agency of spaces and processes. Connection and belonging (see Chapter 4) are also important aspects of helping students and teachers regulate affective factors, providing a basis needed for effective high-level cognitive and interpersonal work.

The following chapter explores specific language learning spaces beyond the classroom. One such specific space to be examined is the language laboratory/language center. Garrett and Liddell (2004: 32) point out the lack of attention given to affective factors in language learning: "where classroom teaching adapted to both affective and cognitive styles of learning, the technology of the language labs remained firmly in the cognitive camp. By the late 1980s, signs of strain in the infrastructure of language learning at the postsecondary level could be roughly summed up as: methodological, technological, professional, and structural." Such spaces adapted over the decades, and now often focus more holistically on factors such as social space, wellbeing, inclusivity, belonging, and access. Built pedagogy, as discussed previously, is a lens through which we can include new insights and research of learning and language learning into the physical space design.

Taylor and Enggass (2009: 79) provocatively state: "Can't learn in Ugly." This is a simplification because of course you *can* learn in unattractive environments. But aesthetics play a role, albeit a more complicated one. Other than focusing on individual perceptions of aesthetics, it is important to focus on agency and autonomy in spaces. "Clearly, how learners feel in a space is important and has an impact on their engagement within that context and their learning. How we experience autonomy and the role our emotions and feelings have in the creation of spaces and places for learning opens up a number of lines of enquiry to be pursued in the future" (Murray and Lamb 2018c: 256). When consulting for a liberal arts college, I asked the local language students to show me their most and least favorite learning spaces. They led me to the newly constructed campus center. Everything was pre-arranged and there was nothing you could change about the space. The new lounge chairs were all the same size and from the same brand, largely immovable, and the movie posters on the wall had been chosen by the designers, impeccably framed, and neatly arranged. This was the language students' least favorite space. Then they took me to their most favorite space, a co-op cafe run by students. The furniture consisted of upcycled, old, and mismatched couches and tables, and posters and flyers were taped to the walls with blue tape. Why was this the students' favorite learning space? Because they had ownership, they could create their environment, they could make it fit with their values and ideals. The space was a place—full of students, faculty, and visitors—full of life. The space was created not by designers but users. "Space is literally *made* through our interactions" (McGregor 2003: 354). These interactions are difficult to plan, especially for informal spaces. But we can more intentionally provide the right environment and conditions for these to happen.

Identity

Language learning differs from other disciplines in that it takes the medium of communication, the L1, away from learners in a way. In other subject areas, the L1 is the modus operandi and allows learners to convey complex thoughts and information. In language education, the absence of that means a loss of identity. "We can only speak the second language when thoughts, identities and self are aligned. In the new culture and language that means the development of compatible identities that do not negate existing ones, nor erode the self. There is a constant struggle for authenticity and voice in the new language" (Van Lier 2004: 128). Physical space, materialities, and the body can mitigate some of that, allowing to convert information, thoughts, and emotions through other, nonlinguistic means. But there is another aspect crucial for conceptualizing how we design spaces around this particular issue: How can we create environments that allow their users to support and even enrich their identities, how can they provide a sense of safety and protection when their identities cannot be fully expressed? This goes beyond the awkwardness that many language learners experience when their L1 is no longer the basis of communication. The social relationships in language learning situations can be between learners, but there is also the "asymmetric power relationship between the teacher, the all-knowing expert" and the learner, especially those with lower L2 proficiency. It "can pose a significant deterrent to fostering the necessary interactions that prime the SLA pump, over and beyond the usual affective barriers engendered by worry over public embarrassment" (Blake 2008: 98). The physical space in both formal and informal settings can strengthen or soften how such relationships are perceived.

Being intentional and inclusive is a good starting point to acknowledge the learner's individuality: "new physical spaces should be developed as an array of social and study spaces, which also cater to students' emotional needs of comfort, relaxation, identity and belonging" (Hobbs and Dofs 2018: 214). Chapter 4 further explores the idea how spaces and materialities can support diverse stakeholders' identities and provide supportive and enriching spaces.

Conclusion

Language learners' and educators' emotions, sense of wellbeing, and identity influence learning processes. Physical spaces can mitigate potentially negative effects and provide positive environments that support language learning. Reducing anxiety and fear can also support interlocutor communication, foster community building, and create more positive associations with language learning.

Interlocutor Communication

Burr (1996: 39) reminds us that language is a social phenomenon: "it is something that occurs between people, whether they are having a conversation, writing a letter or a book, or filling in their tax return. It is in such exchanges that between people that the construction of the person can take place." As discussed in Chapter 2, ACTFL emphasizes the importance of communication in language education and distinguishes between three modes of communication: interpretive, presentational, and interpersonal. In this section, we will take a closer look at how spaces can facilitate or hinder communication and provide a context for such interactions. As we discuss learning spaces through a disciplinary lens in this chapter, it is important to remind ourselves how language education is quite distinct from other disciplines. It is often much more participatory. Fenwick (2015: 83) argues that "[C]onventional metaphors of knowledge 'acquisition' and transfer are being replaced with understandings of 'participation' and active collective engagement in particular contexts." This is particularly true for language education, which relies on collective action and communications between interlocutors. Bax (2011) notes that these interactions often include social and emotional dimensions. When individuals "do" something—for example, have a conversation or write a document—they usually don't do this alone, but rather act together with other entities. This distributed agency extends not only to other people but also to objects (Guerrettaz 2021). It is prudent, therefore, to critically assess all of these co-actants, including the nonliving ones, and determine their appropriateness for language learning.

Interpretive communication includes receiving information in a variety of ways, such as through handouts, a PowerPoint presentation on a screen, audio or video files, or the voice of the teacher. Language education benefits from the possibilities that new media and technology afford by allowing learners to access mediated content in the target language. As discussed in Chapter 5, the lines between physical and virtual spaces are blurring, providing the opportunities to be in physical and virtual spaces at the same time. Physical space design can provide environments that facilitate transmitting this information. As previously discussed, acoustics and lighting are basic considerations. Providing the necessary hardware and technology that is accessible and easy to be used have also increasingly become the norm of learning space design. But beyond standard practices that can be found in discipline-agnostic learning spaces, languages have some more particular considerations. Making materials accessible, especially physical ones, such as realia, board games, books, and teaching props, seems to be mundane. But practitioners rely on these for many reasons, including scaffolding, sparking interest, directing tasks, providing access, and emphasizing the material side of languages. As these tend to take up space, organizing materials can be solved through design. These considerations, as we will discuss in the following chapters, extend not only to formal learning spaces but informal ones, such as language resource centers, as well. Presentational communication relies on many of these considerations. Felix (2007) argues that speaking in front of a whole class can be quite difficult, making students, especially older ones, feel exposed. Spaces can minimize this anxiety through harmonious design.

Interpersonal communication adds challenges to physical language learning space design as it adds to complexity. In more open learning spaces, such as language centers or language cafes, it is difficult to predict how their users utilize the space and how they organize themselves. In those spaces, we also have both the beauty and the difficulty of multiple languages in one space—learners of a particular language cannot communicate with learners of another language, as they often do not know which language others learn and practice. In more formal learning spaces, such as classrooms, we have more control over interpersonal communication. Furniture choice and arrangement is a powerful tool in managing interlocutor expectations and actions. Cranz (1998: 18) asserts that "arranging seats in rows facing one direction has very different consequences for social interaction and the flow of information than arranging them in a circle. Lining up two chairs side by side, face to face, or at right angles to one another produces three different kinds of communication." Training educators in leveraging such choices can be an important tool in fostering different kinds of communicative scenarios. Harmer (2007) lists possible types of seating arrangements, such as circle, solo work, separate tables, orderly rows, and horseshoe, the last of which he argues are the most common around the world. Rajaee Pitehnoee, Arabmofrad, and Modaberi (2020) discuss different seating patterns and classroom layouts for language learning and found that younger students preferred U-shaped (also called horseshoe) arrangements but do acknowledge that Ramli, Ahmad, and Masri (2013) found that it was the students' least favorite one. Context is crucial and much depends on learner age, group size, focus of the course, student expectations and previous experience, cultural considerations, location and locale, etc. The situated nature of learning spaces extends to seating and furniture arrangements and solutions should be found at a more local level. Chapter 4 provides further details regarding such design considerations.

Physical spaces have communication affordances and characteristics that differ from virtual spaces. As previously discussed, using the whole body allows for more ways to transmit nonlinguistic information. Gestures, for example, can amplify what is being said and capture and direct attention. "Gestures express so many meanings directly," Tversky (2019: 113) argues. "[W]ords take time to find and assemble. Words are arbitrary. Except for a few onomatopoeic words ... words bear no relationship to their meanings." In contrast to virtual spaces, there is no lag in communication happening in real-time, and linguistic and nonlinguistic information are finely tuned to each other:

> In actuality, conversation partners do not just coordinate the content and the timing of the conversation, they also coordinate aspects of their behavior that do not at first seem relevant to the conversation. They coordinate their actions, leaning forward to take the stage or backward to yield the stage, crossing or uncrossing their legs. They mimic each other, a phenomenon known as *entrainment*. They adopt each other's words and phrases, even accents. They copy each other's facial expressions, eye gaze, and body movements.
> (Tversky 2019: 29)

This unconscious coordination lowers the level of awkwardness that L2 communication can create and enhances communicative flow and continuity. It can fill a conversation with meaning that would otherwise be difficult to convey or share. This is particularly important as L2 learners "have difficulty establishing an authentic voice … in the target language, because thought, identity and self may clash" (Van Lier 2004: 128). Managing and supporting identity work is part of language learning as meaning is created in communication: "When people talk to each other, the world gets constructed" (Burr 2003: 8). Ackerman (2004) argues that we negotiate meaning through tangible forms, including our expressions and cultural media. Physical spaces can support externalizing communication by intentionally designing affordances.

Conclusion

Interlocutor communication is an important and complex component of language learning. It involves not only cognitive aspects but different physical properties. Physical spaces can provide supportive environments that foster approachability, provide environmental cues, reduce anxiety and awkwardness, and scaffold and inspire communication.

High-Impact Practices and Innovation in Language Education

Language education is remarkably innovative and dynamic. Henshaw and Hawkins (2022: 24) assert that "Language teaching is unlike any other type of teaching because language acquisition is not the same as learning anything else (e.g., dancing, playing an instrument, solving an equation, etc.). It is not about showing learners how to do it, and then helping them master it through repetitive practice. Repetition and imitation are not the driving forces of acquisition." If we look at the different methods, approaches, and visions, we have come a long way since grammar and translation was the norm. Not all innovations are significantly impacted by physical space, but some are. This section examines a few of such innovative, high-impact practices and how they relate to physical learning spaces.

Some of these new ideas in education in general and in language education in particular may even contradict established learning space design. Thomas (2010: 503) argues that "traditional classrooms and lecture halls do not provide the affordances that encourage engaged learning. This does not mean that engaged learning is impossible in such spaces, rather, the argument here is that engaged learning is an emergent property of learning spaces and environments that are designed to provide affordances that actively encourage such engagement."

Learning Communities and Immersion

Immersing learners in language learning through special programs and settings can lead to higher proficiency outcomes (Merrill 2020). Study abroad has long been an established immersion practice. There are also different practices that take place within the home country or institution, such as summer camps or language houses, dorms, or corridors. Residential learning spaces can provide engaging and immersive environments for experiential language learning (Bown, Dewey, and Baker-Smemoe 2020). Chapter 3 further discusses immersive spaces for language learning.

Project-Based Language Learning

Project-based language learning (PBLL) is based on the project-based learning (PBL) framework. It can be defined as:

> a transformative learning experience designed to engage language learners with real-world issues and meaningful target language use through the construction of products that have an authentic purpose and that are shared with an audience that extends beyond the instructional setting. PBLL can be conceived as a series of language learning tasks that are articulated toward a common goal: the construction of a public product representing a response to a challenging problem or question.
>
> (NFLRC)

While PBLL can of course be completely virtual, there are multiple intersections in physical and hybrid contexts. The underlying idea is that projects involve others as an audience. Learning spaces can promote showcasing and sharing these through different design features. Furthermore, many projects are done collaboratively and benefit from not only social and collaborative setups but those that foster creativity and provide necessary materials. Maker spaces are a type that can be particularly beneficial for PBLL.

Community-Based Learning and Service Learning

Coined by Clifford and Reisinger (2019: 6), community-based language learning (CBLL) stems from community-based learning (CBL), "an umbrella term that provides models of how to engage in curricular and co-curricular experiences with local communities." Engman and Hermes (2021: 90) argue that "Second-language learning within schools and the academy is concerned with language as a static object of study, a system of skills to be mastered. Too often divorced from context in language classrooms, learning a second language is traditionally expected to take the form of a carefully measured process of acquisition located in the individual." CBLL is one way of embedding language learning into more meaningful contexts. While the spaces utilized in this practice are usually outside of educational intuitions—in fact that is at the core of their idea—there are instances when the community might be invited in.

Technology-Enhanced Language Learning and Teaching

Technology and learning spaces have a long history in language education. As discussed above, materials in the target language are an important component. Especially the ability to record voices led to the rise of the language lab. Personal computers provided interactive features that allowed for automation and combined media, and the introduction of the World Wide Web provided connectivity, allowed for new forms of ways to connect across distances, and gave access to even more authentic resources instantly. Until this stage, about 2010, these technologies still required some spaces to accommodate them. Since then, ubiquitous computing, mobile learning, and BYOD (bring your own device) rapidly changed technologies in physical spaces. Stand-alone devices, such as camcorders, microphones, cameras, karaoke machines, various gadgets, and physical media that had previously been purchased, stored, and checked through language resource centers quickly disappeared as mobile devices, such as smartphones and laptop, quickly became devices that could do it all. This changed how we can design our physical spaces, freeing up square footage, creating fluidity, and allowing for new usage scenarios.

Individual Pathways

While a lot of attention has been given to virtual spaces in recent years, physical spaces can provide rich environments to support and engage individual learners. Reinders and White (2016: 149) argue that "[S]ocial technologies for language learning draw our attention back to the value of ecological approaches to understanding learner autonomy. They focus on the multiple environments in which individuals pursue their learning, the role of others and their contributions, and the ways in which learners work with and restructure aspects of their learning environments to establish more optimal learning conditions moment by moment." Laurillard (2002: 2) argues that "the individual learner's sense of breaking new ground makes learning something personal, peculiar to the individual, and therefore not so amenable to the mass treatment that a didactic education system tends to adopt. This is the paradox that challenges the teaching profession: we want all our students to learn the same thing, yet we want each to make it their own." Focusing on individual pathways and meeting student's different needs both in formal and informal contexts is a high-impact strategy that can be an institutional or program focus area. Language learning can of course happen outside of formally and informally organized learning physical spaces—"in the wild" (Godwin-Jones 2019). But learning spaces can be designed and conceptualized to add intentionality to these goals. Language resource centers, self-access centers, and social spaces can give structure to these practices outside of the classroom, while classrooms and more formal spaces can use symbolic, spatial, and technological features and materials to encourage instructors and students to increase autonomy in language learning. One way to increase a focus on autonomy and individualization is to consider creating learning *places* rather than learning *spaces*. The following chapter provides more concrete examples of physical spaces that can support individual and diverse learners.

Conclusion

Language learning's particular characteristics, properties, needs, and challenges can benefit from a more nuanced approach to conceptualize and design physical spaces. Guerrettaz and Johnston (2013: 782) argue that "[T]he classroom ecology focuses on relationships between and among *participants, processes, structures* and *artifacts*." Learning spaces' design must consider all four aspects. There is no perfect classroom that will magically make language education better. Educators need to be trained to make best use of the spaces they are given, and all stakeholders must be consulted and involved. Spaces not only develop over time, but they are also created through interactions and actions of people. Creating learning spaces is more than choosing chairs and wall colors—it involves a framework of constantly evolving and adapting processes, structures, objects, and norms. Moreover, learning spaces can be a tool in language educators' toolboxes that can support and enhance language education. We can design them to make them active instead of passive: "Rather than viewing the school building—its various rooms, walls, windows, doors and furniture, together with outdoor 'nooks and crannies,' gardens and open spaces—as a neutral or passive 'container,' architects and educators have considered it to be an *active agent*, shaping the experience of schooling and promoting and even pioneering a particular understanding of education" (Grosvenor and Burke 2008: 10).

Our current physical spaces for language learning are not fully congruent with the many developments in language pedagogy or in technology. Because it takes a long time to plan and create physical spaces, there is often a lag. It is difficult to foresee future developments and create enough flexibility to make sure spaces are useful and resilient in the future. But despite these difficulties, language education benefits from the affordances of physical learning spaces that are difficult to replicate in the digital realm. This includes whole-body education and communication, a sense of belonging, affective benefits, and the use of materials and materialities that aid, support, enhance, and foster language learning.

Much of the previous research has focused on generic physical learning spaces (e.g., Oblinger 2006). Language learning has distinct characteristics, approaches, and needs. A closer examination of these differences, in addition to the characteristics shared with other disciplines, can make language learning and teaching more efficient, more effective, more approachable, and more accessible. Designing such spaces requires joint efforts by educators, students, and design and planning experts to bring together various disciplinary approaches and expertise.

Language education extends beyond the classroom. Much of our institutionalized work centers around formal, instructional spaces. But as newer practices and innovations may become more common, we can leverage physical spaces that are designed to support and enable such practices. The following chapter discusses the possibilities that such language learning spaces provide and gives readers an overview of how we can think beyond the classroom.

3

Physical Language Learning Spaces beyond the Classroom

The term physical learning space often gets equated with the term classroom. As discussed in Chapter 1, classrooms have become largely normalized and the de facto norm for instructed language education. Zheng et al. (2018: 45) claim that "[I]n learning a language in foreign language settings, classrooms are considered almost the only 'place' language learning takes place, except for homework done at home." Calls to think beyond these traditional "teaching boxes" (Skill and Young 2002: 31) are not new, but alternative spaces remain the exception rather than the rule. The focus of this chapter is on specialty and exemplary spaces for *instructed* language learning. One component of instructed second language acquisition (ISLA) is "the systematic manipulation of the learning environment and learning processes, which separates ISLA from what has been called, among other things, uninstructed or naturalistic L2 acquisition; in this, learners are simply surrounded by the target language but make no or little conscious effort to learn the language. Such scenarios might involve immigrants who are exposed to another language as they live in a wider social context, but who are not actively involved in learning the L2" (Loewen and Sato 2017: 2). The spaces presented in this chapter offer different levels of formality, and while they are not all directly instruction or teaching spaces, they all involve a focus on language learning that is not naturalistic or "in the wild," and are institutional spaces that were intentionally planned and designed.

It is worth noting that the spaces highlighted in this chapter are not a representation of all existing language learning spaces but rather a curated list of spaces and types that expand the notion of what is possible. The spaces highlighted are meant to inspire transformation and lead to further innovation. There is a certain inertia and caution within the university ecosystem, as Davidson (2017: 9) points out: "It will not be easy to transform the university from the inside. Many academics are traditionalists, and many institutions revere their traditions and are rewarded for them. They often reject innovation simply because it represents a departure from how things are done."

There is common a dichotomy of formal versus informal learning spaces. Informal spaces are often not regarded as central to language education but rather as peripheral. The classroom remains to be at the center of instructed language education because this is where formal instruction happens. It is embedded in a system that increasingly emphasizes structure, credentialing, testing, assessment, and awarding grades and credits over unstructured and intrinsically motivated language learning. Most university instructors' contracts are guided by how many courses are taught. These courses are specified in length and duration, and usually in location. Grades must be awarded, certain parameters must be fulfilled. This places an emphasis on the spaces that this kind of learning happens in.

And yet, research and newer approaches to learning and teaching languages point to the need to think beyond the classroom, both in a metaphorical and in a physical sense:

> People who achieve high degrees of second language proficiency typically learn and use languages in multiple settings over a prolonged period of time. They learn both in language classrooms and in a variety of institutional and non-institutional settings beyond the classroom. The distribution of their time and effort across these settings also changes over time. We are, thus, coming to appreciate the complexity of the *where* of language learning at both global and local levels, and in relation to time. In addition, because people learn second languages in a single space, we need to attend to the configurations of spaces in which they learn, or the ways in which learners assemble the *where* of language learning in space and over time.
>
> (Benson 2021: 3)

The formal/informal dichotomy might be too simplistic as boundaries have blurred in other domains as well, such as reality/virtuality and private/public life. Boys (2011: 3) calls it a myth that "formal and informal learning are binary opposites." Perhaps a better differentiation for physical language learning spaces is between curated and not curated spaces. The question then arises how we can better and more intentionally choose, design, and curate spaces beneficial for different aspects and scenarios in language education, and how we can bring them closer into the center to elevate their usefulness.

In this chapter, we will look at the rich variety of nonclassroom spaces that have developed. The language laboratory, which has an almost century long tradition, has developed into the language center in the last few decades and can be found in many institutions of higher education in the United States. Social spaces, such as language cafes or dining halls, are a more recent trend. There are also residential spaces, such as language houses, language corridors, or immersion places, that engage students in language learning beyond formal hours of schooling. And then there are those spaces we often do not see as "real" learning spaces. These invisible learning spaces, such as corridors, thresholds, plazas, or offices, are spaces of learning that can be more intentionally designed and leveraged. Furthermore, there are many physical spaces that can be used for language learning, such as museums, libraries, gardens, outdoor spaces, community spaces, etc.

In many ways, these diverse spaces beyond the classroom provide an opportunity to break out of the proverbial silos that are so often lamented in higher education. But they are also a way to build disciplinary community and sense of belonging. Strange and Banning (2001: 165) posit that "[A]mong the physical features that most clearly shape the direction of any community is territory. Communities, by nature, tend to be territorial; they need space in which to exist and to carry out their functions." Creating distinct identities, modeling possibilities, and providing unstructured or semi-structured opportunities of exploration can be achieved through a more intentional approach to physical learning spaces beyond, but not excluding, the classroom.

From Language Learning Spaces to Language Learning Places

While this chapter describes types of spaces beyond the classroom, it also introduces specific places. Places are both individually constructed realities and socially constructed realities (Hutchison and Orr 2004). They are assemblages of "materiality, meaning, and practice" (Cresswell 2019: 201). For Löw (2016: xvii) the defining characteristics of places, contrast to spaces, are that they are "always markable, nameable, and unique." Places are filled with meaning, references, and individualization. These are usually driven by the users of a place and are difficult to be designed by professionals. The live parakeets in the language center at a liberal art college, the constantly changing international hats on another college's mascot, one center's renaming of one of their rooms as "the fishbowl," and the student-generated Day of the Dead altars spilling into the hallways are all examples of placemaking. While those might be dismissed as trivial manifestations of space, they provide an atmosphere of individualization, identity, agency, belonging, and meaning. These factors, further developed in

Chapter 4, are crucially important for learners because of the proliferation of generic spaces devoid of meaning all around us:

> A combination of mass communication, increased mobility, and a consumer society has been blamed for a rapidly accelerating homogenization of the world. More and more of our lives, it has been argued, take place in spaces that could be anywhere—that look, feel, sound, and smell the same wherever in the globe we may be. Fast food outlets, shopping malls, airports, high street shops, and hotels are all arguably more or less the same wherever we go. These are spaces that seem detached from the local environment and tell us nothing about the particular locality in which they are located. The meaning that provides the sense of attachment to place has been radically thinned out.
>
> (Cresswell 2014: 75)

Therefore, any discussion of physical language learning spaces must go beyond the generic and include language learning places. It is in the local, the situated, and the specific situation that places are created and recreated. The examples given in this chapter should therefore not be seen as a blueprint but rather should be adapted to fit an institution's specific situation, users, and needs.

From Language Lab to Language Center

Over half a century ago, Huebener (1959: 126) posited that "[W]hat is not possible in the average classroom can be done in the laboratory." The language laboratory holds a powerful image in our shared history of language learning and is well documented (e.g., Hocking 1964; Salaberry 2001; Roby 2004; Hagen 2017; Lavolette and Simon 2018; Sebastian et al. 2018; Lavolette and Kraemer 2021). Almost a decade ago, Kronenberg (2014: 1–2) wrote that "[W]hile its predecessor, the language laboratory, had a clearly defined mission and purpose, current models of language centers are multi-purpose spaces that manifest themselves in very distinct ways at different institutions and locations."

Historically, there was a real need for lab spaces as they contained specific technology to provide certain functions, namely to play audio recordings, and later to record students' own voices and for them and their instructors to be able listen to later: "The goal was automatized production of selected sentence patterns" (Van Lier 2003: 57). Hutchinson (1967: 356) lists "10 things language laboratory facilities can do," all of which can today be accomplished without a laboratory through ubiquitous, untethered computing.

The audio-lingual method led to the rise of technology-focused audio and later computer labs, which emphasized technology and individual practice over communal or social aspects. Isolation of learners was not simply a result but the intention of the technology (Dakin 1973). When the audio-lingual method was superseded by other methods and approaches, the language laboratory lost its relevance: "In essence, by the late 1980s, there was a growing dichotomy between the face-to-face interactivity on the one hand, and the computer—and tape-based language laboratory on the other" (Garrett and Liddell 2004: 29). The physical manifestation, the built pedagogy, resulted in adding carrels and sound barriers to the space, installing sophisticated technologies that required specialized staff, and in changing schedules whose effects are still found in many programs (e.g., in "lab sessions," sometimes also called the fourth or the fifth hour). From a space standpoint, the lab's powerful influence might even undermine the learning goals that instructors and programs set: the built space influences how we teach and exerts agency in the teaching and learning process. The idea and influence of the lab remains, sometimes in subtle ways, in sociomaterial assemblages until today.

Physical spaces are expensive and durable, and so, many labs were dismantled, repurposed, or taken over by other units (Garrett and Liddell 2004). Other labs in the United States reinvented themselves as what might be generically called language centers: language resource centers, media centers, CALL centers, world languages studios, language hubs, etc. They all have in common that they are curated and organized in an intentional way, and usually have some level of staffing that provides programming and guidance. Van Lier (2003: 54) criticizes that the move to computer labs is "convenient for administrators, profitable to vendors, but not particularly empowering for teachers and learners." And yet, two decades after his comments and in a time of normalized mobile and cloud computing, we still find labs being built or powerfully influencing design and administrative patterns.

Language centers, the successors of the language laboratories in the United States, have been reacting to disruptive changes for decades. What started out as technology-enabled listening and recording facilities with a clearly defined mission have evolved into spaces of multi-purpose support (Bard 2018), face-to-face and online teaching (Giupponi et al. 2018), research (Sun 2017), or social and hybrid spaces. Lavolette and Kraemer (2017: 149) define a language center as a "physical and/or virtual space that supports foreign and/or second language learning and/or teaching within a larger educational institution." The very open nature of this definition highlights a few things: language centers are at institutions and serve them. How they serve them is left open. Many of them support instructors, provide resources and spaces to students. Some conduct research or drive innovation, while others are involved in advocacy, recruitment, advising, and cross- and inter-institutional collaboration. For many centers, these fields of engagement are not static but are slowly shifting and sometimes radically pivoting. It doesn't always take a pandemic like the Covid-19 crisis to change a language center's role more profoundly. Sometimes changing personnel, new institutional or unit strategic plans, structural changes, or a move to a new building can lead to a changed mission and role within the institution's ecosystem.

It is useful to deconstruct the multiple meanings we can apply to the term "center." Since it may be viewed through different lenses and by different constituents, it can be difficult to find common ground. A language center can be a resource center, a self-access center, a social space, a technology space, a teaching space, a community of practice, a virtual space, a professional development space, a research space, an innovation space, or a space of possibility. It can be one or several of these. A language center can be an independent administrative unit, it can be part of a unit, such as a department, or report to multiple units, but managed professionally, or it can simply be a conceptual and physical space that has no administrative function or role. How a language center is conceptualized, structured, and created matters tremendously in setting vision, mission, values, and goals. Its staffing is connected to its ability to adapt: "Language lab directors are often thought of as staff, not faculty, and are seen as managers of student workers and providers of the routine services demanded of them by teachers (though they often teach language classes themselves as part of their responsibilities). Direct access to higher administrators or senior faculty in the LL&C departments may be problematical. In short, they may lack a strong political voice at the academic table" (Garrett and Liddell 2004: 33). As argued above, physical spaces do not exist in a vacuum and are strongly tied to curricular and procedural attributes.

In the United States, most language centers can be found at Ph.D. granting universities, as well as regional universities, liberal arts colleges, and K-12 institutions (Lavolette and Simon 2018). While language labs were quite common at K-12 institutions in the past, few now have dedicated language centers. This is also true for minority serving institutions of higher education, including community colleges. In other countries, language centers are often situated quite differently. In Germany, and much of Europe for that matter, language centers often organize and offer language courses to all university students, not only those majoring in a language, but generally do not, however, offer degrees. They also provide student services, such as L2 writing support, professional development, and social spaces.

Similarly, language centers in Japan, often self-access centers (SACs), place a strong emphasis on learner autonomy (Murray and Lamb 2018a). Thornton et al. (2018: 32) argue that "a feature of many SACs is not simply that they focus on fostering learner autonomy, but that they consider it their driving philosophy around which all their functions are organized." This distinct mission leads to several design considerations for the physical space, focusing more on interactions and collaborative spaces, social spaces, and support spaces rather than classrooms (Mynard et al. 2020). In recent years, a shared interest in physical language learning spaces has manifested itself in new partnerships between the International Association for Language Learning Technology (IALLT) and its overseas partners, such as the Arbeitskreis der Sprachenzentren (AKS) and the Japan Association for Self-Access Learning (JASAL). Diverse models from around the globe show how much these language centers are intertwined with their institutions' structures, missions, values, and historical developments. While it is difficult to change many of these factors, we can learn from these diverse models of success and adopt relevant features and goals into local centers.

Cornfield (1966: 77) lamented over half a century ago that the "choice of the name language laboratory was an unfortunate one since it gives the false impression of its real purpose. A laboratory is usually a place where research or experimentation goes on. Nothing of that nature should take place in the normal course of events in the language laboratory." Interestingly, today's language centers, the heirs of the language lab, have taken on more of a role of a lab in its original sense: as a space for exploration, research, and innovation. Perhaps they should be called labs again for that reason. The labels that the language field has generated have created their own dynamic and expectations, and it is important to frequently reexamine their use and meaning:

> The connotations that attach to different terms, and pervade whole bodies of discourse, are likely to affect people's attitudes to and experiences of certain kinds of buildings (e.g. "tower block" versus "skyscraper") or certain kinds of spaces (e.g. the range of labels, having different social status connotations, used for public eating places, such as "canteen," "restaurant," "mess," "cafe," "deli," "drug store," or "snack bar"). Labels embody a hierarchy of value which need have nothing to do with the merits of specific buildings. Examining the labels used for spaces within a building can alert us to the way spatial divisions become

naturalized, though in fact they are the product of specific cultural/historical developments, and may subsequently be used to enforce those developments more widely."

(Markus and Cameron 2002: 42–3)

Whatever the naming conventions, language centers are not all alike. Many provide excellent physical spaces that support language learning and explore new ways of providing rich environments. Importantly, they can be places, giving their spaces meaning and making them unique. If language labs were mostly language learning spaces, many language centers today are language learning places. They can be hubs for diverse language learners. This transformation happened in some ways in libraries as well, which moved further away from mainly providing resources, such as books, journals, and later technologies, toward shared spaces and places: "People are not coming to libraries only to get work done; they also want an audience and to be part of the performance. They position themselves around other people who are working on their own assignments ... Being surrounded by other productive people is a powerful motivator" (Mathews and Soistmann 2016: 27).

Conclusion

We can regard the language center as a curated possibility space. It is usually managed and can thus actively adapt to new developments. Throughout their history, they have shown their adaptability (Ledgerwood 2017). This kind of flexibility (see Chapter 4) and postoccupancy control (see Chapter 4) are important components of providing more than generic, not optimized leaning spaces. Language centers will need to be designed, reinvented, and organized in the United States to adapt to ever-faster cycles of disruptive technological, institutional, and pedagogical changes (see Chapter 5). Many language centers in the United States have been moving away from massive technology installations to more flexible, adaptable, and curated diverse and social spaces (Yaden and Evans 2017).

Social Language Learning Spaces

"Social learning space" is a vague term. It is based on the view that social processes generate learning (Lave and Wenger 1991) and appears to be the binary opposite of learning spaces that focus on an individual and cognitive view of learning. Social learning spaces are often equated with informal learning spaces, which have received more attention in recent years: "For many educationalists, this requires a move away from formal lecture halls and classrooms towards technology-rich and informal, social learning spaces—a strong driver in many recent building designs and adaptations" (Boys 2011: 2). Cox (2018) argues that informal learning is experienced as embodied and that visual, auditory, and sensory aspects play an important role.

To some degree, we face an artificial, rigid binary of formal spaces that focus on individual cognition and informal spaces that focus on social aspects of learning. Fenwick (2015: 83) argues that "learning cannot be considered effectively if the sole focus is upon individual cognitive processing." This view of learning in general extends to the disciplinary focus of language learning, which should consider both cognitive and social processes (Mills 2013). We may view social spaces also in opposition to closed and tightly controlled spaces:

> We suggest that these problems largely originate in "spaces of enclosure" that characterize the modernist institution of school education. The book, the classroom and the curriculum can be viewed as intermeshed fixed enclosures which operate in concert to separate educational engagement from wider spheres of social practice: substituting reliance on texts for an integrated experience of word in relation to world, and in the process conferring heavy responsibility on the teacher to organize curricular activities and materials, and interpret meaning and experience.
>
> (Lankshear et al. 1996: 154)

Characteristics of Social Spaces

Social spaces are, of course, not necessarily physical. Learning communities do not necessarily need to meet on campus or in formal physical spaces. Communities situate people through networks in relation to each other, but also produce and organize space-time (Nespor 1994). Organizing learning in social spaces includes supporting community building and involves not merely physical design but also designing procedures, processes, and programming. Communities of practice need a level of informality and autonomy (Wenger et al. 2002), which may not be found in more formally or rigidly conceptualized spaces. Language centers, for example, can provide such structures that are helpful to create social bonds and community (Stapleton 2022).

While a physical space is not necessary, it can be helpful in curating and intentionally supporting communities and social spaces. Physical social spaces involve a co-presence: people need to be in the same place at the same time. Social spaces allow people to gather, and their design attributes will differ from those of other physical spaces, such as classrooms or lecture halls. Doorley and Witthoft (2012: 41) distinguish between three categories of gathering spaces: "drop-in spaces, which focus on predictability and a fixed set-up," "curated spaces, such as lobbies or welcome areas" that "allow for a certain degree of variation, which does generally not occur on a daily basis" and "self-service spaces" that "are very flexible and can be customized by patrons and staff." Different design attributes can make spaces more social: "sociopetal" spaces support social interactions and are "socially catalytic" (Strange and Banning 2001: 145). Sociofugal spaces, on the other hand, discourage such interactions, which can be intentionally or unintentionally designed that way.

Third Places are usually sociopetal spaces that provide communicative opportunities: "Neutral ground provides the place, and leveling sets the stage for the cardinal and sustaining activity of third places everywhere. That activity is conversation. Nothing more clearly indicates a third place than that the talk there is good; that it is lively, scintillating, colorful, and engaging" (Oldenburg 1999: 26). Indeed, providing opportunities and environments that support communication and interaction can be deliberately designed. Third Places are more than simply havens of escape (Oldenburg 1999) but are spaces and places of choice that involve at least the potential for connection and social interaction. The term "magnet place" is also a useful label for gathering spots in academic environments, such as libraries, or for specific disciplinary spaces. "We flock to these environments knowing that we can learn from others as well as demonstrate and apply our own knowledge and skills. These locations exude magnet-like properties, attracting individuals with similar outlooks or dispositions" (Mathews and Soistmann 2016: 104). The Covid-19 pandemic increased the awareness that people have agency in choosing spaces that suit them rather than having to accept the default. If we want to attract stakeholders into social language learning spaces, we must design such magnet-like attributes.

Murray and Fujishima (2016a: 2) argue that the defining feature of social language learning spaces is "a focus on language learning through informal social interaction." They provide opportunities for unstructured or semi-structured interactions, both planned and incidental. Physical social spaces address whole humans, their bodies, and their emotions, not just their minds and their disciplinary focus: "As an aspect of social practice, learning involves the whole person; it implies not only a relation to specific activities, but a relation to social communities—it implies becoming a full participant, a member, a kind of person" (Lave and Wenger 1991: 53). Social learning spaces should embrace wider topic areas of mutual interest. Wenger et al. (2002: 9) remind us that "[S]haring tacit knowledge requires interaction and informal learning processes such as storytelling, conversation, coaching, and apprenticeship of the kind that communities of practice provide." A supportive environment should provide multiple forms of participation and the ability to stay on the sidelines, to merely observe, but to also be drawn further into social practices and activities, without barriers. A whole-body focus includes participants' agency to choose their location, their posture, and be able to use their bodies as communicative devices. For example, Tversky (2019: 136) argues that gestures are "social glue."

The three following examples of social physical language learning spaces provide further properties in more concrete terms: residential language learning spaces, food spaces, and immersive spaces.

Residential Language Learning Spaces

Residential language learning spaces are immersive environments where learners live in a place that is, even if only temporarily, connected to their language learning context. Examples for such spaces are language villages, language corridors, language houses, language clusters, and language dorms. Bown, Dewey, and Baker-Smemoe (2020: 11) use the term "foreign language housing," or FLH, which they define as "residences on or near college campuses where speakers of the same L2 reside together. The purpose of FLH is to provide a non-threatening, naturalistic environment, in which learners can practice their L2s and learn about culture." Ericson (2020: 155) comments that "[I]deally, FLH serves not only as a place to speak the target language, but also as a venue of connecting people through multiple layers of cultural and academic experiences." These spaces are not discussed much in the literature or intensely researched (see Bown et al. [2020: 16–17] for an overview). But they provide us with a model for targeting and highlighting specific properties of language learning spaces that can be replicated or used in other types of spaces. There are different levels of permeability in such spaces because they can be more strictly a home, or First Place, or a more open Third Place that can invite people from the outside in. They can also be a place of work, or Second Place: Ericson (2020) reports that some classes take place in their language houses. What kind of place residential space is depends on organizational structures, uses, and expectations. They need to be actively managed to provide relevant formal and informal programming, which is an important part of creating social cohesiveness (Montgomery 2020). Such active management often involves financial resources and staffing, which can be an issue for residential language learning spaces (Bown 2020).

Residential spaces can provide a way to organize and structure common and meaningful activities outside of formal contexts. They "invite sustained interaction and repeated engagement over time—particularly when they foster a sense of acceptance and belonging" (Montgomery 2020: 357). Shared activities and experiences can have powerful effects on social cohesion; for example, through consuming food or drinks together, or through play: "Playful interaction allows a penalty-free rehearsal of the normal give-and-take necessary in social groups" (Brown and Vaughan 2014: 32). Besides games, other materials that provide rich opportunities for social interaction include music, movies, videos, art and craft supplies, props, realia, and toys. Montgomery (2020) provides many concrete examples of materials that are particularly suited for residential spaces and different levels of language learners.

Residential language learning spaces must not necessarily be permanent. First-year learning communities, for example, are a high-impact practice that can have students cluster around different focus areas during a specified time. Their set-up can provide a way of bridging otherwise siloed disciplinary areas. Other residential spaces are permanent, integral units, such as the Oldenborg Center at Pomona College. It is a language dorm divided into six language halls centered around a dining room with many different daily and weekly language tables. The Oldenborg Center employs six graduate-student-level language residents, one per language, and staff to actively provide programming and immersion experiences (Dwyer and Dale 2020).

One caveat that has received more attention in recent years is that as some residential spaces can be more closed than permeable, they can be exclusionary and inaccessible, especially if they cost more than other housing options. Furthermore, students with caregiving responsibilities or disabilities may not be able to choose this option.

Language Learning Food Spaces

Food is a cultural practice that has a distinct physical component. It can function not only as physical sustenance but also has important social and symbolic meanings. Food is both material and practice, and involves various processes around preparation, serving, presenting, eating, and conversing about. Food can be an important part of ceremonies, events, and gatherings. It can function as a symbolic anchor. Having coffee together, for example, provides a framework of acceptable behaviors that can transcend and connect cultures and decrease barriers and awkwardness. It may also signal that a gathering is more than a functional meeting.

Some formal learning spaces may explicitly prohibit food for various reasons, including cleanliness, expected behaviors, exclusion of sounds and smells, and safety. Social learning spaces are usually more permissible when it comes to food. Some of these are deliberately not part of institutional spaces, such as meetings at a local cafe, restaurant, bar, or beer garden. These can be regular events (such as language coffee hour, Stammtisch, happy hour, etc.) or occur only occasionally. For our purposes specifically, there are also institutional and actively designed spaces that revolve around food.

Some language centers provide food spaces and programming as extracurricular language learning opportunities. Language cafes are such a model. For example, the Language Café at the Språkstudion at Stockholm University is built on three principles: language diversity, including those languages that aren't taught at the university; inclusivity by being open to all students and staff/faculty and to all language levels; and a focus on autonomous learning and lowering barriers by requiring no registration and allowing participants to join spontaneously (Kann 2022). Furthermore, it is not integrated into the curriculum and provides its users with agency. The Covid-19 pandemic provided the need to have virtual coffee hours, which allowed for more flexibility, more linguistic diversity, and didn't need available rooms; and this made scheduling easier. It also allowed international participants to join. But according to Kann (2022), the threshold of participation was raised, spontaneity was lower, and some "natural" and communal aspects were lost: the role of coffee, tea, and food "should not be underestimated" as it was a not insignificant motivator for many participants.

Language cafes provide opportunities that set acceptable norms. Like the residential spaces discussed above, they provide frameworks that allow participants take part in other activities beyond L2 communication. When there is an awkward silence, they can pour themselves another coffee or get up and get a cookie or clean up. They can use facial expressions or gestures to convey information about the food. They can also just be there without speaking and just listen. The Oldenborg Center at Pomona College, the residential language learning space described above, provides daily and weekly language tables in its dedicated dining hall. The language residents actively work during lunch hours to bring speakers of diverse levels of L2 proficiency, backgrounds, and roles together (Dwyer and Dale 2020). The lunch hour is curated and involves preparation, attention to all individual participants, and materials. This kind of active curation can create a more inclusive and deliberate environment and a framework for regularly engaging with language learning outside of formal courses. It creates conditions of wellbeing and belonging (see also Chapter 4). Such food spaces provide spaces of possibility and models for innovation in embodied and social learning:

> Social spaces for language learning like the L-café, constituted of spatial elements and human agents, can become complex dynamic ecosocial systems offering learners the possibility to generate a diverse range of affordances for learning. To "occasion" these complex dynamic social learning environments, educators and administrators will have to push the boundaries of their academic imaginary ... and come to see space, place and pedagogical activity in new ways.
>
> (Murray and Fujishima 2016b: 146)

Another innovative and inspirational physical food language learning space is the Global Kitchen at Grinnell College, whose goal it is to "facilitate through theory and praxis the interdisciplinary study of food and its central role in the human experience" (Grinnell). It also builds interdisciplinary bridges to approach issues such as global food issues, food insecurity, and food justice. Instead of merely providing food, the kitchen learning space engages learners also in production processes, making them not mere visitors but active participants.

Designing such designated spaces is, of course, resource intensive. Existing spaces can often be appropriated by re-evaluating existing policies and space designations. Areas in a dining hall can be designated as language tables or lunch hour without building a dedicated space. Language centers, for example, are often in a position to allow food rather than to prohibit it and to create programming that deliberately includes food, such as chocolate tastings or smelly cheese contests. If this sounds rather unacademic and not serious, that is *exactly* the point: it is informal, and it is social.

Immersive Language Learning Spaces

A third example that often overlaps with other social spaces mentioned thus far is that of immersion spaces. It is important to be clear about its definition and acknowledge that the term "immersion" in K-12 settings differs from that at the postsecondary level. In K-12 settings in the United States, immersion programs involve teaching non-language subject courses in a language other than English. In contrast to that, in the postsecondary level, immersion programs generally foster language learning outside of regular, formal classroom settings (Dewey 2004). This section will examine the latter. Merrill (2020) discusses that immersion programs have been found to result in higher proficiency levels when compared to regular classroom settings as well as study abroad. While study abroad might be seen by some as an immersion program, the term usually refers to spaces within the home country. They can range from language summer camps (Schenker and Kraemer 2018) to highly organized summer schools, such as Middlebury Language Schools (Merrill 2020), or the Deutsche Sommerschule am Pacific (Collenberg-González 2020). While there is some research on programming of immersion spaces (see Merrill 2020 for an overview), there is relatively little available for designing such spaces. We can view them as involving multiple social spaces (residential and food spaces, for example), while they may also provide more formal spaces. What we do know about such spaces is that they provide opportunities for frequent engagement and communication, allowing them to build community more effectively: college students "who had more opportunities to be closer together, whether in their dormitories, apartments, or classes, more often tended to form friendships and like one another" (Mehrabian 1981: 113). Designing such physical spaces depends greatly on programming, guidelines, expectations, and rules (e.g., a language pledge), structures, and opportunities for interaction. Ambient, spatial, and technological, in addition to procedural, attributes can support immersion language learning goals, as outlined in Chapter 4.

Design Considerations for Social Spaces

Designing social language learning spaces differs from designing more formal learning spaces. Social spaces need not be very open, agora-like spaces; rather, they should provide various spaces for different users and situations, allowing for multiple ways of participating in social acts. Doorley and Witthoft (2012: 132) suggest that "[H]iding places offer a crucial respite from an open, collaborative environment." They suggest immovable furniture so that no decisions need to be made, and that the space is hidden, laid back and small to feel cozy and secure. Parker (2018: 69) discusses why people gather and explains that density is an important factor to consider: guests at a party often congregate in the kitchen because "people instinctively seek out smaller spaces as the group dwindles in order to sustain the level of the density." For the context of learning spaces, Cox (2018: 1088) suggests users construct *"learning atmospheres,"* which stem from not only social convention but also architecture, furniture, and signage. To make deliberate choices in how to structure and plan social spaces, Crook and Mitchell (2012: 22) suggest distinguishing between different levels of varieties for social engagement, ranging from intense and deliberate to simply providing a space without direct engagement: "Focused collaboration," "Intermittent exchange," "Serendipitous encounter," and "Ambient sociality." It is also useful to consider supporting multiple communication channels through design attributes, as Mehrabian (1981: 112) discusses:

> The concept of "environmentally facilitated approach" refers to one important effect of spaces in which people meet and/or interact. It refers to the extent to which a setting facilitates mutual sensory stimulation among persons within it and is measured in terms of the spatio-temporal proximity or by the number of "communication channels" available to the individuals in that setting. Communication channels are the means by which we convey our thoughts and feelings to another—words, facial expressions, tone of voice, postures, movements, and so on. Greater approach tends to be associated with communication in more channels and the resulting increase in information has been found to be arousing.

Conclusion

Social learning spaces are a promising but often not fully leveraged concept that can provide affordances that are complimentary to more formal learning spaces. These spaces can take on different forms, including immersion, residential, and food spaces. Social language learning spaces benefit from postoccupancy processes (see Chapter 4)—as spaces are created through people's social interactions, physical social spaces should be able to change and adapt. Social interactions are difficult to directly plan for; rather, they must be cultivated by providing the right, rich, fertile environment, and ambiance.

Invisible Language Learning Spaces

This section deals with spaces that are usually not seen as learning spaces—they are invisible, or zero spaces, which have other primary functions. Examples of such spaces are hallways, offices, nooks, patios, waiting areas, plazas, or other miscellaneous spaces that primarily serve other purposes. And yet, language learning happens in these spaces all the time. From a sociomaterial perspective, it is interesting to examine what actually happens in them rather than merely looking at their affordances. This can help us make better choices and be more intentional when designing these spaces.

First and foremost is the question of "ownership": it is often not clear to whom many of these spaces belong. While offices are designated to one or more staff or faculty members, it is harder to determine authority for the hallway that leads into the office, the threshold into the building, or the patio just outside of the building. As will be discussed later, they are all part of a larger ecosystem. Usually, buildings are segmented and siloed, with room numbers designating a sense of ownership by a unit. But invisible spaces often lack such designations as they often do not have clear boundaries and thus are not considered in some language learning space design projects.

Thresholds

Thresholds are a type of in-between space, a liminal space. Most people don't give them much thought. But the entrance into a room or a campus building can already promote or hinder learning (Strange and Banning 2001). They mark a transition from one space into the next: from the outside to the inside, from the hallway into the classroom, from the lounge into a professor's office. "Thresholds signify change, and they are easy opportunities for leveraging intuitive behaviors. People frequently expect to act differently when exiting one space and entering another" (Doorley and Witthoft 2012: 42). The change in expectations can be unconscious and subtle. The various spaces discussed in this chapter have different properties, rules, and conventions. Thresholds also have a temporal dimension. For example, entering a classroom ten minutes before class starts or ten minutes after will lead to two different behaviors. The same goes for entering a busy social space during a peak time or an empty one during an off-peak time. Depending on the time, behaviors might change radically or not at all.

There can be physical markers that reinforce behavior change. For example, if the door is closed to a space, whether that is a classroom, an office, or a gathering space, the change is more noticeable and observable through sound or visuals. Opening a door might also be felt by a change in temperature, or one might feel a draft. What kind of a door or other closing feature is installed also matters. Is it visually permeable or solid? Does it open automatically or not? Does it swing or slide? Does it require much effort or is it easy to open? Are there possibly even multiple doors or thresholds? Doorley and Witthoft (2012) argue that thresholds should not be afterthoughts but should be consciously designed and suggest that signage and wayfinding cues are examples of good threshold design. It should be noted that thresholds have different cultural conventions. In Germany, for example, it is common to close doors and, depending on the space, expect people entering to knock beforehand. In the United States, it is more common to leave doors open in some cases to signify availability or transparency.

Within the context of language learning, thresholds are an opportunity to encourage certain behaviors and set mood and atmosphere for certain language learning activities and expectations. They also allow them to switch their minds to the L2 and set different expectations and policies (Imamura 2018). Thresholds can signal to visitors that they belong (see also Chapter 4) to the space they are entering, and thus, they can potentially signify place as well. The different languages on the stairs in the image indicate that one is entering a language space. Some spaces do not have clearly defined thresholds, they are more gradual. While doors are very common, other types of thresholds and transitional areas exist. For example, open areas might lead into other open areas. Transitions can be signaled through different attributes, including changing flooring materials, patterns, or colors; a different ceiling; stickers on the wall or the floor; different wall colors; etc. Furthermore, delineation can be achieved through front desks. The placement and type of desk can influence how a new space is entered. If it is in the entering person's path and potentially big and immovable, it might make it less likely for people to come in. If they are smaller and not in the direct path, they are likely perceived to be a smaller obstacle. Front desks can even be flexible and be adjusted to changing needs. Last, a common kind of threshold feature found is locking mechanisms: do you need a key, a swipe card, or key fob to enter? If an unlocking device is needed, then policies regarding how and who will receive access must be set, which can present to be an obstacle. Often this is desired, for example, for security reasons. It should, however, be an important consideration to clearly define access policies when designing thresholds.

Hallways

There are many names for this type of space: transitory spaces, circulatory spaces, pathways, liminal spaces, corridors, etc. For this book, they will be referred to as hallways. They are crucial for connecting different spaces and allowing users to move in-between them. They can have different shapes and lengths, ranging from just a few yards with little attention paid to major installations, like the 251-meter (823 ft.) long Infinite Corridor at the Massachusetts Institute for Technology (Hapgood 1993). The most common design in educational facilities

Figure 1 Stairs with different languages signifying threshold and boundary.

is that of a corridor leading to classrooms (and in some cases offices) on both sides of it (Hutchison and Orr 2004).

Hallways might be liminal and often not much noticed, but they are also learning spaces themselves. As discussed above, David D. Thornburg highlights different primordial metaphors for learning spaces. The Watering Hole metaphor is appropriate for various social spaces; but it also includes transitory spaces, as the path to and from the watering hole is an opportunity to talk among peers. Maybe students exchange information about the upcoming class or discuss plans after class to work on a project. Instead of abruptly ending, hallways provide a transition zone that does not have a strict boundary. This differs from a video conference call, as interlocutors are immediately gone once they hit the "end" button.

Hallways can be gathering spaces: "It is not unusual for students to gather outside a classroom before class begins or to linger in the hallway after class. This is a great opportunity for students to connect with each other and for instructors to engage with students" (Folkins et al. 2015: 56). Their in-between and more public agora-like characteristics signal less formality and thus a change in expected behaviors. Such hallway encounters can provide serendipitous moments and the possibility for incidental learning. While those learning moments might not fit in with formally established and stated learning outcomes, they can provide necessary opportunities to connect on a more personal and perhaps informal level. They lower the threshold to engage in conversation. Compared to scheduling a meeting with a professor or coming to an official office hour, hallways can provide the opportunity for a quick question or comment: "Establishing a safe and trusting relationship between students and teachers can be greatly facilitated if the learning environment encourages learners and teachers to interact before, during, and after formal class meetings" (Skill and Young 2002: 25–6).

Hallways are usually sociofugal spaces that often do not have favorable characteristics for prolonged conversations and lingering (Montgomery 2020). They may be drafty, cold, and loud. They usually lack furniture and seating options, often due to fire codes or safety regulations: "In older buildings, it's common to see students camped out on the floor studying outside a lab or classroom waiting for the instructor to unlock the door" (MacPhee 2009). While they can be a type of Third Place, they often do not have favorable features.

Intentionally designing hallways and other liminal spaces should not be an afterthought. Designers can encourage the lingering effect mentioned above by making hallways more active. Passive hallways are merely there to provide space for people to move from point A to point B. Active hallways provide additional space, such as "conversation-friendly alcoves connected or adjacent to the more formal teaching and learning spaces" (Skill and Young 2002: 26), seating areas in the middle or the side of the hallway, or gathering spaces in hallway corners or bends. As gathering areas between classes can be noisy (Folkins et al. 2015), it is important to consider creating quieter buffer

Figure 2 Hallway with student sitting on the floor with laptop.

zones or nooks. Dittoe (2006) calls active corridors "pathways": expanded "spaces that normally function as hallways" to "support continued learning opportunities, promote impromptu gatherings, and provide individual places for quiet reflection." They also allow those that do need to just pass through not be blocked. Furniture is likely to be heavy, unmovable, or fixed, to not interfere with the circulatory properties and safety regulations.

Chapters 2 and 4 discuss how agency and autonomy can enhance a sense of ownership and belonging. Hallways are useful spaces to post student work and make learning visible and tangible (OWP/P Architects, VS Furniture, and Bruce Mau Design 2010). Language classes in particular can benefit from displaying student projects (Pettit 2022). Selingo (2018) suggests adding writable surfaces to unused wall spaces in hallways to engage this current generation of students. Overall, conversations or work that originated in the classroom should be able to be continued and transitioned to hallway areas easily (Skill and Young 2002).

Offices

Learning space design often focuses predominantly on students, but McGregor (2003) reminds us that space also matters to teachers and instructors. It is, after all, their workplace. For K-12 teachers in the United States, it is not uncommon to have their own classroom, which is often also their office space. They have more agency to make spatial choices within the rooms. In other countries, it is more common for teachers to circulate and students staying in one room except for subject classes taking place in particular rooms (e.g., a laboratory, music room, or gym). In higher education, it is common for students and faculty to change rooms. Faculty often have their own offices or a shared office space.

These office spaces are learning spaces. For language learning in particular, students might come to office hours to get help with a particular problem, discuss an essay, or even just talk in the target language. Visiting a professor's office and going to office hours can be stressful and intimidating, especially for first-generation students, even though they are an important aspect of learning success (Laiduc et al. 2021). Increasing the likelihood of such visits can be supported by removing barriers, training students and faculty, and improving access. Physical space design and even subtle design changes can make offices more approachable. Signage, decorations, materials, and ambient features can provide important cues. Lighting, furniture arrangements, and closed or open doors and window shades all matter in a student's perception. Faculty should balance concerns of openness and transparency against needs for confidentiality when deciding on when to close a door. Glass doors can provide a way to shut out auditory information while providing visible fluidity.

A more intentional design can support policies and expectations. Offices differ because often faculty have more agency in how such spaces can be set up, decorated, and personalized. Even the waiting area outside of offices is important to consider. If students must camp out in front of a professor's office and perhaps sit on the floor, that sends a symbolic message (see also Chapter 4 for a more in-depth discussion of furniture and chairs). The office, its entrance, and the immediate area outside provide a rich canvas for conveying language-relevant information and a possibility to display learning materials, visuals, quotes, articles, etc. It might be the space most instructors have sole agency over.

Storage Spaces

The last learning space to be discussed, storage space, is usually completely ignored and invisible because of its auxiliary and rather mundane nature. Nonetheless, storage spaces play an important role in the ecosystem of language learning spaces. As previously discussed, languages in particular benefit from various materials—such as books, games, and other media—realia, teaching props, technological devices, etc. If there are no suitable, not visible, or not enough spaces to store such things, they tend to not be used. Doorley and Witthoft (2012: 42) argue that "[W]e always need more space than we have, and Support Structures [sic!] never really count as space for people and activities. Thus, they often end up underrepresented in the final floor plans." When designing learning spaces, it is important to include storage areas and spaces and be conscious of their procedural attributes. Who has access, who has the power to borrow or check out items, and who purchases new materials or discards old ones are necessary considerations. There is often a regulatory vacuum which results in either completely unused materials and empty storage spaces, or completely overcrowded ones.

Ecosystems

None of these language learning spaces should be seen in isolation. When we think of classrooms, we cannot ignore hallways or thresholds. We should consider how offices and storage spaces relate to classrooms. In short, we need to see them as connected, not individual entities, and thus as an ecosystem. An ecosystem is a structure or community of living and nonliving entities. Other attributes of ecosystems include the flowing and movement across and between areas and boundaries, and the ability of living and nonliving things to adapt. One only has to think of crabs that use a soda can as their shell, a shipwreck full of sea life, or a coral reef. Ecosystems are healthy and flourish when there is balance and diversity. Most importantly, we should remember that spaces are not mere physical containers but are created by people within environments and their actions. In many ways, places share many of these same characteristics as they "also exist on a horizontal axis. They are connected to other places and, in part, derive their identities from these connections. They overspill their bounds, giving them width and a distributed presence" (Cresswell 2019: 185).

In regard to language learning spaces, we have students, faculty, staff, visitors, etc. interacting with nonliving things, like classrooms, hallways, offices, restrooms, lounges, etc., along with all the items in them, like bulletin boards, electrical outlets, benches, trashcans, and so forth. Ecosystems do have boundaries, but they are usually more or less permeable and connect to other ecosystems. In our case, the outside of a building might have different properties than the inside, but it is also connected. The patio outside of the doors of an educational building is both a part of the system as well as separate. A campus is in itself a larger ecosystem, connecting smaller systems. In order to create a sense of belonging in new or redesigned spaces, it is advisable to create links to existing buildings, structures, landmarks, or other features. This can be done through several means; for example, by linking styles or materials (Dober 1992).

Middleton (2018: 67) discusses the concept of "interstitial space" which "is about the connection between spaces: for example, how the classroom idea connects with the café idea; how home connects with work and with study; how the digital connects with the physical. It creates both frisson and teaching challenge. It reveals opportunities for engagement and the potential that one space gives to another." If the sum is greater than its individual parts, then a systems approach is crucial when considering design or redesign projects. This includes discussions about disciplines and subject areas and how they relate to one another. Interdisciplinarity is frequently the subject in higher educational discourses. From a spatial perspective, however, we often find buildings separating the disciplines and departments. Davidson (2017: 249) argues that the "major in a traditional discipline no longer maps to the complex ways students encounter the world or the jobs and careers of the present and the future, and so we must champion relevant interdisciplinary projects, missions, programs, and goals, across departments and silos of knowledge and expertise." The question then is how space design can support such complexity and interrelatedness? If language learning spaces are only frequented by language students and language faculty, how will those outside of those groups engage with ideas around language? This chapter's section is entitled "invisible language learning spaces": we must ask ourselves how we can make them visible within a larger ecosystems' context.

Addressing the complexity of such systems is more difficult than dealing with distinct, individual, and contained spaces. It is advisable to create gaps and leave some areas to be filled with meaning at a later point, as users change and adapt. It is important to consider the functions and goals and provide spaces for different kinds of social engagement (Crook and Mitchell 2012) and different modes and types of learning activities. As previously discussed, thresholds can signal boundaries between and within ecosystems. Other zone and boundary marking possibilities include different colors or materials, either on the floor or the walls, and signage. Even simple floor lines, as Doorley and Witthoft (2012: 212) suggest, "can create surprisingly powerful partitions that can be used to change behaviors & define boundaries." Chapter 4 provides more detail and concrete ideas about design processes, attributes, and considerations.

Conclusion

There are different physical spaces that are not usually seen as language learning spaces. These invisible spaces, such as thresholds, hallways, offices, and storage spaces, do play an important but often overlooked role in the educational enterprise. They are part of an ecosystem of spaces that can provide important functions that more formal learning spaces afford. It is important to pay attention to these often-neglected spaces during various stages of language learning space design processes.

Alternative Language Learning Spaces

The spaces mentioned thus far in this chapter are more or less categorizable. The purpose of this section is to summarize several other alternative spaces that should be considered when designing language learning space ecosystems. Zheng et al. (2018: 45–6) argue that the "classroom has typically been the main site for language learning, in which 'input' is mainly from teachers, textbooks and peers. Focusing learning on the linguistic system and the collateral consequence of decontextualized results neglects powerful learning environments outside of the classroom." Similarly, Benson (2021: 134) calls for more research on these other spaces for language learning:

> Much out-of-class language learning research is conducted in schools and universities and involves custom-designed facilities such as self-access centres, computer laboratories and other kinds of learning spaces. Although the design

of these spaces deserves more attention, there is also a need for SLA research to spread out into a much wider variety of settings. Within educational institutions, these might include libraries, extracurricular clubs, open spaces and "schoolscapes."

This section provides an overview of diverse space possibilities along with design considerations to encourage a more expansive view of what kinds of language learning spaces are possible.

Studios

Studios share characteristics with and are similar to other spaces described thus far. Hart-Davidson (2020) defines studio environments as spaces "where learners, guided by a teacher, learn with and from one another. The other learners in the room are the most important resource they have." A studio is a safe space "where learners can see others like themselves, fellow learners, and watch as they attempt to do similar things, calibrating their own efforts. The mirrors in the studio are just as important. There learners can see themselves and reflect on where they are succeeding and where they might improve." The term *studio* is a useful physical space label and descriptor for communities of practice. Studios are usually associated with the arts, art studios, photography studies, dance studios, etc. Their design attributes usually support an apprentice system and foster goals of community building (Lave and Wenger 1991), sense of belonging, and collaborative learning.

Programmable Space

Programmable space—for example, displays or exhibits—can really be in any space—in hallways, in language centers, in sitting areas, etc. We can see them as learning spaces within spaces, providing opportunities to reach potential learners that do not even necessarily consider themselves language learners, such as passersby, visitors, support staff, etc. Mathews and Soistmann (2016: 32) liken physical spaces in libraries to those in the virtual space: "I view library buildings in the same manner: It is all programmable space. We can move book stacks, computers, or study carrels and arrange them differently." These temporary features are not static but curated and programmed. Sometimes these can be an afterthought because most language educators are not trained in designing such spaces. Furthermore, considerations of agency, authority over the spaces, access, and lack of guidelines sometimes lead to programmable spaces that either have not changed over a long period of time, or they even remain empty.

Language Outdoor Spaces

Outside spaces at an institution are not unusual, but they tend to be conceptualized as social and informal language learning spaces rather than formal spaces. Examples are plazas outside of language centers and residential or food spaces. Schenker and Kraemer (2018) report that language summer camps use outside spaces. There are some clear drawbacks to outside spaces, however, particularly when used for formal language education: the weather is unpredictable and, depending on the geographic region, these spaces cannot be used for parts of the year. They make planning difficult, provide limited affordances and technology options, provide challenges around security and acoustics, and are thus rarely found.

Commonly outdoor classrooms are associated with younger learners; for example, forest classrooms and forest preschools, or *Waldkindergärten* (Huppertz 2004; Schwarz 2017). The pandemic led several institutions of higher learning to experiment with designing specific outdoor learning spaces (Felix 2021) in order to make airborne virus transmission less likely. This provided some useful experiences to reframe our thinking about how and why we might use such spaces. Jones (2021) quotes one biology professor, for example, who remarked on new possibilities for group cohesion and work due to changes in thresholds, boundaries, and directions: "In the context of group work, when people are done they can leave, even when it's not the exact end of class," he said. "I liked the idea of people being able to walk out in roughly 360 degrees of direction … it sort of made it less of an event when someone walked out the door. I liked that from a pedagogical point of view." The lack of walls forces a reconceptualization of normalized expectations and increases the horizon and scope of the surroundings.

For language courses in particular, we do not have many examples of outdoor language learning experiments, but the few we do have provide a glimpse into understanding ambient and spatial attributes for language learning better. For example, S. Sterling (2021, personal communication, 1 March) reports via email about of two projects at Indiana State University, a pop-up outdoor language classroom for migrant workers as well as an RV-based language learning space. During the pandemic, the outdoor classrooms at Pomona College provided a mask-free alternative to indoor spaces which required masks. Prof. Bana Dahi describes her experiences as having both advantages and disadvantages (Pomona 2021):

> My students and I really enjoy being outside teaching and learning beginner-level French without a mask. The students were very engaged and loved meeting each other without barriers, while keeping social distancing in mind. Learning a new language can be very challenging and intimidating for students who are learning new phonetics and sounds and need to pay attention to how they are produced. Creating a close community and a safe space is a must for the students to feel comfortable enough to speak a new language. I can't imagine being able to do this when facial expressions are hidden behind masks.

In my interviews with language faculty who taught outside during the pandemic, they remarked on several features. On the positive side, there is the heightened awareness of the surroundings, the extended horizon, the bidirectional visibility and openness, elements of risk and surprise, the noises, the more immersive and not sterile surroundings, the changed mobility and inclusion of movement, and the much-increased use of mobile technologies (in contrast to fixed ones). One faculty member reported that it was by far the most connected class she had taught. On the negative side, common disadvantages included acoustics and street noises, issues with technologies, such as the inability to hide cables, glare on TV screens, relatively small screen sizes, etc. The sunlight was sometimes too bright, and unshaded parts were too hot. They also reported that the outdoor spaces were much more public, which may have caused some anxieties for the teachers and the students when speaking in the L2. This was also perceived as positive, however, because the classes were much more visible to passersby and made language courses public to those who weren't enrolled. Faculty reported that exams were still conducted inside.

While results were clearly mixed, there are interesting takeaways for conceptualizing not only outdoor spaces but also creating better indoor spaces. The experimental spaces were of course born out of the emergency situation that an external event, the pandemic, brought about. They were not designed from the ground up for that purpose but rather provided a temporary solution. Furthermore, the courses themselves were not designed with outdoor teaching in mind. This resembles the experiences with emergency remote classes in virtual spaces, which also differed from intentionally designed online courses. To pursue this, a robust faculty training system should be in place to more deliberately use the affordances that the outside provides and design courses and lesson plans differently. Location, geography, and climate are also considerations—what works in Southern California would not be feasible in Michigan for much of the year.

Another example of outdoor language learning spaces is the Japanese garden that is part of the Asian Languages House at Colorado College. The garden, which is focused on authenticity and involved students in its creation, is "a focal point for conversation practice, cultural activities, and community building. The Japanese garden serves to create a sense of Japan within the students' home campus, making the house an inviting place to be" (Ericson 2020: 155). It invites "interaction among various communities of practice" and serves "as a culturally sensitive 'text'" (Ericson 2020: 141).

A final example in this exploration into outdoor language learning spaces is how nature and the land itself, in this case the forestlands of what is northern Minnesota and northern Wisconsin in the United States today, are an integral part in Indigenous language reclamation: "particularly for language reclamation, the land is more than a learning environment and more than a text. The land is a living dialogic resource that can be consulted with all of a learner's senses. The land is an interlocutor, capable of contributing to the co-construction of knowledge about phenomena that are, were, and will be" (Engman and Hermes 2021: 101). These natural spaces are places full of meaning and context. "The land is a participant because its participation in the interactions around inquiry, wondering, and knowing is required" (Engman and Hermes 2021: 101).

Outdoor learning spaces must not, of course, be used only in formal ways. They can simply be transitory or liminal, in-between spaces. They can provide a reason for students to gather before class and not disperse afterwards, offering community-building and placemaking aspects. MacPhee (2009) suggests planting shade trees and providing sitting areas that make these spaces more usable for students to linger before going inside for class. Departments "claiming" spaces outside of their buildings can extend the square footage and support an ecosystems approach as outlined above.

Learning from Outdoor Places for Indoor Design

Outdoor learning spaces offer many benefits. Connecting with nature is deeply integral to being a human being. It "gives our supply of mental resources an opportunity to renew and regenerate," (Paul 2021: 97) provides better lighting, and allows us to be more in tune with our physical bodies, provides opportunities for awe, and extends the bounds rather than restrict us to confined spaces.

In recent years, biophilic design has received growing attention not only in workplace and healthcare settings but also education. It uses design cues from outdoor spaces inside of buildings; for example, through fractal patterns often found in nature, more windows with views of natural spaces, and use of natural materials and plants. Determan et al. (2019) report that middle school students had less anxiety and stress and higher learning outcomes in biophilic learning spaces. Another solution might be overcoming the dichotomy of indoor-outdoor spaces by considering hybrid, in-between spaces. Olsen (2020) suggests a hybrid category, "mid-doors," which combines advantageous attributes from each.

Bonner and Reinders (2018: 36) discuss virtual reality (see also Chapter 5) and its affordances in language education. They argue that "[T]here are no distracting classroom windows to stare out of when students are directly immersed into the topic they are investigating." From a biophilic perspective, the removal of natural light, naturally occurring fractal patterns, and natural movements is not helpful in the learning process, at least not for extended periods of time. While staring out of the window might be seen as a distraction, it might also be a way for learners to process complex information and regulate emotions and behaviors.

Nonlanguage Learning Campus Spaces for Language Learning

Most classes take place in the same space throughout a semester. If the registrar assigns room A123, then it is common practice to gather in that room during every class session. There are benefits about changing locations occasionally and having class sessions in other places. Parker (2018: 62) argues using the term "Displacement" which "is simply about breaking people out of their habits. It is about waking people up from the slumber of their own routines." This can often happen within the same campus and allows for leveraging interdisciplinarity. It can also create more memorable, embodied experiences, foster motivation, and increase group cohesion through shared experiences. Spaces can include but are not limited to libraries, on-campus museums, botanical gardens, lawns, and other outdoor spaces, community spaces, the international center, rare books rooms, game rooms, maker spaces, exhibition spaces, dining halls, or campus cafes. Not all institutions have all of these campus spaces, of course, but educators can be encouraged to explore these spaces and create new synergies across common disciplinary lines. Setting up partnerships, like the Michigan State University CeLTA and Abrams Planetarium Partnership (Cornell 2023), can set pedagogical and logistical frameworks, allow partners to coordinate lesson plans and support mechanisms, and increase visibility.

Off-Campus Community Spaces

Much of this book is about institutional learning spaces. But there are many spaces outside of campus boundaries that provide rich opportunities for language learning in particular and learning in general. Utilizing community spaces is one way of acknowledging and bridging this divide. Lave and Wenger (1991: 53) stress the embodied nature of learning:

> As an aspect of social practice, learning involves the whole person; it implies not only a relation to specific activities, but a relation to social communities—it implies becoming a full participant, a member, a kind of person. In this view, learning only partly—and often incidentally—implies becoming able to be involved in new activities, to perform new tasks and functions, to master new understandings. Activities, tasks, functions, and understandings do not exist in isolation; they are part of broader systems of relations in which they have meaning.

Dislocation pedagogy can address some of the shortcomings of institutionalized and contained types of learning. Godlewska (2013: 384–5) defines dislocation as "the removal of students from what has become familiar to them, disrupting their geography (where they and others belong in the community that is home to the university) and their assumptions about life course and the authority of academic knowledge. This kind of learning is difficult in a classroom but entirely natural in everyday life." As such, life places can "disrupt the narrowness of focus in the demographically simplified context of the university" (Godlewska 2013: 385). It replaces these contexts with other experiences, communities, and groups of people and activities. Whether language students visit the local elementary school, a community center, library, cafe, or park, leaving the safe and familiar confines of the physical classroom dislodges learning from its familiar routines.

Conclusion

The goal of this chapter was to map out language learning spaces beyond the classroom. They all have in common that they are what I would call "spaces of intentionality." They are designed with a specific purpose in mind, and view language learning as a more holistic activity. They are deeply connected to institutional structures and preconditions and are locally manifested. As already discussed earlier, successful spaces turn into places, which Burbules and Callister (2000: 161) see as a "condition for the formation and maintenance of communities." Meaningful language learning spaces can thus be the basis for places that support language learning communities. It is important to stress the procedural and unplannable nature of places, which are not uniform in their meaning. That meaning is recreated collectively and individually, formally and informally, officially and unofficially. "Places are where stories gather. Individual stories (telling a story without a place would be experimental in the extreme), collective stories, official stories, subversive stories" (Creswell 2019: 181).

There are certainly many other spaces not mentioned in this chapter, which is not meant to be a complete list. Other specialized language spaces range from more common spaces, such as spaces for language testing to more unique ones, such as language theaters and movie theaters, prayer nooks in social language spaces, musical performance spaces, and language video game rooms. There is unfortunately relatively little research about such spaces, and it would be useful to study these further in the future. But the often-hidden diversity of language learning spaces, or rather places, is also an encouraging starting point for those who wish to explore this topic further.

There is a danger in categorizing spaces. As the example of the language center illustrates, no one center in that category is the same. When we view spaces as processes and constantly evolving and adapting, as a multitude of functions, affordances, and possibilities, we can create spaces that matter. We should acknowledge that spaces are not the same to all stakeholders and users. This then leads us to consider how we can design within such a framework, how to create parameters and processes that enable not just the design of generic, categorizable spaces but specific places for language learning.

It should also be acknowledged that the spaces introduced in this chapter are quite US-centric and focus on institutional settings. Guerrettaz (2021: 60) reminds us that "[W]hile not all language learning occurs in Euro-Western-style classroomscapes … the broader and more flexible concept of 'space' is applicable to diverse pedagogical settings." This may include the briefly discussed incorporation of the land and nature, different cultural conventions—for example chair sitting versus not chair sitting cultures (see Chapter 4)—and the role that community spaces can play. It is also important to consider that language learning in settings other than institutional programs and classes is common practice: "If FL education is to take learners seriously as legitimate users of the language, scholars and instructors must consider the different ways in which their students could imagine engaging with the world beyond the context of classroom" (Warner and Dupuy 2018: 124). Learning differs from education as it can take place "in a multiplicity and diversity of sites" and not only in "educational spaces of enclosure" (Edwards and Usher 2008: 90).

The following chapter then frames language learning spaces less as concrete types of spaces, but rather as processes and attributes. It thus will blur architectural boundaries and situate them beyond common representations and labels. Boys (2011: 48) argues that:

> What is most interesting here is that the kinds of "spatial" terms being used by educationalists—concepts such as liminal or transitional spaces, boundary crossings and thresholds, centripetal movements, and the call for spaces that are "safe," enabling belonging but not reinforcing comfort zones—do not easily offer the kind of simplistic associative social-spatial metaphors of "informal" learning. Most importantly, the very underlying structure of ideas, which makes formal and informal oppositional, precisely through an assumed sequence of associated and analogous spatial/aesthetic differences (e.g., uncomfortable/comfortable, one-directional/multi-directional, teacher-led/student-led, serious/playful), just does not work for more complex conceptual spaces such as liminality or transition. These ideas may link to, but cannot be so easily represented through those seemingly obvious design tropes such as "niche" or "cluster," "street" or "hub," as described in the previous chapter.

Resisting labels and planning beyond overly simplistic categories is important when designing truly innovative and effective spaces for language learning.

4

Design and Administration of Language Learning Spaces

So far, we have examined learning spaces themselves: which kinds exist, which are possible, and how they fit in with educational philosophies and methodologies. In that sense, spaces are often passively accepted by their stakeholders rather than actively created. That aspect, the design of learning spaces, is what this chapter is about.

Most educators and students are never directly involved in designing the learning spaces they use. But being active participants, drivers, and initiators in this process can lead to more optimized and intentional design of physical language learning spaces. Those involved in learning space design are usually professionals, such as architects and designers, and from the institution's side, facilities managers (Skill and Young 2002). Educators, students, and other stakeholders usually are not deeply involved in the design and redesign of learning spaces. Yet buildings and spaces are not merely aesthetic or technical objects but social ones and can thus be critiqued and analyzed through a social lens as well (Markus and Cameron 2002). The first section of this chapter discusses who is involved in which administrative processes and who is in control of various aspects of physical learning spaces.

Design should be based on the educational mission. Institutional and community values are an enduring foundation that can provide a basis of resilience and allows for necessary adjustments later as technologies, pedagogies, and organizational structures change. OWP/P Architects, VS Furniture, and Bruce Mau Design (2010: 69) remind us: "It seems obvious but is often forgotten: Teaching and learning should shape the building, not vice versa." An intentional design process that includes all stakeholders at all stages and in all aspects is a necessary ingredient in creating learning spaces that are truly aligned with the educational mission and values. There are many large and small decisions that must be made for each space project. From wall colors and treatments to furniture selection, from wiring to lighting, from acoustics to aesthetics, even a small space requires many choices. Because such institutional spaces need to serve a diverse group of stakeholders, compromises must be found, and best practices should be consulted. The "Design Attributes" section in this chapter provides an overview of design attributes with special attention paid to language education.

Once built, educational buildings usually last decades if not centuries; there is a certain inertia in our built environment. Major updates and redesigns happen rarely and are generally more incremental: "transformation is painstakingly slow in the world of school design" (Nair and Fielding 2005: 1). While it is exciting to be a part of the process of designing new spaces, most of a building's life is in the postoccupancy phase after its users have moved in. The "Post-Occupancy Processes" section in this chapter details how spaces can be not only maintained but be continuously worked on to thrive, adapt, and innovate.

The final section of the chapter discusses how learning spaces can be created to be more equitable, accessible, and inclusive. It is important to create spaces that do not merely provide a functional container but one that diverse people choose to spend time in, in which they feel not only comfortable but feel they belong.

Control and Administration of Language Learning Spaces

Who controls our physical educational spaces? Who gets to make the decisions, who controls the money flows, who oversees guidelines and processes? Who "owns" these spaces? While the curriculum is generally at least partially controlled by the department and its educators, learning space design is often controlled by different entities or offices, including in the initial design as well as post occupancy.

Space and power correlate, as the use of physical learning spaces at the University of Missouri campus in Columbia in the novel "Stoner" illustrates. While the depicted spaces are conventional, the novel also shows that the physical and the mental worlds are not mutually exclusive as shown in Stoner's love affair. At some point, Prof. Stoner is forced by his nemesis department chair, Prof. Lomax, to teach at undesirable times and in terrible rooms. The room assignment is a physical manifestation of power, influence, and politics:

> The building was an old one, with wooden floors, and it was used as a classroom only in emergencies; the room to which he had been assigned was too small

for the number of students enrolled, so that several of the boys had to sit on the windowsills or stand. When Stoner came in they looked at him with the discomfort of uncertainty; he might be friend or foe, and they did not know which was worse. He apologized to the students for the room, made a small joke at the expense of the registrar, and assured those who were standing that there would be chairs for them tomorrow. Then he put his folder on the battered lectern that rested unevenly on the desk and surveyed the faces before him."

(Williams 1965: 221–2)

Physical spaces symbolize power structures through different criteria, including office sizes, classroom assignment priorities, and agency over furniture selection. Power differences can also be found within classrooms, which usually assign different (and larger) furniture to instructors in contrast to students. Because there isn't a single entity in charge of learning spaces, different entities often have different goals, priorities, values, and expertise. Sometimes communication and alignment between these entities is minimal, leading to sub-optimal learning spaces in the predesign phase, the design phase, and the postoccupancy phase.

Predesign Phase

Before any language learning space design or redesign project, someone needs to start the process. This can be a top-down process, initiated by a strategic plan or a campus plan, or by individuals in the administration. It might come from a self-study. In such cases, the language department(s) is informed that newly designed or redesigned spaces are to be expected in the future. In some cases, the department(s) has little say in the matter; in other cases, they might be deeply involved in the whole process. The initial conception phase can also be triggered through a bottom-up process. For example, a department or a committee might develop the idea that the current spaces are inadequate, outdated, do not serve the unit's goals, or are simply non-existent. Sometimes this is driven by highly motivated individuals, such as the department chair, language center director, or a faculty member. The department might approach such a project in this phase in a number of ways; for example, by looking first for funds through grants, foundations, or donors. It might hire a consultant to help navigate this phase. Donors might also trigger this initial conception phase if they wish to fund a whole building or individual language learning spaces.

Often, the process is not as clear-cut. It might be a mix of different triggers, an iterative process that can in many cases span a long timeframe. Plans might be on ice until adequate funding is secured or until an administrator is willing to substantially support and back such an endeavor. At this point, the project can be driven by different interests and needs. For example, the administration simply might want to move departments into different buildings or cluster certain units. It might want to adjust the space available to the needs of the units. This phase might have nothing to do with language learning goals, outcomes, and priorities if it is conceived in a top-down process. The goals of the faculty and the department do not necessarily align completely with those of administration or donors.

Design Phase

During the design phase, more entities are involved. It is usually a siloed process and includes professionals and experts, such as architects, designers, technologists, media specialists, IT personnel, financial experts, advancement staff, and campus building professionals. Meaningful participation of all stakeholders is not always guaranteed in this phase. Especially those who use the spaces the most, students and faculty, are oftentimes only consulted briefly through surveys and listening sessions. Sometimes representatives or committees are appointed in order to keep the process moving forward and not become too costly. But designing physical spaces in itself is an act of shaping and influencing educational processes and practices. Leaving key stakeholders largely out of the process, or sidelining them, can lead to not optimally designed spaces. For example, in one project I consulted for, the architect's team had assumed the language department wanted a computer lab. They asked how many stations were needed in their surveys. Everyone assumed that a computer lab was needed. It was only through individual conversations that it became clear, well into the design phase, that a computer lab would be a waste of money as most faculty did not want a dedicated lab. But the normalizing power of the survey and assumptions of what language learning spaces a language department should have almost led to a very costly mistake. The architect, designers, and campus planners were not familiar with current language pedagogy trends and research. Their frame of reference came from other campuses they had seen previously. In a way, the powerful stereotype of the language lab had a large influence on the process.

Postoccupancy phase

The network of stakeholders changes during the postoccupancy phase and now includes the registrar, cleaning personnel, maintenance workers, IT and media support, and teaching/learning specialists. Many of these stakeholders cannot or will not make major decisions on changes to the space, either because it is not their job or because they lack access to funds or specific expertise. There are many people involved in this constantly shifting web, and nobody is formally or informally in charge or control of many of them. This can result in spaces that stay largely inert.

Inertia

Inertia is commonplace in education, and learning spaces are no exception. Miller (1998: 18–19) writes that "*everyone* working in the academy already knows at some level … that all teaching occurs within the context of a deeply entrenched bureaucratic system that exercises any number of material constraints on what must take place in the classroom, on who and what may be allowed in that space, and on how those entities and materials may interact." The larger institutional context and its power structures are slow to react to new trends and tend to avoid unnecessary risks and uphold the status quo. Without considerable energy spent by individuals or smaller units, learning spaces often do not change appreciatively, and transformation is very slow (Nair and Fielding 2005). But not only is the initial effort important, it is crucial to set up sustaining mechanisms that keep the spaces effective and efficient. This includes rules, staffing, managing expectations, ongoing financial support, and professional development. In short, language learning spaces must be curated. Otherwise, newly built spaces may fall back to their uncurated, normalized state.

Loosely Coupled Systems

It can be argued that institutions of learning are loosely coupled systems (Weick 1976). Each component and actor, such as departments, units, faculty, etc., has a relative degree of independence compared to tightly coupled systems. If the Spanish Language department makes changes, the Physics department or the Campus Maintenance office is usually not affected much. This provides a "sensitive sensing mechanism" and allows for "localized adaptation" (Weick 1976: 6) and autonomy. This is important as the goals of a language program or department differ from those of other units or programs. The tension with learning spaces is that they are a tightly coupled system, run and managed by a professional team with quite different goals, such as scheduling, cleanliness, security, efficiency, cost-effectiveness, etc. This leads to standardization, which is the opposite of localization. Control of learning spaces is further curtailed by access to funds and expert knowledge. While faculty and departments have great control over the curriculum, learning goals, pedagogical approaches and methods, and so forth, they wield almost none over the system of managing, maintaining, and designing learning spaces.

While this can explain some of the problems in the design of specialized learning spaces, such as those for languages, loose coupling can also be beneficial. It shields one unit from the other as the actions and decisions of one unit often do not affect another unit. Regarding learning spaces, it means that one unit can design innovative or radical spaces while the other one keeps traditional ones in place. Each unit can be unaffected by the other's decisions, allowing room for experimentation. On the flip side, however, loose coupling also prevents distinct units from coordination of their space design projects.

Finances

Learning spaces are a structural, political, and financial issue. In the fictitious newspaper "The Campus Scribe" in the novel "The Shakespeare Requirement," (Schumacher 2018: 1–2), the physical building symbolizes the institution's power and value structures:

> The Economics Department's portion of Willard Hall now includes state-of-the-art technology-enhanced classrooms, a fully equipped computer lab, elegant seminar and meeting rooms, faculty offices, and a café. Stunning mosaic tile floors and skylights were underwritten by the Morse Foundation; digital LCD wall displays were donated by philanthropist-alum Bill Fixx. Asked to comment on the nearly completed project, University President Nyla Hoffman praised Payne's corporate and private donors and said she looks forward 'to a renewed era of growth for the Department of Economics, a jewel in the crown here at Payne.' Willard Hall is also home to the Department of English, which occupies the lower floor.

The fictional treatment of the topic reflects that in the United States, donor contributions are an important part of financing building projects. The value attached to a discipline or a focus area is linked to which new buildings are financed and which ones are priorities in the remodeling pipeline. There is a territorial aspect at institutions that extends to the physical as one of the most precious resources. It is often not well-defined which spaces "belong" to whom. In such a vacuum it is unclear who can make meaningful space decisions, and this often results in inertia.

Of course, not all such building decisions are made by donors. But how they are financed is a crucial component of understanding learning space design projects. Institutions create strategic plans to emphasize their values, prioritize building projects, and make strategic decisions about allocating scarce funds. But departments also have limited avenues of securing their own funding by applying for grants, courting donors, or working with foundations. They can also use processes that do not rely on large sums of money (see Chapter 4) to make less costly but effective choices within existing learning spaces.

Adaptation

Even though spaces may have been designed with certain goals in mind, the lived reality usually does not match these intentions. No matter who has control over a space, its users can change it and exert their own control over it. "Residents of an architectural space adapt their activities to fit the space, and adapt the space to fit their activities—the relation is always both ways, and it is in this reciprocal adaptation that a space becomes a place". (Burbules and Callister 2000: 162). Here are four examples of such adaptations in language learning spaces: The example from the photo shows a language student who is not using the video viewing room as it was intended by using university-provided tapes or DVDs on the provided players. Rather, the student streams the movies on her own laptop.

The room's initial function is no longer used, but the users adapt to the new medium of streaming. A second example are students not using the provided desktop computers in a language computer lab, but rather pushing the keyboard and mouse away with their laptops. In a third example, a table was installed in a corridor outside of the classrooms on the second floor. The intention for building it was for students to use it as a standing desk. During the postoccupancy phase, however, students used the tables as seats, which prompted the administration to tape signs stating "Risk of falling: Do NOT sit" to the tables. The students were not using it as intended for several reasons. There were no seating opportunities in the hallway, where they usually congregated after and before classes. The tables also had no electrical outlets, which forced some of them to sit in a different corner on the floor (which was also not intended for congregating). Burbules and Callister (2000: 162) give another example of space adaptation: "many college campuses lay out a pattern of sidewalks, designed in advance, to connect various buildings, only to find that the grassy areas in between are often worn down by new paths that the residents of the campus actually use in getting from building to building."

106   *Physical Language Learning Spaces in the Digital Age*

Figure 3 Video viewing room at a US language center.

In the last example, facilities' office and cleaning staff posted a note on the door leading to a flexible, active language learning classroom. The piece of paper states: "Attn: Instructors If you re-arrange the furniture in this room, please return it to 'CLASSROOM STYLE' before you leave. Thank you." The sign illustrates that the goals of the educational users (collaborative work facilitated through new and flexible setups) differ from those of the cleaning personnel (which is to efficiently clean and maintain the room). The act of setting up the room back to a "classroom style," as defined by the facilities' coordinator, competes with what the normal and intended use and pattern of the space is. It actively undermines the pedagogical mission and philosophy, its built pedagogy.

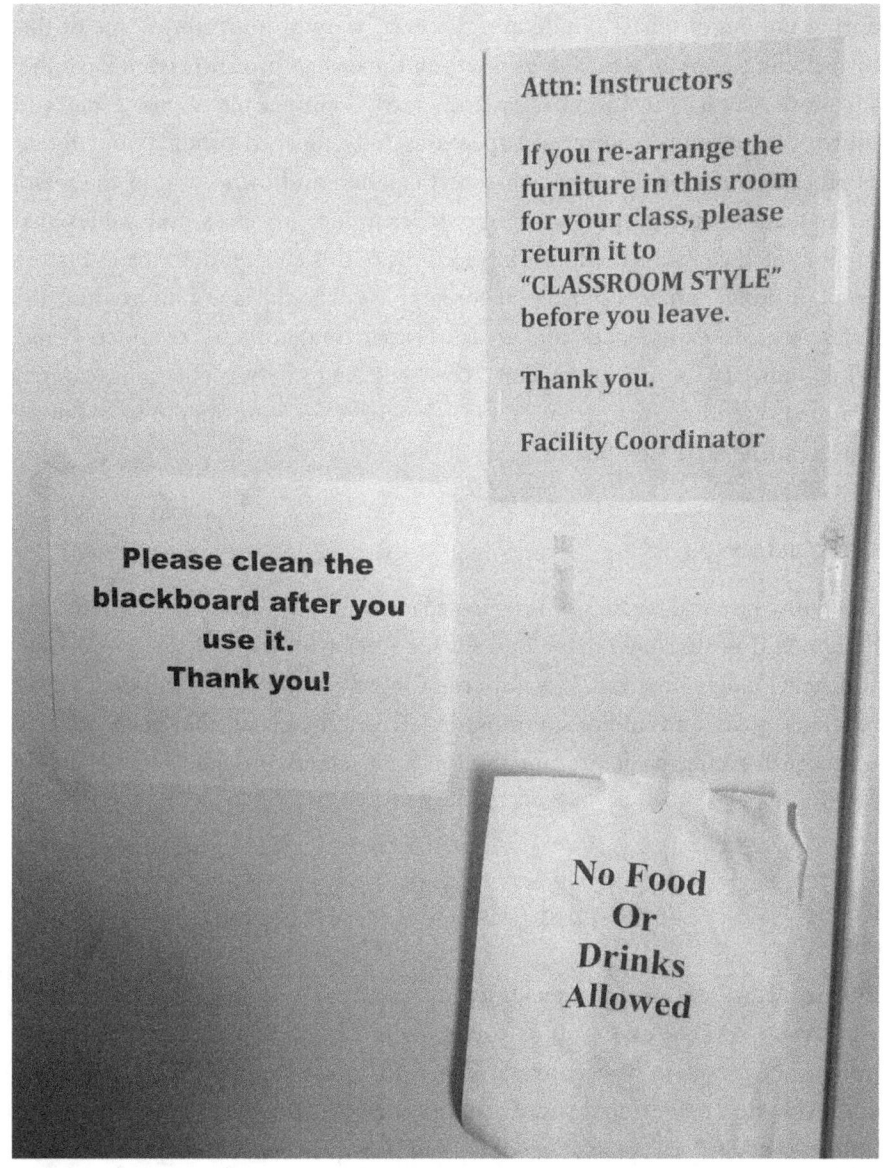

Figure 4 Language classroom door with notes posted by maintenance staff.

One can also deduct, however, that faculty and students tend to move furniture around, and thus have a different concept of what "classroom style" might entail. The example shows that all stakeholders should be included in learning spaces, including the maintenance staff.

All these examples illustrate that, in different scales of space, users turn spaces into places through reciprocal adaptation processes. They always make unintended changes to their spaces, and it is difficult to foresee actual usage during the design phase. There are, however, ways of mitigating some of this by including users in a meaningful way in the design process; create flexibility and leave space to intentionally adapt; clearly defining intentions, goals, and control issues; and to never see spaces as fully finished products but rather as processes. If we want to increase participation and ownership in the realm of language learning spaces, we should examine processes and values that support such goals. As the following sections of this chapter describe in further detail, a design process during all three phases should take into account the different goals, experiences, and areas of expertise that the stakeholders bring. While many factors are important—cost, building safety, regulations, campus planning, branding, maintenance, etc.—language learning should be a central aspect during all design phases.

Conclusion

Designing physical languages' learning spaces involves three phases: predesign, design, and postoccupancy phases. Each comes with its own set of processes and stakeholders involved. It is important to be mindful of the different power relations, goals, and interests of those involved. This means that pedagogy and language learning goals are not the only considerations that a space design project involves.

Value- and Mission-Driven Design

On the surface, designing language learning spaces seems to be about functional and structural choices: choosing furniture and technologies, determining the number of people to be accommodated, finding solutions for space problems, and allocating resources. Many concerns drive the design of learning spaces: building codes, acceptable vendors, bidding processes, safety and health precautions and regulations, financial priorities and restrictions, registrar and enrollment data, branding decisions, efficiency considerations, etc. They are all important, and many of these are not negotiable in a design project. But while structural features of spaces are important, we must also pay attention to their symbolic features. Spaces project a system of values, and therefore we should be mindful and intentional about our values and align them with the design project.

Earlier it was discussed how built pedagogy is the architectural manifestation of educational philosophies. Physical learning spaces are more than just four walls that adhere to rules and guidelines: they are reflections and manifestations of our values (Doorley and Witthoft 2012). The effects of built pedagogy can also be found in the macro unit of the school, as Grosvenor and Burke (2008: 8) remind us: "Like other buildings, schools are the products of social behaviour. They should not be viewed merely as capsules in which education is located and teachers and pupils perform, but also as designed spaces that, in their materiality, project a system of values. In turn, the ways in which the buildings are used and experienced give them meaning." If we view and read learning spaces as texts, we can understand that beyond their superficial language lie deeper layers of meaning.

While educational mission and goals may change and adapt, values are a very durable dimension which can provide a strong basis for a learning space design project. As physical spaces tend to outlive changing trends and departmental needs, it is useful to ground any project in a shared understanding of what truly matters within an educational program and unit. The functions of space, and the many design decisions and details, should only be approached after the values foundation is firmly established.

Values

Values are fundamental building blocks that do not change frequently and that, in the case of institutional space design, are shared by a group. There are multiple layers of explicitly stated or implicit values: institutional values, unit values, sub-unit values, program values, individual values, etc. For example, in the case of Michigan State University (MSU), the university's values are collaboration, equity, excellence, integrity, and respect. MSU's College of Arts & Letters values are equity (inclusivity, diversity, social justice, equitable access, accessibility), openness (transparency, open process, candor, accountability, open source), and community (collaboration, collegiality, empathy, respect, connection). Within the college, the Center for Language Teaching Advancement's values are to connect, innovate, and transform. All of these, while not aligning perfectly, project a stable value system that can inform fundamental decisions during times of shifting priorities, competing interests, and individual goals. While they are intentionally vague, they nonetheless form the first layer of what is truly important long-term for the institution and unit. An institution or department can enact its values through the process and the "product" of learning space design.

Values and their manifestations are not always consciously and openly visible. While on the surface an institution or program might professes certain aspirational labels, there are underlying beliefs that Tyack and Cuban (1995: 88) call "the grammar of schooling": the "unexamined institutional habits and widespread cultural beliefs about what constitutes a 'real school.'" Many physical learning spaces are part of this grammar of schooling and might undermine aspirational values. To enact such values, we must first determine, examine, and understand the underlying values and structures before beginning the design process.

Symbolic Features

Rajaee Pitehnoee et al. (2020) found that elementary EFL learners paid a good amount of attention to symbolic features. They also argue that structural features are diminished when there is a lack of symbolic features. Such features can exist either because of conscious or unconscious decisions. A classic example of symbolic features in language learning spaces is flags. Often chosen with the good intention of highlighting the international dimension of language education, they are easily recognizable, inexpensive, and flexible. When students, educators, or visitors see a room with flags, they will subconsciously and perhaps even consciously associate that space with international education and languages rather than a different disciplinary area, such as math or music. The issue with flags as a symbolic feature is that they emphasize a national view of languages: French is spoken in France, German is spoken in Germany, etc. This leaves out other countries where these are also majority or official languages. In that case, Austrian and Swiss flags might be added because Germany is spoken here as well. This leaves out other countries, like Liechtenstein and Luxembourg. Even if those are added, this still doesn't acknowledge that these languages are spoken by a diaspora of people throughout the world, by migrants, refugees, bilingual and heritage speakers, etc. The picture is further complicated by Indigenous languages that are not associated in the traditional sense with a nation-state. It also leaves out dialects and variations. How do we symbolize dormant, dead, or extinct languages? There is also the political dimension of flags of countries that are contested or not recognized. Furthermore, flags divide people into in-groups and out-groups. Does this align with the department's or program's values? As this simple example shows, the symbolism behind certain features is not as simple as it might seem.

Ostensibly structural features often also carry symbolism. The fictional "Willard Hall" example from the previous section shows that location, facilities, and configuration can carry immense symbolic power. Strange and Banning (2001: 15) argue that "[F]or example, the symbolic message of a second-floor location may communicate that the institution does not give serious consideration to the users of the service nor their needs for accessibility and convenience." Many structural features also carry symbolic weight and provide non-verbal cues for behavior. Such non-verbal messages, whether deliberately designed or not, may be seen as more truthful than written or verbal ones (Mehrabian 1981). These features are not always directly visible ones but can be found in sounds, smells, temperatures, textures, absolute, relative locations, etc. From a sociomaterial perspective, we should also include the many organizational features in building design. For example, the timetable of courses and assigning of individual, closed rooms, which is the norm in most educational institutions, projects a system of values that segments learning into units, into expectations of punctuality, of beginnings and ends. This type of factory model in which sometimes a bell signals the beginning and end of different class shifts enacts a system of values: efficiency, segmentation, siloization, punctuality, etc. This might not align with the values and goals of an institution or department, which might favor student-centered learning, openness, flexibility, responsibility for one's own learning, intrinsic motivation, etc. Skill and Young (2002: 28) argue that "[S]ince time on task involves activities that include all forms of learning, the design of physical spaces to support time on task requires a systems view of the learning environment. The outmoded Industrial Age model of education as a series of seat-time requirements stands as a significant barrier to learning— but not an insurmountable one." Indeed, the question is how do we better design spaces, idealistically and realistically, that support and reflect values around language learning? How do we balance architectural efficiency with educational effectiveness?

If a program highly values in-person interaction and engagement, spaces that support such values should be considered. If openness and interdisciplinarity are values, spaces should reflect a certain porousness and inviting design. That doesn't mean computers cannot be a part of these spaces. But they should not be the driving force when conceptualizing a specialized, localized language learning space. Unfortunately, this happens in many projects, resulting in underutilized spaces that do not align with the values and mission of the language programs.

Value- and Mission-Based Design Examples

To make these abstract participatory design principles more concrete, here are three actual examples of how language learning space designs were designed using a values-based approach.

Example #1: Language Center

This language department at a US liberal arts college started out without dedicated language learning spaces but felt it was lacking adequate physical space. The project team, which included faculty, had seen what other peer institutions had built and wanted something of their own. They started with functions that were common at those peer institutions: they wanted something to make their teaching more digital and include new technologies, so they planned for a dedicated computer lab. This is what they had seen and what seemed to be common practice. Their program, however, valued social, face-to-face interactions and prized communication and activities not only in the classroom but also outside of it. Their values included openness and inclusiveness. When surveyed, it became clear that the faculty did not wish to use more technologies, nor did they think the current computer labs were inadequate. They preferred to build on their extracurricular strengths, be more inviting and welcoming, and foster their community in the physical space. In the end, their values and goals did not align with the seemingly obvious goal to build a computer lab.

In the end, the department decided on a social space that emphasized their values. The space resembled more a cafe and a lounge than a computer lab. While classes could take place in the space, it was more geared toward multiple usage scenarios, including those outside of typical class times. Procedures and policies were aligned, so that, for example, food was allowed (and even encouraged), that students did not have to formally check in, and that after-hour access was available for students via card swipe. The space symbolized trust (trusting students with access, with their activities, with being responsible), ownership (including them in design processes, listening to their ideas), openness (through design and policies, by deemphasizing a front desk), and open interaction (its main goal weren't language activities, drills, testing, or other tightly defined institutional processes).

Example #2: *Space of Possibility*

The Center at Rhodes College, which this author designed and directed along with a diverse group of stakeholders, was built around the value of sustainability and flexibility. Initially conceptualized around 2009–2010, it incorporated the notion that not only technology but also pedagogical innovations were changing fast. Mobile technologies were rapidly maturing and becoming normalized, and the initial goal of building a technology-focused space was adapted to not design this with the present in mind but with the future. The future, of course, is very difficult to predict: "What is new today will become the old of tomorrow, so that in developing a new language-learning environment, one should be wary of promoting this as the panacea for every problem identified in the current situation, for it will inevitably become the 'traditional' language-learning environment of the future" (Conacher and Kelly-Holmes 2007: 19–20). So the space concept incorporated sustainability and stewardship principles and a gap-mentality to continuously adapt. Procedural elements were an advisory board with rotating members consisting of faculty, staff, and students.

Example #3: *Testing Room*

A third institution was completely remodeling a whole building for the language departments and wished to build a brand-new language center. The old language center was mainly handling testing. The departments wanted to emphasize other aspects of their curriculum and not just testing. Their vision was to rethink what might be possible along their values of a more open, connected, and expansive notion of education along Davidson's (2017: 8) argumentation: "Right now, our educational system focuses on tests and outputs, standards and institutional requirements. Redesigning higher education demands institutional restructuring, a revolution in every classroom, curriculum, and assessment system." The departments wanted to emphasize learning over credentialing, openness over strict control, and motivation and flexibility in language learning over accuracy. The departments first had to self-reflect on the misalignment between their de-facto testing culture and their more open values. Resolving this was a crucial first step before embarking on what type of language center they actually wanted and needed. Importantly, they wanted to get away from creating spaces of fear that were only used for testing purposes.

Mission and Goals

Mission and goals are another building block for dedicated language learning spaces. If architecture "is about configuring spaces that both anticipate and direct activity" (Burbules and Callister 2000: 162), then we must first determine what said activities are. Since not all language programs have the same goals, it is a crucial conversation that stakeholders should have prior to embarking on a project that might quite literally largely be set in stone once built.

For some programs, this is quite easy as they have already done that work. But if they haven't, it is crucial to be completed before spending large sums of money. Questions for language programs to reflect on might include: Why do we learn languages? Why should or must we learn languages? What should students be able to do at different stages and at the end of the curriculum? Which aspects have priority, and which are not as important. How do we best teach our students?

These seem like fairly basic questions, and most language educators could answer them individually. But to answer them collectively, programs need to have identified the most salient features, goals, and even beliefs. A very common mission discussion is whether language learning is technical, vocational skill development or rather an important component of liberal education with goals that emphasize critical thinking, general communication skills, and empathy. Another is around the view of the learners, either placing them "in the role of a participating social agent in the language acquisition process" (Mills 2013: 346) or as an individual agent. The curriculum currently in place is another important consideration. Engman and Hermes (2021: 90) argue that "[S]econd-language learning within schools and the academy is concerned with language as a static object of study, a system of skills to be mastered. Too often divorced from context in language classrooms, learning a second language is traditionally expected to take the form of a carefully measured process of acquisition located in the individual." Whether a program views language education in this traditional view or if it has a more open curricular view and goals will determine what kinds of spaces are actually needed. Goal questions abound: are stable and perhaps even higher enrollments the goal? Focus on form? Lifelong learning and love for language? Creativity? Interdisciplinarity? For some physical language learning space projects, a lack of or disagreement on questions around values, mission, goals, and ultimately vision can derail plans well into a design project.

Design Processes

The processes, the *how* we approach design, are an important aspect in physical language learning space design. Most language educators, students, and even administrators have little to no experience or expertise designing physical spaces. They may have personal experiences with home remodels or even personal building projects, but only a few may have been involved in a previous campus building design, planning, and construction project. Such projects do not occur very often for language academic staff or students, and usually they have not received any training in architecture. "Many institutions have relegated the design, renovation, and maintenance of learning spaces to facilities people, but we have found that many of the individuals in these operations are very eager to work with faculty as equal members of the design team in an effort to arrive at solutions that are both cost-effective and highly engaging for our learners" (Skill and Young 2002: 30). When non-design professionals become part of a design team, they are often only people with subject matter expertise in language education. Markus and Cameron (2002: 69) point out that the "authoritative knowledge produced by professional architects and planners, and codified in such forms as buildings and planning regulations or design guides for certain types of building types, has enormous power to affect people's everyday lives." These professionals, in contrast to faculty, students, and most staff, are constantly involved in building projects, most of which are not specifically concerned with *language* learning spaces. Since most of them will not have expertise in the latest research, trends, and pedagogies in language education, they will likely base their assumptions on limited knowledge from their own language learning experiences, from previous projects which may have been years ago, or from other language learning spaces they may have superficially seen on other campuses. If they saw a computer lab for language learning on several other campuses, they might consciously or unconsciously assume that that's what is currently the norm in physical language learning space deign. "Designers tend to react to environments in perceptual terms (which are *their* meanings), whereas the lay public, the users, react to environments in associational terms" (Rapoport 1990: 19). They will also try to be very efficient in their projects—it is faster to design standardized rooms rather than implement several customizations. Kroll (1984: 167) argues that "[R]elationships between people in space that suits them, that is architecture. An empty box is not architecture. Construction finds its meaning only in the social relations it supports." Users such as faculty and students are in the best position to understand such situated social relations.

Stakeholders

In specialized projects, such as learning spaces specifically for languages, it is useful to include a wide variety of stakeholders. Taylor and Enggass (2009: 115) argue that "[W]hen we approach design problems with predetermined spatial solutions already in mind, we limit creative possibilities for new design, and we shut out student, teacher, and community input as well. Many of the strongest architectural designs for schools arise from deep understanding of the particular client, place, and usage, and are site specific." Kroll (1984: 167) posits that architecture's language addresses the unconscious: "If it is designed entirely by specialists, if it is fixed and untouchable, it cannot possibly respond to the diversity and creativity of those who use it." Including experts and practitioners from a wide variety of domains (Schratzenstaller 2010) is key to building learning spaces that are sustainable and have the future rather than the past in mind.

Extensive involvement of stakeholders is not common practice. Grosvenor and Burke (2008: 157–8) ask "how many architects today are able to follow the advice of pioneering collaborations of educators and architects from the past and actually spend time in schools, carefully observing how they function in order to understand how best to support good practice?" Ideally space designers are "simultaneously a cultural translator and a builder" (Doorley and Witthoft 2012: 38) to be able to leverage the profound knowledge that language specialists and stakeholders bring to make not merely a generic space but an optimized language learning place.

If we accept the notion that there are multiple levels of official and unofficial control agents in the design process and the postoccupancy phase for any given learning space, we can more intentionally design with change in mind by including not only language faculty and students into the whole process but also all those who interface with the space. That means including administrative staff, cleaning staff, media technicians, IT professionals, etc.

Faculty

Getting language faculty interested in a building project can be difficult. Two arguments that have been well received in two decades of working with universities on language learning space design are proposing a sense of ownership and viewing buildings and spaces as language or texts. Convincing faculty of the benefit of being able to have a level of control and a sense of ownership is a good strategy to get buy-in from this group. Because they normally do not have any stake or control in learning spaces, they tend to not engage in this area. If spaces can be places relevant to their needs and can be manipulated, influenced, and optimized, rather than generic learning spaces, there are motives for participation in the design process. It should be noted that some faculty are neither formally trained in architecture and design nor in language pedagogy: "The dominant North American pattern has been that almost all tenure-track faculty members in LL&C departments were trained exclusively in literary criticism but might do as much as two thirds of their teaching in language classes. Their preparation for this consisted of little more than being language assistants in their graduate school years, often with little or no formal training" (Garrett and Liddell 2004: 33). In some programs, this can provide a significant professional development challenge, but also an opportunity to be more intentional around the topic of student learning.

A second strategy is to frame learning spaces not as architectural entities but as language or texts. Markus and Cameron (2002: 1) assert that language is a "neglected subject in discussions of architecture, which is conventionally regarded as a visual rather than verbal activity." They argue and explain that there are multiple connections between architecture and language, and that writing and speaking about physical spaces is a crucial component of speaking and making sense of our built environment. Language faculty in particular are keenly aware of the communicative and influencing power of language, and many will understand that learning spaces are texts that can be created, edited, read, and interpreted. Markus and Cameron (2002: 15) assert that "[B]uildings themselves are not representations. They are material objects which enclose and organize space. However... buildings often do this (or more exactly, their designers do it) on the basis of texts which *are* representations." Writing about language learning spaces can be a process that can give language faculty a more meaningful participatory role and design tool. It would allow them to be more mindful of the symbolic and functional features and the messages they send. Boys (2011: 27), however, warns that treating built environment as texts can also cause issues:

> Metaphor then is a useful but dangerous tool for designers, their clients and users. It can represent a social-spatial idea and give it the appearance of "obvious" and "commonly agreed" reality, especially where it becomes a well-recognised convention through time. But this does not mean that the resulting space is interpreted by all its occupiers in the same way, or that other ways of expressing spatial and social relationships are not possible which are not generated from metaphor; and—most crucially—that the representational image necessarily or transparently translates into an equivalent everyday lived experience.

Students

Ackermann (2004: 18) reminds us that influential educators, educational philosophers, and psychologists have long framed learning as "collectively designing a world in which it is worth living." Students spend a large part of their time in formal and informal learning spaces, but paradoxically they are rarely involved in shaping this part of their own world. But "if campus environments are to be educationally purposeful," Strange and Banning (2001: 110) argue, "they must also involve students in effective learning experiences that require taking on meaningful roles and responsibilities." Including students can happen from a young age on: "To honor the natural history of place in education is to honor *all* those who have a stake in the place of education in society as we forge school buildings, learning settings, and place pedagogies of the future" (Hutchison and Orr 2004: 150–1). Even children can have a "legitimate presence" (Grosvenor and Burke 2008: 168) to work along with professional designers and architects to design meaningful, situated, and appropriate learning spaces.

Design work can even be integrated into language curricula; for example, through independent study, clubs, 1-credit courses, etc. As discussed above, learning spaces can be seen as texts. During design processes, language is an integral part, manifested in the many documents and discussions that happen during all phases. For example, there is a participatory design activity that asks participants to write job descriptions for whole learning spaces or parts of them. This is a fascinating activity that designers use to elicit purposeful thinking about what we expect of our spaces. It personifies spaces, it makes them agents, it creates intentional expectations, and it puts lay designers into a position of control and generates a sense of possibility.

It is important to give students opportunities for meaningful participation that go beyond surveys or token participation. If there is one student representative on a design committee, the student might not be in a position of power to effect meaningful influence. Students in design projects can be full partners, and this involvement itself can be a true learning opportunity for them (Strange and Banning 2001).

Cleaning Staff

Cleaning staff and other physical plant employees that interface with learning spaces are often overlooked in design decisions and processes. And yet, they spend considerable time in each space and manipulate and control it in certain ways. They move furniture to spots that they think are appropriate. They might "straighten out" out the room, determine what is trash, and what the space should look like. They also must be efficient and take care of a large number of spaces. So, designing with their work in mind, and listening to their ideas is important. Beyond these functional considerations, they are stakeholders, and in the age of paying closer attention to DEI (diversity, equity, and inclusion) issues, it is not only wise but also ethically appropriate to include them meaningfully in this process, listen to their ideas, and likewise make sure they understand the educational philosophies behind a space that might be designed considerably differently than other learning spaces. Since designing language learning spaces through a sociomaterial framework includes processes and postoccupancy frameworks, including this group of staff will lead to better conditions and fewer conflicts beyond the initial design phase.

Media Technicians and IT Staff

Physical spaces for language learning house visible and invisible technologies, which have to be maintained, replaced, and updated. Faculty and staff also must be trained to use these tools and supported when something is not working properly. Language education has its own set of technology needs, including audio and video projection equipment, interactive technologies, and mobile technologies. Some programs might even experiment with video games, virtual reality, or maker space tools. IT staff and media technicians play a vital role in modern language learning spaces and should thus be part of the initial design process as well as post occupancy. Furthermore, it is important to use their expertise to design with future possibilities in mind. Retrofitting a space later is very expensive, so future-proofing and building flexibility and adaptability into the spaces are crucial.

Administrative Staff

There are many invisible processes and procedures behind learning spaces, often handled by administrative staff. For example, the registrar schedules formal learning spaces, such as classrooms and labs. Other administrators, such as language center staff, might schedule dedicated language learning spaces, such as self-access language spaces, social spaces, etc. Because there are a myriad of small tasks, decisions, responsibilities, and policies that must be considered, it is vital to include those involved in the administration in the design of spaces.

For example, will the registrar or the language center administrator handle reservations for the language center computer lab? Will students be able and allowed to swipe into the space after hours? Who handles checkout? Cleaning of equipment? Who handles conflicts between faculty members who wish to reserve the space at the same time? The list of those details is long, and while not all of these issues can (and should) be resolved during the design phase, it is important to include those who will deal with them during all stages of the process.

Participatory and Inclusive Design Processes

Including all stakeholders in a design project sounds good in theory. But in practice, how can this possibly be achieved? Participatory, collaborative, or co-design processes can provide a framework that is more inclusive and can create stronger bonds: "The underlying argument is that co-design enables people to take ownership of their environments, services or products and, therefore, creates stronger and more meaningful connections among people and these creations" (Zamenopoulos and Alexiou 2018: 24). Lundström et al. (2016: 423) argue that we need collaborative design approaches in order to create "spaces that meet the needs of users at all levels (emotional, practical and infrastructural)." A useful theoretical foundation for participatory design can be found in situated learning theory (Lave and Wenger 1991), involving stakeholders within a community of practice. Not all of those involved have a static role, and some may only participate in the periphery while others are more centrally involved in the process. Sanders and Stappers (2008: 6) see co-design as referring to "the creativity of designers and people not trained in design working together in the design development process," and thus including stakeholders "with a high level of passion and knowledge in a certain domain" (Sanders and Stappers 2008: 12). The above-mentioned groups can all be included in some way at all or certain points of the design process.

Zamenopoulos and Alexiou (2018: 10) posit that co-design "is becoming important in the face of complex social, political, environmental, educational and technological issues, where no one person has the knowledge and skills to understand and solve them, and where a different approach is needed to empower people to participate and take control of their own life and environment." Indeed, language learning spaces exemplify the complexity that is inherent in such projects. With costs in higher education growing, it is crucial to be mindful of why a design project should be started, and if underway, how the new spaces can be utilized as much as possible and provide maximum sustainability. In this sense, it is advisable to start not with a finite product in mind (e.g., with the goal of building a computer lab, or three smart classrooms). Instead, the goal might be left intentionally open for some time. Co-design processes can facilitate this: "The front end is often referred to as 'fuzzy' because of the ambiguity and chaotic nature that characterise it. In the fuzzy front end, it is often not known whether the deliverable of the design process will be a product, a service, an interface, a building, etc." (Sanders and Stappers 2008: 7). Witham et al. (2019: 3) provide a useful summary of why we should seek out more inclusive, collaborative design practices:

> We understand collaborative design research practice as seeking new ways of connecting people to shared and individual futures, unlocking, amplifying and catalysing individual creative potential, and contributing to broader, systematic shifts in governance, politics, and social practice. This expansion of design intent away from its well-defined and well-equipped pathways of products and projects, service provision, briefs and stakeholders, criteria and critique offers a new landscape of possibilities for the designer. This work is frequently underpinned by a recognition of the complexity and diversity of challenges that the world faces, the entanglements of knowledge and technology needed to address such challenges, and the heterogeneous perspectives of individuals implicated in them.

Architects and designers are *not* experts in language education, and their personal experiences as former language students may mean that they have a different understanding of what the theory and practice of language education is. And usually, they do not have the time to carefully observe language classes and other learning opportunities in action. In order to balance these concerns, active and meaningful participation by language educators and other stakeholders throughout the process is important when designing optimal language learning spaces.

Practical Strategies for Collaborative Language Learning Spaces' Design

Kronenberg and Schwienhorst (2021) propose a long-term co-design process for physical language learning spaces that includes all stakeholders; is inclusive, permeable, situated, and organic; creates sustainable stewardship and sense of ownership; and is more attuned to local cultures, diversity, and social needs. Their I7 model for language learning spaces is based on intentional, open, iterative, and evolutionary design processes. They argue that clear communication channels and strategies are keys to building momentum and effecting sustainable change. Taylor and Enggass (2009: 116) stress that:

> [S]ince administrators and teachers should play a key role in planning and should work closely with architects, they must be properly educated in architectural processes and visual language so that their educationally valid ideas are included in the design. Preprogramming can help fill this gap through design studio workshops ... and through presentations and walking tours that introduce stakeholders to exciting architecture.

New language learning spaces do not have to wow an audience or aspire to unrealistic goals. It is better to continuously and intentionally work toward achievable and realistic goals. Other strategies include building a community around the design or re-design process, being open to many different stakeholders' viewpoints, including those of students, faculty, and staff outside of the unit, stakeholders off-campus, etc., actively listening to experts and non-experts alike, not rushing the process, not viewing the learning space as a finished product but rather an iterative process, embracing ambiguity and partial successes, and sharing progress on an ongoing basis.

Conclusion

There are many stakeholders involved in the administration and design of physical language learning spaces. Not all of these are always included in decision-making processes before, during, and after creating a new space. Because there are different interests, goals, and types of expertise involved, it is important to situate design projects in a transparent system of vision, mission, values, and goals. Including diverse stakeholders leads to a more participatory process that will make it more likely to create useable and meaningful language learning spaces.

Design Attributes

Every language learning space design project involves a myriad of choices, large and small. The goal of this section is to provide an overview of possible design attributes that might need to be considered. It is not intended to provide specific answers, solutions, or products because each project requires individual and situated decisions to be made, and there are many professionals that could and should help with these. The following, rather, provides some shared attributes that are of concern and important so that lay designers can use a common language and address particular wishes and concerns.

There are many classification systems for interior design attributes. Peker and Ataöv (2020) argue for seven categories: layout, flexibility, color, size, accessibility, comfort, and safety. Yang et al. (2013) divide classroom attributes into three categories: ambient, spatial, and technological attributes. Ambient attributes include acoustics and lighting, temperature, air quality, etc. Spatial attributes refer to room layouts, furniture, and visibility, whereas technological attributes include hardware and software. This categorization is useful albeit rather technical. For a more comprehensive list of attribute categories, I suggest adding procedural attributes that include postoccupancy processes (see the "Post-Occupancy Processes" section in this chapter) to the list to emphasize that spaces are processes, not complete products, and that they are created by interactions of people.

This section of the book is primarily written with language educators in mind, providing a limited overview of best practices. To use a languafe metaphor, "space design has its own grammar that can be tweaked to bolster desirable habits" (Doorley and Witthoft 2012: 38). Understanding some fundamentals is important before making concrete decisions. As previously discussed, a view of design as language and of learning spaces as texts is a useful approach to creating meaningful outcomes. Boys (2011: 19) similarly emphasizes the power of language and metaphors for spaces beyond the normalized classroom:

> These new kinds of learning spaces offer both design metaphors and physical arrangements, centred on a certain set of associated ideas ... Spaces are envisaged as enabling collaboration and interaction (both educational and social), articulated, for example, as "atrium," "street," "hub," "drop-in centre" and "learning café"; particular spatial layouts for enabling a range of group and individual study combinations in space, such as learning "nooks," "pods" and "clusters"; a tendency to informal, "softer" furniture such as beanbags, asymmetric furniture layouts, bright colours and "landmark" elements such as special features or artist commissions; and finally, what are usually called technology-rich environments.

It should be noted that while most of the discussion in this book and chapter is focused primarily on higher education, it is important to consider that learning space design must take the learners' age into account (Rajaee Pitehnoee et al. 2020). Furthermore, it is important to remind ourselves that learning atmospheres are created not only by the ambient attributes, furniture, layouts, and technology, but also by a space's users (Cox 2018).

Ambient Attributes

Ambient attributes, such as acoustics and lighting, temperature, air quality, etc., create and contribute to an encompassing atmosphere in learning environments. These attributes may be easily recognizable, such as bold colors, while others may be subtle and are not consciously or easily recognized. Some of these can be difficult to share in a mediated way, such as air quality, ambient sounds, or smells, while visual attributes are more readily shareable and transmittable. Ambient attributes remind people of what's expected. Rapoport (1990) writes that textures, music, sounds, colors, flooring materials, etc. all contribute to behavioral outcomes and prime their users for certain types of behaviors.

Light is important not only because it enables students to be able to read, see each other and objects, and write, but it also affects mood, wellbeing, sociability, and expected behaviors. For example, harsh bright lights carry different connotations than soft lighting with different hues (Casciani and Musante 2016). Burke (2005: 140) argues that light "as an object of material culture, was and continues to be a fundamental part of the makeup of the school." Lighting can be natural (see also the discussion on biophilic design in the next section) or artificial. The latter has seen several technological advances in recent years, allowing for finer calibration, automation, and adjustability. For example, new airplane lighting systems subtly adjust hues and intensity over the length of a flight, changing the mood and supporting expected behaviors. Similar systems have become more user-friendly, and smart lighting gives more options for teachers and students to effect lighting changes. Frequently additional lighting is added to the "front" where the teacher is supposed to sit, underlining and "setting in stone" this power relationship. Transparent design allows for openness and letting in natural light but creates acoustic separation (Nair and Fielding 2005: 47). Furthermore, additional lighting in the front of the room where the teacher desk is located can further support power dynamics.

Acoustics is an important issue to consider for language education, especially in more open learning spaces. L2 learners who cannot understand parts of a sentence may not be able to fill in the missing information the way a native speaker could. Placing sound-absorbent materials, such as flooring, carpets, or panels, in spaces may lead to better understanding. There are different sources of sound that can be distracting; for example, street noises or HVAC (heating, ventilation, and air conditioning) systems (Dockrell and Shield 2006). Sounds can be blocked out, of course, but they can also be intentionally added. Degrave (2019) reports that music playing in the background can reduce anxiety and support L2 conversations. Chou's (2010) findings indicate that the type of music may affect the degree of distraction.

Visual ambiance features can include different wall and floor textures, materials, and colors. Glass elements can have different degrees of opacity, and writable surfaces can be added as installed boards, as areas painted with whiteboard or chalkboard points, or as mobile units. Decorations can be centrally planned, or aimed at involving users; for example, by providing pinboards and other manipulatable installations. Ambient features can signify expected behaviors; for example, by highlighting transitional areas and boundaries. Doorley and Witthoft (2012: 42) advise to not "shy away from calling attention to thresholds with bold visual strokes like changes in flooring or wall color."

Ambient design can signal that a space is focused on language learning. Words in different languages and fonts, for example, are a simple way of creating an atmosphere that contrasts the spaces from generic ones or those focused on other disciplines. These can be shown through a number of media, including wall stickers, signage, posters, floor treatments, or pillows. Such elements can support producing a "linguistic landscape," which "refers to any display of visible written language" (Gorter 2013: 190). The ambiance created in such linguistic schoolscapes can foster placemaking as well as feelings of belonging and shared interests. Strategically placed, such elements can also signify boundaries and thresholds.

It is useful to consider that spaces and their ambiance influence and shape our thinking, our activities, and our attitudes:

> Consider how these ideas might reshape the way we talk about knowledge and learning: the way I make meaning when I'm sitting in the local bar arguing with someone about knowledge is different from how I make it right now as I'm writing this. In the bar meaning is constructed in conversation and it varies according to whom I'm talking, our level of sobriety and so forth. In my office I can consult books, articles, fieldnotes, interview transcripts and earlier drafts of this text. The difference between what I "know" and in the two settings isn't in my ability to articulate some head-knowledge, nor do the books, people, or other elements of the contexts simply "add to" some knowledge that already exists in my head. Rather, in the two settings I'm part of different cognitive systems (I'm a different "I"). My "psychological" state is integrally connected to, indeed is a product of, my "social" situation (which includes inanimate "tools" as well as

other people). Finally, my experiences in each setting alter me, my individual mind, in some durable way (I internalize something) that shapes future activity.

(Nespor 1994: 8)

Different attributes in a space for language learning provide different cues for behaviors and mindsets. Learners might be more talkative in a social space than in a tightly controlled and rigid space.

Spatial Attributes: Focusing on Flexibility

Spatial attributes are often at the core of what lay designers consider when designing new language learning spaces. Creating flexible layouts and environments that can adapt and choosing appropriate furniture are crucially important strategies for maximizing learning spaces and creating resilient, adaptable, and sustainable setups.

Flexibility has certainly been a buzzword for quite some time when it comes to learning space design. The distinct possibility that our educational system, its practices, and tools will change within the next few decades is nothing new. Wright and Gardner-Medwin (1938: 109) wrote nearly a century ago: "The lesson of the all too solid schools of the last century should teach us that it is unreasonable to expect a school building to serve an effective, useful life of more than forty years at most. In this space of time we must anticipate important changes, some of them beyond prophecy, in social conditions, educational theory, teaching equipment." They stress the importance of adaptable and scalable design because it is nearly impossible to predict necessary and desired changes. Forty (2000) claims that the word "flexibility" and its use in architectural contexts evolved in the early 1950s. As modern life is seen as increasingly complex and changeable, it is difficult for designers to anticipate future functions and needs:

> The notion of sharing is fundamental to the construct of decentralized or distributed control. The construct is an essential ingredient for emergence. In educational contexts, affordances for learning emerge through the learner's interaction with the environment … If the environment is too tightly regimented, there is little room for unanticipated possibilities or randomness.
>
> (Murray and Fujishima 2016b: 145)

This view aligns with a view that design is an ongoing process, never finished, and that it includes more than just professional designers but rather all stakeholders. It is a type of emergent design akin to emergent engineering, which "embraces uncertainty as a fact of life that's potentially constructive" (Flack and Mitchell 2020).

The term flexibility is a rather vague one and ill-defined when it comes to learning space design. While some might refer to "flexibility" as being able to move furniture around, others might think of it as the ability to make a space bigger or change its function. Deciding that a physical language learning space should be flexible is not sufficient. Rather, more specificity is required in order to better align design goals. Is the goal to encourage physicality and movement in language classes? Is it to build with future expansion in mind? Or is it to be able to use spaces for different purposes? Each of these questions would be addressed through a different property of flexibility. Monahan (2002) provides a useful framework by dividing the term "flexibility" into five related yet different properties: "fluidity, versatility, convertibility, scalability, and modifiability." Fluidity refers to the level of porousness and the ability of different entities—people, light, sounds, etc.—to traverse spaces. Versatility means that spaces have multiple functions; for example, a language classroom that can be turned into a social space after class hours. Convertibility is the level of ease with which a space can be reconfigured in the future. Scalability refers to the ability to expand or contract a learning space to suit different needs. In that way a larger space can easily be created if needed. And finally, modifiability is the flexibility to allow for quick reconfiguration of a space. For example, modifiability is high in a space in which chairs arranged in rows for a presentational format can quickly be moved around so that group work can take place.

There are several arguments for flexible learning space design. One reason is that physical spaces require immense financial and time resources in order to be adapted. Kern (2020: 33) refers to cities when she explains that "[B]ecause the built environment is durable over long time spans, we're stuck with spaces that reflect outdated and inaccurate social realities. This, in turn, shapes how people live their lives and the range of choices and possibilities that are open to them." Flexibility and adaptability then are crucial not only from a logistical standpoint, but also from an ideological and pedagogical one. As previously discussed, the power of built pedagogy reinforces no longer wished for educational activities simply by being there. If an institution owns a language laboratory, then there are tendencies to try to still make use of it. If a classroom is set up in a traditional pattern, then faculty tend to fall back into more traditional teaching models. Uses and needs also change. Hutchinson (1967: 356) lists "10 things language laboratory facilities can do." All of those can be accomplished without a laboratory today. Flexible spaces allow for a recalibration, for a new start.

Flexibility can signal ownership of a space. If things are fixed and unchangeable, its users are unlikely to see themselves as having control. Agency is a crucial condition for placemaking (Middleton 2018). Providing reasonable possibilities of manipulation involves users in a meaningful way: "Ultimately, space most likely to contribute to involvement must be flexible in its design. The ability to move walls and to rearrange seating capacities and designs allows for the maximum use of space and the accommodation of the greatest number of needs" (Strange and Banning 2001: 146). Ownership extends to different groups of stakeholders, from administrators to faculty to students and visitors. Designing a space that is not completely finished and that allows for bringing in personal and local adaptation provides a placemaking possibility:

> Two things seem clear from the above. First, that much of the meaning has to do with personalization and hence perceived control, with decoration, with movable elements rather than with architectural elements. Second, that architects generally have to be opposed strongly to this concept; in fact, the whole modern movement in architecture can be seen as an attack on users' meaning—the attack on ornaments, on decoration, on "what-nots" indwellings and "thingamabobs" in the garden, as well as the process of incorporating these elements into the environment.
>
> (Rapoport 1990: 22)

Clearly, meaning is created by the space's stakeholders, and will constantly change.

Another argument for flexibility is that our *zeitgeist* demands it. Selingo (2018: 31) argues that to "teach Gen Z, flexibility is key. That's to allow for individual and group work, as well as technology and other forms of active learning. Campus leaders should consider updating classroom space accordingly." Generational work patterns are constantly shifting, due to technology, insights, and new mobilities. As learners and instructors have more tools and agency for creating, accessing, disseminating, and communicating information than previous generations, our spaces should be able to adapt to provide maximum usability and require as few resources as possible. This includes the ability to shrink the physical footprint in the future. For example, if dedicated computer labs for languages are no longer necessary because any computer lab can now be used due to cloud computing (or not at all because of mobile devices), flexibility includes the acknowledgment that perhaps fewer square feet of real estate might be needed for a language program. Giving up ownership to other units on campus is a taboo among administrators and educators. But in the twenty-first century we should be more concerned with network patterns rather than territoriality. Furthermore, there have been discussions of decreasing the physical footprint of institutions due to changed usage patterns, especially in the aftermath of the pandemic.

Fixed and Closed Spaces

Flexibility has been such a buzzword that it seems it has to be included everywhere. But there are advantages to more static and immoveable design features as well. Sometimes rearranging is not called for; for example, in transitory spaces (furniture might block the flow of people, or create fire safety hazards). Some architectural features, such as built-in cabinets or booths, can add character to a space and distinguish it from other spaces. In some circumstances, static design features can add an air of permanence and reassurance to a space and provide grounding. Furthermore, specific spaces that require certain dedicated technology setups also frequently have to rely on fixed installations. Also, hiding spaces that allow users to retreat from open and collaborative spaces (Doorley and Witthoft 2012) can benefit from more fixed and closed setups. There are good reasons not to create everything with utmost flexibility. Rather, it is important to be mindful when choosing different levels of flexibility.

Furniture

Furniture plays a significant role in language learning space design considerations (Kronenberg 2016). It not only allows spaces to be updated without major construction efforts and can have considerable influences on learning activities. Like the built pedagogy of learning spaces discussed in Chapter 1, furniture influences pedagogy by making some behaviors more likely to occur than others:

> School furniture in general, and school desks in the various forms taken over time, in particular, have always been a key, essential element of school equipment. Their design and layout reflect the different conceptions held of communication relationships within the classroom itself, contribute to the creation (or not) of a pleasant, informal, relaxed and friendly atmosphere, as well as encouraging practice in line with traditional, intellectual or active, innovative currents.
>
> (Moreno Martínez 2005: 89)

Symbolic and Cultural Functions of Furniture

Beyond its mere functional and aesthetic properties, furniture also holds symbolic and cultural importance. A chair, for example, embodies meanings beyond its affordances (Fiell and Fiell 2000). Cranz (1998) argues that chairs, in contrast to other sitting furniture, such as benches, platforms, or sofas, usually are only intended to be used by one person. Its back provides directionality, so that its user and observer know where the front and the back is.

Who gets to sit, who sits in which seat or chair, signifies order, rank, and importance. Whether in an opera house, an airplane, a train, church, palace, parliament, or a classroom, seats and chairs either explicitly or implicitly carry a number of connotations. In an academic setting, the term chair or chairperson (or in the German *Lehrstuhlinhaberin/Lehrstuhlinhaber*) still holds the meaning of the person in charge of a department or academic unit. One-room schools often ordered student grade, rank, or year by their relative positions. The instructor in a classroom still usually has a different chair than the students do. A commonly found alternative to the teacher's chair-desk combination is the lectern, which increases the student-teacher contrast even more. The height difference of standing versus sitting not only signifies the power structure in the classroom, but it also enables the teacher to be more mobile and be better prepared to exert control over the immobile students. Who gets to stand or sit, and how many people are allowed to be in the in-group can be regulated through the manipulation of the number of chairs (Cranz 1998: 17). Eickhoff (1993) argues that furniture as a whole, its arrangement, and its sizes create a communication system that can enable or hinder interactions between people. If the goal of language education is to teach communication, furniture is worth a more prominent level of intentionality than it is usually given.

Indeed, there is a cultural component in what furniture we use, when we use it, and who uses it. Furniture reinforces those acceptable behaviors. For example, in many cultures in which sitting is expected in educational situations, classrooms signal that sitting is the norm, and that standing or sitting on the floor are not acceptable. Cranz (1998) estimates that a third to a half of the people in the world use a right-angled seating position. Postural variations are determined by culture, not anatomy. The furniture and layout clearly mark and strengthen sitting conventions.

> A chair in a room of floor-sitters is a rude intruder. Conversely, sitting on the floor among chairs is socially acceptable only when there is no other place to sit—and then only under circumstances such as in a crowded auditorium or airport waiting room. Sitting on the floor among chair-sitters disrupts the order of things, which is probably why teenagers like to do it. For precisely the same reason, sitting on the floor was fashionable among the European avant-garde in

the 1920s, among the Beats in the 1950s, and among student protestors in the 1960s—it upset convention.

(Rybczynski 2017: 44)

These often subconsciously accepted norms and standards can serve various social purposes. Fiell and Fiell (2000: 6) argue that, for example, "chair design is connected with different ideologies, approaches to making, and economic theory" and is "invested with its own degree of social significance and set of conventions" (Fiell and Fiell 2000: 7). Over time, floor-sitting and chair-sitting cultures have adapted in different ways to these social conventions, but so have bodies. Differences in muscle development have made some postures more uncomfortable than others, which can reinforce certain conventions (Rybczynski 2017). Students in chair-sitting cultures often tire quickly after prolonged periods of standing or floor-sitting because their bodies have not adapted. Eickhoff (1993) argues that sitting has become so normalized that it is no longer seen as something cultural but as a natural thing that humans do.

Ergonomics of Furniture

Ergonomics are important when deciding on furniture. On the one hand, existing conventions cannot be ignored, simply so that students' (and instructors') bodies are optimally accommodated in order to provide the best setup for learning and instruction. There is an equity argument to be made here, which is further elaborated on in the "Inclusion, Accessibility, Wellbeing, and Belonging" section in this chapter: how can we accommodate the many different bodies, and the different cultures that they may come from, equitably? How can we make learning space accessible to all? For all types of bodies, sitting is an ergonomic challenge.

> We are good at walking and running, and we are happy lying down to sleep. It is in the in-between position that is the problem. This is true even if we sit on the ground—as attested by the variety of pads, bolsters, armrests, and cushions used by floor-sitting cultures. It is even truer when we choose to sit on a chair. Every chair represents a struggle to resolve the conflict between gravity and the human anatomy. Sitting up is always a challenge.
>
> (Rybczynski 2017: 56)

In our own homes, we can choose our furniture. In most classrooms, its users do not have a choice. Usually, there is only one type of chair available. This lack of choice reinforces the ideological tendency for standardization, lack of individual choices, and educational optimization. It also simply does not provide learners with options and choices that are *optimal* for *their* bodies. Furniture can be used to control bodies, as discussed in Chapter 1. Eickhoff (1993) argues that school age children's bodies grow into chair-sitting, along with its physiological effects of reduced breathing and muscle tensions. Moreover, he argues that chair sitting sedates learners and creates physical and mental boundaries. From standing desks to ergonomically designed chairs and stools, there are many types of furniture that, if intentionally chosen, can accommodate and support diverse types of learners and instructors.

Language courses in particular can benefit from different furniture choices and arrangements because they often involve different forms and patterns of communication, from pair work to group work, individual work to plenum discussions, and technology-enabled learning to virtual spaces. Ideally, furniture can support all of these, and is flexible enough to accommodate different learners, different instructors, various modes, modalities, and approaches to learning and teaching languages.

Chairs

Mathews and Soistmann (2016: 27) argue that "[I]n essence, a chair is more than just a place to sit; it is an instrumental part of the larger ecosystem and has a direct impact on the pursuit of learning." Chairs create physical and psychological connections with students, and provide a framework for learning and communication: "No other type of furniture offers the possibilities of making and facilitating connections in the same way or to the same extent" (Fiell and Fiell 2000: 6). On an individual level, the material, texture, and temperature can be directly felt, and might result in positive, neutral, or negative feelings and associations. There are individual preferences among chair sitters, and designs with multiple seating options can not only accommodate students' individual needs and preferences, but also foster a sense of agency.

Chairs also "place" students in the room. Often, they function as an anchor, as a location-fixing device. In many higher education classrooms, it is implicitly understood that once students have chosen "their" chair, or rather their chair location, they will stay there for the rest of the semester. Sometimes, especially in primary and secondary education, there is a seating plan, which helps educators remember names and impose a certain order or structure, or to prevent undesirable behaviors or interactions among students. In general, chairs can be used to organize rooms, control activities and communication patterns, set expectations, and alter a space's ambiance.

In recent years, it has become more acceptable and even desirable in higher education to provide a larger variety of seating options. New forms, textures, colors, and functions have been introduced by the educational furniture industry. Some institutions have also experimented with using non-educational furniture. Especially in less formal language learning spaces, furniture choices are more reminiscent of cafes or hotel lobbies than traditionally educational spaces. Montgomery (2020: 344) suggests that different ideal seating options are those that "accommodate a variety of body shapes and have textures that appeal to diverse sensory preferences are ideal." Offering a variety takes into account that not all bodies are the same size, and that diverse learners have diverse preferences and needs.

Chairs can have different degrees of mobility. They can be fixed and attached to floors or walls, heavy or light, large or small, or with or without wheels. Depending on their properties, they are more or less likely to be moved. It is important to weigh the trade-offs. What level of control of students is important? Is it desirable that students are encouraged to move chairs, or should this be avoided? In very public spaces, such as airports, fixed chairs can make sense. In smaller spaces with fewer people, and in those where creativity and agency are valued, more flexible seating options are more suitable.

Tables

Tables and desks provide crucial functions in learning spaces. They offer a surface for students to write, and place their materials, tools, and technologies. Like chairs, they organize a space and give it structure. According to Moreno Martínez (2005), desk design has been influenced by several factors, including hygiene, technique, and pedagogy, and has not been a linear or stable process. Tables can be anchored to the floor or walls, rendering them immovable. Larger and heavier tables without wheels can be difficult to be moved by a single person, making it more likely that they stay in place. Smaller tables on wheels allow for quick and spontaneous reconfiguration, but might be less stable, provide smaller surface areas, and often lack specialized features, such as charging ports or cable management. Standing-height tables, which are less common in learning spaces, allow for working while standing. Height-adjustable tables allow for flexibility and individualization but may require effort and time to adjust. Tables can provide specialized features, such as privacy screens, keyboard trays, cable management, cupholders, input plugs and charging ports, writeable surfaces, and stow-away folding or stacking options.

While these options can provide additional functionalities, they can also complicate spaces that are used by different people. Their affordances also prevent other functions, so it is important to rely on values, goals, and mission when choosing tables. For example, tables with extensive cable management capabilities limit the number of sides that are usable, which makes shared table space much less feasible. Tables can be attached to chairs, which has certain advantages and drawbacks. While individual student movement might be easier when the chair-table combinations have wheels, they can also be unwieldy and overly emphasize students as discreet units and deemphasize collaborative expectations. There is also the option of having fewer tables or not having any at all. There have been deskless language teaching experiments and projects (e.g., Rankin 2018), which leverage students' use of mobile device and explore the advantages of more space and flexibility.

Other Furniture

While chairs and tables are the most common pieces of furniture in learning spaces, there are many others to consider. Moveable writing surfaces and marker boards have become increasingly popular. They can also be used as presentation spaces (using magnets, clips, or push pins), sound barriers, and visual barriers and dividers. Storage solutions, whether temporary or permanent and even lockable, are also increasingly found. As language learning often involves materials—realia, games, props, teaching aids, books, technology, etc.—there needs to be a space to keep all of them. Language resource centers have long been repositories for such physical artifacts. Storage capabilities are an unspectacular but crucial component in language space design projects. For lay designers and language educators, deciding among all these choices can be overwhelming. Trying out furniture that already exists elsewhere on campus can be useful before making long-term purchasing decisions. But furniture can be a relatively inexpensive way of redesigning a space without costly and lengthy capital projects.

Furniture Arrangements

It is useful to think of all furniture in educational spaces as an ecosystem (Mathews and Soistmann 2016) and communication system (Eickhoff 1993). What matters is not only what kind of furniture is in any particular learning space; its arrangement and relation to each other is also of importance: "Social scientists have proved that arranging seats in rows facing one direction has very different consequences for social interaction and the flow of information than arranging them in a circle. Lining up two chairs side by side, face to face, or at right angles to one another produces three different kinds of communication" (Cranz 1998: 18). Rows are by far the most common and normalized pattern, partly due to its efficient use of space and partly due to its orderly, organized, and structured nature. Rows also promote hierarchical arrangements and produce a front and a back, signaling that the instructor is the center of knowledge concentration (Bendele 1984; Stang 2016). It is a common arrangement also found in other built environments, such as churches, courts of law, and theaters (Koutamanis and Majewski-Steijns 2012: 204). Woolner (2010: 37) similarly argues that this pattern promotes a view of students as individual rather than collective and communicative learners:

> The discussion of differential student involvement when seated in rows and the findings that rows are particularly appropriate for individual work, suggests the importance of considering the purpose of the learning activities attempted. Such classroom organisation will not be as appropriate for whole class discussions or group work, and may actually impede learning in these ways. Thus the aims and intentions of the teacher for some parts of the session may conflict with the classroom arrangement which has been chosen to support other learning.

Desired learning activities and communicative structures in language learning situations can be supported through more intentional arranging of furniture. Van Merriënboer et al. (2017) suggest that more research needs to be done to find out how language teacher cognition and behavior is impacted by seating patterns.

Even the choice of furniture can have an effect on spatial arrangements: "Stools, without directing backs, promote a star or network pattern of communication, whereas chairs promote a centralized or pyramidal pattern of communication. Obviously, stools lend themselves to more democratic, egalitarian social life and chairs to more hierarchical social structures" (Cranz 1998: 33–4). Stools are also a good example of furniture with a smaller footprint given their usually smaller size. Some models can even provide multiple functions, such as a chair, side table, or footrest. How much furniture is in any given space changes the level of fluidity and modifiability. Simply removing chairs or tables can provide more of an open canvas, more options, and types of arrangements. Smaller and more versatile pieces of furniture can increase the available space.

It was previously discussed that furniture places bodies and has the tendency that relative seating structures are chosen by students. If chairs are not in fixed locations, then there is an effect that allows students to break up expected seating patterns. This has the benefit of students sitting next to different interlocutors throughout the semester, providing language learners with more opportunities to listen to different voices, negotiate meaning with different partners, and create more opportunities for social engagement. Instructors of course can use pedagogical actions to change seating patterns by actively changing up pairing patterns. But furniture and its arrangement can support these different pairing opportunities and make them more likely to occur. There is no optimal arrangement in formal learning spaces. Rather, it depends on the situation and the type and nature of the task (Wannarka and Ruhl 2008). What matters is the ability to create the desired arrangements and train educators on how to best manipulate spatial attributes to adapt to the learning situations. Van Merriënboer et al. (2017: 265) suggest that during participatory design processes, "educators, teachers and students on the one hand, and architects, interior designers, ICT specialist and educational publishers on the other must align pedagogies with seating arrangements and physical learning spaces." For existing classrooms, Taylor and Enggass (2009) suggest a five-step program to transform a regular, frontal classroom into a more student-centered and empowering learning space. This program proposes recognizing the mismatch between classroom configuration and student-centered learning, moving student desks, replacing the teacher desk, establishing and expanding a technology zone, diffusing technology use, and creating display spaces.

Technological Attributes

Technological attributes have received a lot of attention in the area of language learning spaces in the last hundred years. Of course, technologies are changing fast, and physical spaces are often not able to keep up with these developments. Technologies can be a polarizing issue, especially before they are established or normalized (Bax 2011). An extreme enthusiasm for new technologies and dismissal of older, more established ones has shaped education for a long time, often without necessary evidence. Saettler (2005) cites Edison in 1913 as follows: "Books will soon be obsolete in our schools ... Our school system will be completely changed in ten years" (p. 98). In language education and language learning space design today, there are disagreements whether large computer labs are still necessary in the age of ubiquitous and mobile computing and new options for hybrid language learning. Making design choices in times of change is difficult. Cost of technology is an important factor that should be considered: "Yet there is still a problem of enthusiasm about the teaching and learning potential of a new technology blinding us to the costs of implementing it, and causing us to overlook cheaper, 'lower-tech' alternatives" (Woolner 2010: 32).

Finding middle ground between enthusiasm on the one side and fear of new technologies on the other can be difficult, especially during a building design project that presents its own timelines and constraints. Instructors sometimes have strong opinions and beliefs, but physical spaces will have to serve all stakeholders. In these decisions, future colleagues will inevitably use these spaces, but their views cannot be included in design deliberations. Other factors include the institution's technology strategy, its image and brand, its infrastructure, technology support mechanisms, and contractual obligations. Technology is not independent of its social embeddedness: "the term 'sociomaterial' is a bold reminder that when we talk either about technologies or organizations, we do well to remember that social practices shape the materiality of a technology and its effects" (Leonardi 2012: 33). Lawn (1999: 71) discusses how the "interrelatedness of technologies creates complex problems that affect how schooling is designed or evolves." Indeed, technologies should not be seen as separate entities but rather in a more holistic and integrated way.

The language laboratory is an example of this combination of forces and domains: while new technological advancements made it possible, its emergence happened in conjunction with the considerable financial incentives of the US government brought about by the Cold War political situation (Hagen 2017). At the same time, the drastically new audio-lingual methodology reciprocally supported the need and implementation of lab installations. As a discipline-specific space, the language lab was largely driven by its technological capabilities. Spatial and ambient attributes were often secondary as the lab's design revolved around the specifics of the equipment. The shortcomings of the language laboratory were recognized after an intense building phase in the United States: "chiefly, it is at its weakest without the humanizing influence of the teacher over the machine" (Hutchinson 1967: 358). As computers replaced tape recorders, a more nuanced view emerged on the role of technology in the language education, and with it less rigid forms of physical learning spaces, such as multimedia language classrooms:

> The multimedia classroom in which these learning interactions take place is set up with the goal of making a dichotomy between technology and classroom obsolete. First of all, the classroom is not set up as rows of individual seats at which information-absorbing learners sit and behave in institutionally expected ways. Rather, the space is set up so as to facilitate collaboration and face-to-face communication, with the technology out of the way below the surface so that

it is available as a tool but does not interfere with the social activity of learning. Further, two or more students work together at one computer, and there is sufficient space on the desk to put books, papers, clippings, etc.

(Van Lier 2003: 58)

The use of digital technologies has become more nuanced and sophisticated in recent years, and is more integrated into language curricula. But at the same time, massive technology installations have become less important due to mobile and wireless technologies and cloud computing. Beyond basic infrastructure, such as providing electricity outlets, internet access, and projection capabilities, built-in technology in physical language learning spaces is less important than in past decades.

There is a flexible, adaptable view of technologies in spaces that integrates the rooms themselves as technologies (while also housing and accommodating other technologies): "it is possible to see the classroom in a further way. As a unit within schools, it is not just the home of technological processes; it is also a designed technology itself. As part of a building designed for a purpose, it contains particular forms, spaces and functions, all of which express intentional usages by teachers and pupils" (Lawn 1999: 72).

Conclusion

There are many design attributes to consider in language learning space design projects. These attributes include ambient attributes, such as acoustics and lighting, temperature, air quality, spatial attributes, such as furniture and layouts, and technological attributes. In a way, designing a physical learning space is designing a technology, and this includes constant vigilance to improve its software, to test its capabilities, monitor its potential obsolescence, and adapt it to new developments and capabilities. Technological attributes in physical language learning spaces are never finished or fixed, but rather a process. The following section deals with exactly such procedural attributes.

Postoccupancy Processes

Spaces are not static, but processes: "Inasmuch as we have begun to think more in terms of relationality, to develop relational concepts of space, and have ceased to regard space as something at rest" (Löw 2016: xiii). Most of our learning spaces are designed with the present, not the future in mind: "Almost no buildings adapt well. They're designed not to adapt; also budgeted and financed not to, constructed not to, administered not to, maintained not to, regulated and taxed not to, even remodeled not to. But all buildings (except monuments) adapt anyway, however poorly, because the usages in and around them are changing constantly" (Brand 1994: 2). Optimizing adaption and setting up structures and processes for postoccupancy should begin already during the early stages of design and be an integral part of space design. One language center at a liberal arts college, for example, built an expensive, state-of-the-art new computer lab. After about five years, the computers needed to be exchanged for a newer model, but there was no budget for this refresh planned. The initial purchase was written into the building budget, but there had been no considerations for future financial needs for such a sophisticated space. Furthermore, it was not clear who had the decision power to initiate the computer refresh and make the choices of which new models should be purchased. Finances are an essential of any learning space design project, and they should include not only the cost of the initial build but also ongoing processes, including staffing, refreshes, changes, adaptations, assessment, and updates.

Procedural attributes are often invisible, especially in contrast to ambient, spatial, and technological attributes. Viewing learning spaces through a sociomaterial lens includes the consideration of not just *what* we design, but *how* we make decisions and manage spaces, *how* we put procedures in place that allow for a space's adaptation. This extends beyond merely designing with flexibility in mind, which is a necessary but not a sufficient attribute when resilience and adaptation are intended to continue a space's relevance.

If we see a space as not ever truly finished, it relieves pressure to get everything right the first time. It is impossible to foresee future developments, whether they be technological, social, cultural, economic, structural, political, or environmental. Institutions change departmental or governance structures, natural disasters or accidents occur without notice, new educational trends and priorities emerge, new technologies are developed, or disease outbreaks shut down whole institutions. Many changes, however, can be more subtle and gradual, such as a department slowly growing or shrinking, newly hired instructors bringing specific expertise to a department, or students on campus asking for spaces for more social engagement.

It is not possible to design fully finished and complete spaces. One possible solution is to design incomplete spaces: "When designing a space, leave some of it unfinished. Don't solve everything; instead, leave room for things to evolve.

Ambiguity serves as an invitation. See how the blank space gets used and then let that inform further development. This allows you to uncover unpredictable directions and to address unanticipated needs" (Mathews and Soistmann 2016: 134). This gap design is not common but will keep the design phase from being fully finished; it blends it with the postoccupancy phase, blurring the boundaries that are common in design processes. Grosvenor and Burke (2008: 16–67) discuss architect and educational designer Bruce A. Jilk's concept of a "montage of gaps" which draws "attention to the significance of the spaces and places in between the formal learning environments; these can be left incomplete in order to stimulate a continuous design response among the users of these spaces over time." Extending the timeframe of the design process significantly is a strategy to be able to observe and analyze how spaces are actually used, which is difficult to predict. As sociomaterial assemblages, learning spaces are dynamic and never finished.

> Things themselves are not stable, identifiable objects and subjects, but teeming masses of particles or waves, energies, ideas, signs and boundaries, that are interesting in terms of the relations that hold them together, pull them apart, reorganize and shape them. This means that educational processes are not simply about forming particular subjects as learners, or using particular objects, such as texts, or understanding objects such as a policy. Sociomaterial approaches trace the shifting webs of dynamics that hold these processes together and shape their properties and interactions. Rather than simply asserting that practices are complex or messy, sociomateriality provides us with ways of engaging that complexity in detail to understand better its implications for learning, education and change.
>
> (Fenwick et al. 2011: 166)

Attention to continued postoccupancy processes means to not only conceptualize new buildings and spaces. Rather, focusing on the "after" rather than the "before" in designing spaces, this process becomes relevant to all departments and programs and not only those in the position to start from scratch:

> Whilst it seems plausible that the participatory approach described here could be adapted to the interior re-design of classrooms, it seems that the changes would be major and that further research would be necessary to render it suitable for that purpose, given the challenges of legacy environments. Perhaps the problems here are not so different from those concerning innovation in education: designing new programmes is much easier than re-designing existing ones. This seems like a worthwhile endeavour, not only because there are more

existing schools than new ones, but also because, in time, the newness wears off, pedagogies evolve, and buildings become inhabited by different cohorts of teachers and learners.

(van Merriënboer et al. 2017: 266)

Spaces of Possibility

In video game design, the term *space of possibility* is "the space of all possible actions that might take place in a game, the space of all possible meanings which can emerge from a game design" (Salen and Zimmerman 2003: 67). For designing language learning spaces, the term can be adapted to provide a framework and environment that allows for possible futures: "Language teachers are very much working within a complex system of opportunity and constraint. Normalization then becomes a process of understanding the infrastructure, the support networks, and the materials, and working effectively with them" (Levy and Stockwell 2006: 234).

Ambient, spatial, and technological attributes can provide such possibilities. Areas of active manipulation and user input can yield creative results. A space with all wall surfaces covered in whiteboard paint, found in some language centers, for example, provides a seemingly limitless canvass and invites users to participate in active, never-ending manipulation. Doorley and Witthoft (2012: 191) encourage writable surfaces everywhere to "create opportunities for capturing serendipitous sketches and outbreaking brainstorms." An outdoor example is the rock at Michigan State University, which students and other stakeholders can paint over to write a new chapter in the institution's narrative. It is not controlled by the administration, and thus a powerful tool for all stakeholders to engage in creating the future of the space. Kroll (1984: 167–9) contrasts this possibility approach with the processes with predetermined outcomes:

> There are two ways to create space for plants, just as there are two ways of organizing social space. The first aims at a single, predetermined objective. It is authoritarian, rational, and reductive. It corresponds to the desire to control events and people on the part of those whose task it is to conceive, organize, and produce. It contains an unconscious will to enclose life within geometrical schemes, to leave nothing to chance. At best, this approach to design divides the richness of life and reorganizes it by subject, like the books in a library. At worst, it turns the world into a kind of storehouse of replacement parts ... The other way of making social space (or, for that matter, a green space) is a living process

which implants only key centers of activity in a clear spatial configuration and with an intensity of form and meaning that favors (and expresses) what we believe essential: living relationships and activities which spring from diversity unexpected initiatives, and, above all, that something in social man that leads to the creation of community. This way of working is at once subjective, holistic, and spiritual. It uses rationality, but recognizes its limitations. The other is objective, normative, egocentric, and utilitarian. These two views coexist: their counterpoint evolves with the times.

Designing language learning spaces as anarchitecture is a radical proposition, and there is an in-between approach that finds a balance. Notice that the MSU rock example does not mean that students paint all over the campus. Rather, by providing a participatory space for stakeholders, it allows a co-existence between official and subversive narratives, or official and unofficial narratives, and of collective and individual narratives. Intentionally leaving unfinished space also means providing space for emergent discourses and new pathways. It eschews perfection and leaves room for creativity: "Neat is the enemy of creativity. If everything is too orderly, too perfect, then it inhibits our imagination. But if the space is a little open-ended (unbounded) and, perhaps, has a touch of chaos, then that frees our thinking about what is possible" (Mathews and Soistmann 2016: 132).

As mentioned before, flexibility can make it more likely for certain behaviors to occur. And providing an environment "rich in evocative objects—whether it's a classroom or a museum—triggers active learning by letting students pick what to engage with" (OWP/P Architects, VS Furniture and Bruce Mau Design 2010: 67). Curating learning spaces does not equal dictating what should be learned. Rather, finding the right balance between being overly prescriptive and strict on the one hand, and providing too much freedom on the other hand, can create engaging spaces of possibility.

Evolutionary Design and Building a Culture of Participation and Adaptation

Iterative and participatory design for physical language learning spaces (Kronenberg and Schwienhorst 2021) requires creating a culture in a language department or unit that constantly allows spaces to adapt and evolve. Mathews and Soistmann (2016: 134) posit that "[E]volutionary design is healthier than visionary design." Circumstances change all the time as the world changes around us, new technologies emerge, goals change, and new pedagogies replace older ones: "schools can and should be invented anew by each generation of teachers and students" (van Merriënboer et al. 2017: 260). Developing a culture of adaptation and participation involves clear processes, multiple ways of collecting and submitting input, and transparent decision-making structures. In loosely coupled systems, it is important to determine who is in charge of certain spaces.

Small, incremental changes provide a sustainable, less risky, and less daunting process of modernizing a learning space. Parsons (2017: 30) lists several examples that are exemplary of what small steps can be taken immediately, without large budgets or input from professionals:

> Revisions to a traditional classroom need not consist of a complete overhaul of the room. Lee and Tan (2013) have suggested that, because of the substantial cost and risk associated with redesigning classrooms, evidence and stakeholder input is necessary before making changes. User councils can suggest inexpensive, thoughtful adaptations that will improve the quality of each classroom on an annual basis. Simple changes such as replacing older chairs, replacing light fixtures, removing naps or snags in the carpet, repairing thermostats, removing clutter, and buffering noise distractions with acoustic pads can greatly improve the comfort and enjoyment of a classroom.

This also works for other, non-classroom spaces. The key is to start conversations about what changes yield the biggest results with the smallest amount of resources. Papert (1980: 173) uses the term "tinkering" for active building and manipulation: "in the most fundamental sense, we, as learners, are all *bricoleurs*." Co-designing a physical space is a learning opportunity for all involved, and the process itself not only builds community but also brings all stakeholders to be more mindful about learning outcomes, educational goals, and shared values. Once changes are occurring, the program or department gains experience in how to even start modifying spaces and builds prioritizing skills and a shared vocabulary for all stakeholders. One promising way of explaining spaces and their affordances to students and faculty is through scripts. Kollar et al. (2014: 7) argue that:

> Scripts can be understood as flexible, individual memory structures guiding our understanding and actions, but also as instructional interventions that help students use the affordances offered in new learning spaces. In study 1 ($N = 82$), the authors observed that when thrown into an unfamiliar, new learning space, students showed low individual learning and low satisfaction with the learning space, compared with students who received basic hints concerning how to use the affordances of the learning space. Study 2 ($N = 77$) demonstrated positive effects of an external script to guide collaborative decision-making in

the new learning space, compared to unstructured collaboration. Thus, a script perspective helps to understand why it is so difficult to use new learning spaces effectively. Script theory can also guide the design of support to overcome these difficulties.

Assessing Learning Spaces

If we want to build a truly innovative space, we face a chicken and egg problem: in order to test what works, we first have to build it. But if we want to build a new space, we need to know what works. Assessing that spaces are successful is not easy because of the many, sometimes contradictory, goals and measures of success. This is compounded if spaces frequently change. There are some assessment systems that can assist with evaluating the successes of learning spaces. The LSC rating system, now in its third version (Learning Space Rating System), provides a scoring system for general learning spaces. Regarding language learning spaces, there isn't a customized, discipline-specific version available. The International Association for Language Learning and Technology (IALLT) developed the Language Center Evaluation toolkit (Simon et al. 2017), which not only addresses physical learning spaces in a limited way but provides a general framework that is adaptable and can help with assessing basic needs. But because of the diversity of possible learning spaces as well as goals and outcomes, assessment options are still limited. Boys (2015: 102) criticizes that "current learning spaces evaluations are still mainly quite poor and that we urgently need better ways of understanding the relationships between space and the activities that go on in it, to improve both our ability to judge the effectiveness of learning in different kinds of environments, and actual learning space design." It is important to create a manipulable language learning space that can provide a research basis for identifying and studying different affordances and possibilities. The Center for Language Teaching Advancement (CeLTA) started a co-design project, but it was delayed due to the pandemic (Kronenberg and Schwienhorst 2021). Overall, there is clearly a need to develop more nuanced and robust learning space assessment mechanisms, and to be able to get more reliable data.

Conclusion

It is important to continue to actively work on learning spaces during the postoccupancy phase. As pedagogy, technology, institutions, goals, stakeholders and their expectations, and the world around us change, physical spaces must continue to be adapted to changes. Procedures, rules, and other processes are intertwined with ambient, spatial, and technological space attributes and have considerable impact on how a space functions. It is important to design these processes intentionally, and to openly and continuously assess the functioning of a space.

Inclusion, Accessibility, Wellbeing, and Belonging

Diversity, equity, and inclusion (DEI) are currently topics widely discussed in higher educational circles. They are also an important lens through which we can investigate better language learning space designs. This section examines inclusion and diversity, accessibility, wellbeing, and belonging as they relate to the design processes; the stakeholders involved; and the spaces that are created. These concepts are related and should not be seen in isolation.

Inclusion and Diversity

Institutions of higher learning are often exclusive by design. Despite aspirational language around the vision to be more inclusive, and many actual projects to widen access to learning, many colleges and universities are selective in who gets to enroll, who gets to take part in classes, and who is awarded credentials or degrees. This can be found in terms in educational discussions, symbols, and metaphors that are often spatial in nature, such as topographies of enclosure (McGregor 2003) or places of enclosure (Edwards Usher 2008), walled gardens, college gates, the town and gown polarity, silos, and the ivory tower.

The physical features of our campus and of our learning spaces shape and influence what is possible, what is expected, what is desired, for whom, and how. This is true for spaces, as it is for places, in general. Kern's (2020: 14) analysis of the city through a feminist lens argues that the built environment is not neutral:

> What sometimes seems even less obvious is the inverse: that once built, our cities continue to shape and influence social relations, power, inequality, and so on. Stone, brick, glass, and concrete don't have agency, do they? They aren't consciously trying to uphold the patriarchy, are they? No, but their form helps shape the range of possibilities for individuals and groups. Their form helps keep some things seeming normal and right, and others "out of place" and wrong. In short, physical places like cities matter when we want to think about social change.

Our educational spaces, including those for language learning, contain many processes and attributes that exclude and include: class times, faculty offices, various cultures (campus cultures, office cultures, national cultures, regional cultures, group cultures, etc.), and curricula. Many of these can be exclusive, and institutions consist of boundaries marked by "culturally concentrated knowledge" (Edwards and Usher 2008: 91). Creating a more inclusive, and thus equitable, diverse, and accessible environment for students and other stakeholders is a goal that has recently risen in importance in higher education. Gee (2004: 79) argues that "creating spaces wherein diverse sorts of people can interact is a leitmotif of the modern world." Strange and Banning (2001: 145) posit that intentional design can be "an important antecedent to involvement." This is not easy, and space design itself does not guarantee intended outcomes: "Perhaps the best we can do is set a tone and invite people in. We can craft perceptual cues and offer some context, but ultimately what a space becomes and how people feel about it is out of our hands" (Mathews and Soistmann 2016: 101).

Physical spaces can reinforce symbolic and conceptual spaces. Campus areas, pathways, digital access codes, room assignments and priorities, or invisible and visible boundaries and thresholds are all examples of space and place marking culturally expected behaviors and relationships and can either include or exclude. This encompasses language used in our spaces, such as signage, posters, flyers, markings, info panels, etc. Spaces and places can be intentionally designed to include. Language learning places, especially those that are often referred to as informal, can use symbolic, atmospheric, and spatial attributes to create a welcoming environment. Third Place (Oldenburg 1999) is an in-between space, located between personal spaces, the home, and formal spaces, such as the workplace, which could also be a classroom. Third Places are less formal meeting places for diverse people that might not meet in the other two. Oldenburg (1999: 24) argues that "[A] place that is a leveler is, by its nature, an inclusive place. It is accessible to the general public and does not set formal criteria of membership and exclusion." Such spaces and places can be created within exclusive spaces, such as institutions of higher education.

Inclusion and diversity do not only have an ethical dimension but also have proven benefits for learning. More voices generate more and better ideas and perspectives, create empathy, and can even help with expanding enrollments (Heidrich Uebel, Kronenberg, and Sterling, 2023). Diversity in learning can be found in many spaces, including diversity of assessment. How spaces, conceptual or physical ones, are designed, and the cultural messages they convey, can create and reinforce inequalities and exclusion, often even unintentionally (Costello 2000). Edgell and Kimmich (2015: 122) acknowledge that architects "may use language in a manner that minimizes the sharing of voice with other participating subcultures." As discussed above, an inclusive design process fosters more diverse voices by actively listening to and including all stakeholders. Fitzpatrick (2019: 34) describes the concept of "generous thinking" as a way "to think *with* rather than *against*, whether the objects of those prepositions are texts or people." Open processes, as well as more open and connected space designs can challenge traditional views "of the university as being a well-demarcated and immovable space" (Middleton 2018: 72).

Accessibility

One tenet of disability justice is an expectation of difference. This may refer to various kinds of differences, including but not limited to physical, mobility, learning, intellectual, mental health, neurodiversity, and sensory differences. Addressing this expectation can be approached in a passive and reactive way, or through proactive approaches to accessibility; for example, through universal design for learning (UDL) (Cornell 2020). UDL allows us to create inclusive physical learning spaces with all stakeholders in mind, with them and for them. It may be a way to prevent othering by providing equitable opportunities and access for all. Inclusive design and postoccupancy processes and raising awareness are good starting points. But because there are many disabilities that lay designers and even professional designers might not be aware of or trained in, it would be good practice to consult with an expert and consider an accessibility audit not only for an initial design but also for ongoing improvements in existing spaces. While flexible set-ups can help with improving spaces, some kinds of flexibility may also represent obstacles. Diversity in space design is an inclusive practice that allows equitable access to participation in language education. It includes intentionally reviewing ambient, spatial, and technological attributes. Procedural attributes are also important in deliberately setting expectations, policies, and processes. For example, what are the movement and placement options permissible in various spaces? Do students have to sit, or can they stand, and at what times and which spaces? Are they allowed to fidget or is movement to be avoided? Fidgeting and other displacement behaviors are coping mechanisms that allow students to self-regulate and alleviate anxiety (Paul 2021), but they can also be regarded as unpleasant by others (Carbone 2001). Other considerations include lighting, sounds, furniture choices and arrangements, and threshold design. Intentional discussions about expectations, values, and processes can be a good starting point to be more mindful about accessibility issues.

Access

Access, which is also another tenet of disability justice, is an inclusive concept in learning space design that allows all users to approach and enter spaces and places. Approachability is often neglected in space design, as it includes stakeholders knowing about the space, its location, its rules, and its expectations. The threshold of entering a physical space does not begin at the doorstep but in a space's perception of access. There are also physical attributes that can foster or hinder access to varying degrees. Some language centers, for example, require students to sign in (via a paper list or a digital device), and in some cases even ask them to pay a semester usage fee. These practices intentionally set access limitations. Others may be more subtle, such as placing a front desk into the direct path of entry or keeping the door closed. While these practices do not bar users from entering the space, they do make it less likely for some users to even attempt to enter. Features inside spaces can also create conditions that make it more likely for users to leave a space: environmental and ambient features, such as sounds or lighting, or symbolic features, such as images, posters, signage, etc. Belonging to a place, which is further discussed below, can be a condition that may be perceived as required for accessing a space. Referring to public spaces in the city, Kern (2020: 13) argues that "[M]ale power and privilege are upheld by keeping women's movements limited and their ability to access different spaces constrained." Likewise, certain spaces on campus can exclude members of some groups, either overtly or not overtly, and make them feel that they don't belong.

Importance of Belonging

Fostering a sense of belonging has become a buzzword in higher education in recent years. Gopalan and Brady (2020: 134) argue that "[I]n college, feeling a sense of belonging may lead students to engage more deeply with their studies, leading to persistence and success." Belonging is something that can occur naturally, of course, but it is not something that happens automatically for all students and other stakeholders. In fact, the annual National Survey of Student Engagement (NSSE) reported in its 2020 results that "Building a Sense of Community for All" is a key finding that can help improve intuitions of higher education (NSSE 2020). The "for all" is an important addition here, as it emphasizes the inclusive and equitable treatment of the issue that many students do not feel a sense of belonging and are thus likelier to not gain from its benefits. It shows that sense of belonging is not merely a vague concept that cannot be supported, planned, and designed for.

A sense of belonging can help with improving mental health and regulating stress (Baumeister and Leary 1995). It is linked to a sense and attachment of place, which is subjective and emotional (Cresswell 2014). Middleton (2018: 66) uses the term "Emplacement" to describe "a sense of common identity and place." There is a good argument for creating meaningful places rather than generic spaces to involve students more as active participants of the learning process, which in turn provides more opportunities for creating belonging:

> We become attached to places because of what they enable us to do ... A place (rather than a space) encourages students to be active residents who define, interpret, search, and modify the settings for achieving personal goals. Whether it is a quiet nook or a high-energy collaboration hub doesn't matter. What does matter is feeling a sense of ownership and camaraderie that elevates the experience.
> (Mathews and Soistmann 2016: 24)

The built environment does not automatically make a space a place. People, interactions, and programming all matter to create a deeper identity and involvement. "What is most relevant to the notion of setting is not the particularity of events (which may be of great interest in other ways), but the ways in which their regular occurrence stamps spaces with a particular character over time" (Benson 2021: 103). For example, a weekly language coffee hour benefits from its regularity and its dependability. Frequent encounters between people strengthen social bonds and support commonalities. The design of a space does, however, also contribute to creating positive emotions and attachment to a place, as Graetz (2006: 62) argues: "It may become a place where students love to learn, a place they seek out when they wish to learn, and a place they remember fondly when they reflect on their learning experiences." This connection can positively contribute to life-long learning goals.

Communities of practice provide a multitude of "intangible outcomes": "the relationships they build among people, the sense of belonging they create, the spirit of inquiry they generate, and the professional confidence and identity they confer to their members" (Wenger et al. 2002: 15). Spaces and places of belonging foster communities of practice, and vice versa, if they allow newcomers to initially observe other members of a community before contributing themselves and moving further into the center of the community: "An extended period of legitimate peripherality provides learners with opportunities to make the culture of practice theirs" (Lave and Wenger 1991: 95). Learning spaces can be deliberately designed to allow for different levels of participation and peripherality, for example by providing a variety of seating options, different areas with different levels of openness, and nooks that allow users to retreat and be by themselves. Emphasizing fluidity means to provide affordances for people to easily move into, out of, and through different areas, and to create visual transparency. Physical learning spaces can simply provide sociopetal conditions and proximity to other people (Mehrabian 1981).

Ideally public places weave social identities and provide opportunities to build community:

> It is within a community, whether in the form of a class, a student organization, a peer training program, or a residence hall floor, to cite a few examples, that participants experience a complete sense of membership in a setting. They become part of the history and culture of the setting such that, when they leave, they are missed, for they have imprinted the environment with their unique mark, in effect, leaving a trail for others to see.
>
> (Strange and Banning 2001: 110)

Groups of people find spaces on campus, and they may avoid others depending on how they feel they belong. Middleton (2018: 44) suggest that "Zoning" can "foster belonging by developing connection between the built environment and its users and by creating opportunities for social interaction and emotional engagement within a community." There are ways of measuring levels of belonging and visualize them (Brown 2016) to better understand student's place choices. For language learning, this matters to diverse people for different reasons. Fritzsche et al. (2022: 46) argue that:

> [B]y providing an actual space for a wide diversity of languages—a space where all types of language learners with different needs, goals, and perspectives can meet and create community—LCTL [less commonly taught languages] programs embody the DEI commitment of institutions of higher education. A diverse WL [world language] curriculum with LCTLs and Indigenous languages allows more learners to see themselves as represented, respected, and acknowledged.

Even though this refers to conceptual spaces here, physical spaces can also be inclusive to allow learners and stakeholders to feel included, to see themselves, and to be able to be their whole selves. Bringing whole selves, which is also emphasized in accessibility advocacy, and ways of building a sense of belonging and community does not necessarily mean that spaces are always perfectly comfortable:

> We need to explore how different learning spaces can make participants (tutors as well as learners) feel safe or uncomfortable, and the impact this can have on their learning. If a space is very "recognisable," for example a lecture theatre, then is it likely that students will fall into standard assumptions about their "place" as a passive rather than an active learner, and may in fact prefer such a location, since it represents what they already know. On the other hand, the strangeness of having "standard" routines shifted, without clear alternative rules being offered, may undermine confidence. This suggests that we need to know much more about our conventional routines for producing and recognising the accomplishment of "doing" learning—and to understand how these can be positively and appropriately adapted and translated across both different physical and virtual spaces. There is no simple one-size-fits-all answer here. Envisaging specific learning spaces that enable both a sense of belonging, and also "push" participants beyond their particular comfort zones, seems to hold in tension contradictory trends.
>
> (Boys 2011: 46)

Wellbeing

During the Covid-19 pandemic, the term "wellbeing" became increasingly popular in various contexts, including higher education. Simons and Baldwin (2021) argue that it's an ill-defined term that is either too simplistically equated with feelings and states of being happy, healthy, or with nouns such as health, wellness, and welfare. They propose using associated adjectives like "flourishing" and "thriving" (positive), and "languishing" and "poor" (negative); determinants like "system resilience," "social capital," "positive psychology," and "resilience" (positive); and "system failure," "social isolation," "negative psychology," and "lack of coping strategies" (negative). Wellbeing is measured and perceived differently in different cultures and can focus on individual or collective aspects of wellbeing.

Physical comforts are not necessarily needed for wellbeing. Selingo (2018: 5) reports a generational shift in building design: "During the height of millennial enrollment, many institutions went on a building, hiring, and programming spree. But Gen Zers tend to want fewer comforts and more supports; they may be fine with simpler housing while benefiting from more flexible spaces that promote interaction with classmates and professors." Gen Z would also profit from more guidance regarding wellness (Selingo 2018). Examples for language learning include the many programs that social spaces can support, from the previously discussed food and game events to yoga in the L2 (Stapleton 2022). In general, to promote wellbeing and mental health, Selingo (2018) suggests encouraging more face-to-face interactions.

One aspect of wellbeing is a sense of safety and the absence of danger. Safety includes not only a physical but also emotional and cultural dimensions (Hobbs and Dofs 2018). Including lessons learning from trauma-informed classroom design (Frey et al. 2020), physical spaces can create environments that reduce stress and take users' different levels of fear and anxiety into account to provide a productive learning environment for all.

Conclusion

Creating spaces that are accessible and inclusive requires wide stakeholder participation in design processes. Not all spaces make all users feel welcome or feel that they belong. Yet such design considerations are not only ethically the best approach but can also promote better conditions for all users. Design considerations should not only include functional aspects of space design but also incorporate symbolic and procedural attributes to create truly inclusive, equitable, and accessible learning spaces.

It should also be mentioned that there is an increasing emphasis on creating environmentally sustainable learning spaces. Physical spaces require an enormous amount of energy and resources to be built and to be maintained. In any design project, it is important to consider existing spaces and resources, reusing materials, and installing energy-friendly appliances and technologies. Repurposing furniture and installing motion sensors are examples of minimizing impact. But perhaps even more importantly, it is important to consider sharing existing spaces instead of building new ones, increasing existing spaces' uses, sharing spaces with other units and programs, and not unnecessarily increasing the physical footprint.

Designing physical learning spaces that serve language learning is a complex process that cannot only be done by professional planners, it requires all stakeholders to be included. It is not enough, and sometimes harmful, to focus on superficial and subjective attributes, as Sutherland and Sutherland (2010: 59) remark:

> [M]any architects are interested in buildings as monumental objects. We suggest that such an image-based approach to designing schools could be limited in

terms of the way in which a school actually needs to work as a complex set of interconnected learning space. Such a "wow factor" approach to the design of buildings is the visual equivalent of the "sound bite" selling of a product or an idea, and this simplification and commodity approach to designing large schools is incompatible with the spatial complexity required for modern learning environments.

Design processes are not merely technical considerations that happen before a space is built and end thereafter. Rather, they need to be sustained and should thus be iterative, procedural, and require ongoing curation in order to be spaces and places rather than mere learning containers. It is often people who create places out of spaces (Burbules and Callister 2000), but placemaking can be supported by spatial attributes as well as intentional processes (Middleton 2018).

Language learning spaces can be more than merely classrooms and specialized rooms. If we want them to optimally support language learning, it is important that shared learning goals are clearly defined. These goals should, along with shared values, mission, and a clear vision, form the basis for the many space decisions for the initial planning but also the space's lifespan.

5

The Physicality of Hybrid Language Learning Spaces

The title of this book suggests that there is something special about physical language learning spaces during this time of ubiquitous computing—*in the digital age*. Indeed, digital technologies and their rapid developments in the last few decades present new possibilities that pose the question: do we still need physical spaces for language learning? The previous chapters laid out an argument for physical spaces: from extended cognition to creating a sense of belonging, from different affordances to motivation. Arguments for physical spaces are not in opposition to or at the expense of digital or virtual spaces. Rather, it is important to be mindful of the different affordances and situational advantages to make more deliberate use of both. This chapter then looks at how physical spaces, in the digital age, should be designed more intentionally to benefit from the advantages and affordances of both. This kind of hybridity, with a focus on its physical aspects, will be discussed in more detail in the following sections. The chapter concludes with a reflection on the developments during the pandemic, when many L2 learning activities went fully virtual, and on the lessons we learned in order to envision a better future for L2 hybrid space possibilities.

The Hybrid Spectrum of Learning Spaces

Physical and virtual (also sometimes referred to as digital) learning spaces are sometimes presented as opposites, with hybrid spaces constituting the spectrum in-between the two poles. This section discusses how we can leverage the synergies between physical spaces and digital spaces rather than seeing them as binary opposites.

Polarized views were discussed in previous chapters within the context of normalization, and how acceptance is located in-between. Binary opposition of the physical and the digital has been common in many educational contexts and scenarios: printed book or eBook; pen and paper or laptop; live presentation/workshop or webinar; board game or video game; online course or face-to-face course; etc. Each supposed opposite end of these pairs has its own set of characteristics, with different affordances and advantages.

The example of printed versus electronic books illustrates how after an initial polarized view, a co-existence has become normalized and the gap has disappeared. After a period of dividing opinions and beliefs between proponents of the new (eBook) and proponents of the old (printed book), we have reached a phase of normalization. Many educators and students now use both, but within different contexts and for different purposes. For example, when doing research, one might conveniently download several eBooks to save time and quickly get an overview of which texts and authors might be most useful. The eBook allows its users to copy citations with ease, save time, and minimize mistakes. On the other hand, readers might choose to buy a book for other scenarios, such as when a book has special meaning to an individual, it is from a favorite author, it is read out of personal interest, or if a reader cherishes the tactile (and even olfactory) sensation that comes from a physical copy. There are many reasons for either, and they differ from person to person and situation to situation.

Similarly, we should overcome the false physical space/virtual space binary: "Hybridity dissolves existing dichotomies such as physical-digital, formal-informal, learning-teaching and individual-collective" (Kohls 2019: 228). The physical-virtual dichotomy is a false one because all learning is embodied. Purely virtual learning spaces separated from the physical world don't exist (Savin-Baden 2008), but are rather all hybrid in nature. Likewise, purely physical learning spaces are increasingly less common as virtual and digital spaces are increasingly ubiquitous. For instance, a student might use a digital textbook, a recording or dictionary app, or an online video or article during a face-to-face class. It is not an either/or scenario:

> What this boils down to is the idea that when we act we're simultaneously interacting with the people and things in the immediate environment *and* with people and things in the immediate environment spatially and temporally removed from us, but none the less present in the situation in some way. To understand how activity is connected to learning and knowledge we have to deal with *both* threads of interaction.
>
> (Nespor 1994: 3)

Therefore, it is useful to deconstruct the possible attributes of both virtual and of physical spaces to better understand the possibilities of hybridity.

Virtual Spaces

Virtual spaces differ from physical ones especially in one regard: a person can only be in one physical location at any one time. The person cannot simply disappear or be invisible, and in most situations there is a reciprocal relationship with the people in the same space. If the person wants to be in a different space, they usually have to expend energy, time, and resources to move and to cross boundaries. Physical spaces place many obstacles that cannot be changed: walls, doors, restricted areas, linearity, borders, and the time of day in a given location all share the relatively static nature of physical spaces.

Digital spaces fundamentally differ from that, which makes them so useful for learning and especially language learning: "Place and time therefore no longer signify the firm boundaries of the possible that they once were, with rhizomatic practices taking precedence over linearity. To put it another way, boundaries have become more permeable, porous and traversable with greater ease. In cyberspace there are networks with fewer borders, limits, or even rules" (Edwards and Usher 2008: 121–2). There is a simultaneity in digital spaces that the physical world does not allow. In cyberspace, a student can, for example, listen to a Zoom class call, write notes in a collaborative notes document, browse a shopping site, *and* listen to music at the same time. Other students or the instructor only share one or a few but not all of those spaces with that student. The multiplicity of spaces can provide certain advantages, but it also limits truly shared spaces. Digital spaces provide a certain freedom (Savin-Baden 2008) by upending the laws and limitations of the material world. This can have an equalizing effect: in order to "see" the Eiffel Tower, in the past a person had to expend considerable amounts of resources and time to travel to see it. Today, there are multiple ways to experience it through different types of representations and digital recreations, through photos and videos, digital models, three-dimensional (3D) renderings, and increasingly through immersive virtual reality (VR) simulations. Similarly, sounds and voices can not only transcend time and distance but may also be digitally created. Digital spaces are often a lot cheaper than physical ones, both in their creation and in their consumption and use. There is also a rapid proliferation of digital spaces at a speed that is not possible in the physical world. The number of choices can be both freeing as well as overwhelming at the same time, and it is difficult to discern authenticity and reliability in digital spaces.

Digital spaces "dematerialise communication" (Edwards and Usher 2008: 118) as distances and physical entities are no longer essential in this process. This can be beneficial for language learning, as texts can be produced, shared, and mediated with ease. Savin-Baden (2008: 81) argues that "[D]igital spaces demand that we confront the possibility of new types of visuality, literacy, pedagogy, representations of knowledge, communication and embodiment."

On the other hand, physical space concepts discussed previously are not as easily replicable in digital-only spaces: bodily sensation, embodied learning, extended cognition, placemaking, whole selves, and sense of belonging.

Hybrid Spaces

The term "hybrid" is vague and has been used in many different contexts by educational scholars. It has changed over time just as other, related terms have come into existence. Ducate et al. (2012: 68) argue that the terms "hybrid learning" and "blended learning" are often used interchangeably, but define it for their purposes as follows:

> With respect to language classes, this definition generally implies a learning space where instruction takes place in a traditional classroom setting and is enhanced or supplemented—sometimes even replaced—by computer-based or online activities. Such activities can, but do not necessarily, replace classroom seat time, but the implementation of a hybrid approach implies that students interact with the instructor and other students both in person and virtually.

Caulfield (2011: 4) focuses on the learner: "Hybrid courses place the primary responsibility of learning on the learner, thus making it the teacher's primary responsibility to create opportunities and foster environments that encourage student learning, rather than simply telling students what they need to know."

There are many other, related terms that each emphasize different aspects of hybridity: blended synchronous, blended asynchronous, integrated learning environments (Skill and Young 2002), "phygital" spaces (Gaggioli 2017), polysynchronous, blended polysynchronous, and HyFlex (Beatty 2019). Even though definitions for each exist, in practice they are usually not used in a concise and agreed-upon manner. Robert (2022) provides a useful acknowledgement of this lack of consistency: "We recognize that instructors, students, administrators, instructional designers, and other stakeholders have not come to a consensus on the way instructional modalities are labeled and operationalized. Terms such as 'online,' 'online synchronous,' 'online asynchronous,' 'hybrid,' 'blended,' 'HyFlex,' and 'face-to-face' continue to mean different things to different people."

A way forward then might be to use the concept and noun of "hybridity" rather than "hybrid" as an adjective. Middleton (2018: 68) argues that "[H]ybridity embraces the polycontextual nature of learning." Murray and Lamb (2018b: 2–3) posit that "learning places can be polymorphous, sometimes being hybrids of physical, virtual and/or metaphorical spaces." Perhaps the more open concept Löw (2016: xv) provides, "spatial overlapping and intermixing," shows that concepts of hybridity cannot be neatly divided but are all related to one another. In this view, learning spaces can be seen more as a spectrum along different axes: physical-digital, formal-informal, internal-external, immediate-lifelong, and planned-incidental.

Conclusion

Digital spaces and thus hybrid spaces have seen tremendous growth since the end of the twentieth century, and the current generation of students has not known a purely analog world. They are not only comfortable with hybridity, they also expect it: "This is a generation accustomed to learning by toggling between the real and virtual worlds" (Selingo 2018: 5). For the purposes of this book, it is useful to remind ourselves that hybridity always involves physicality. Taylor (2002: 42) posits that "[U]sers do not simply roam through the space as 'mind,' but find themselves grounded in the *practice* of body, and thus in the world. Much like offline life, our sense of self, other, and space is constantly reinscribing itself as structures and relationships change." There are synergies between the two abstract poles that we can leverage to overcome simplified dichotomies.

Extended Reality

Extended reality (XR), sometimes also called mixed reality, encompasses a range of digital spaces that connect with physical spaces in different ways, such as augmented reality (AR) and VR. They are hybrid spaces in the sense that both domains, the physical and the virtual or digital, are necessary and important parts of the whole. This "convergence of the physical dimension and the virtual dimension," which (Gaggioli 2017) refers to as "phygital," is becoming increasingly common and sophisticated. These new hybrid spaces differ from more traditional forms of cyberspace in that the body and the physical world play a crucial role in these. Traditionally, the disembodied nature of cyberspace has been stressed: "Unlike other forms of space, exploring, and getting around in, cyberspace does not require any physical movement beyond pressing keys on a keyboard, using a joystick or moving a mouse. Once connected, a variety of activities become possible and it is these that constitute the network of relationships that are cyberspace" (Edwards and Usher 2008: 117). XR utilizes physical objects, movements, location, and physical space to create new possibilities for immersion, for additional information, and new communicative affordances and experiences. Selingo (2018: 4) argues that for the newest generation entering college, XR and hybrid space is already normalized: "Growing up entirely in the era of the smartphone and social media mean that Gen Zers see technology as an extension of themselves with respect to how they communicate, manage friendships, consume information, and learn. They expect a high-tech educational and campus experience but don't want to live entirely in the virtual world."

Augmented Reality

AR is "the viewing of digital information that has been superimposed or augmented onto a live view of our physical environment" (Gorter 2013: 204) and thus "allows people to visualize videos, pictures, and 3D objects, or play an audio file upon scanning a trigger image on a mobile device" (Karacan and Mollamehmetoğlu 2022). In addition to scanned images and QR codes, there are other triggers, such as location-based triggers or timed triggers. Bonner and Reinders (2018: 34) argue that AR enables "enhancing reality with digital resources." AR can alter our physical environment in a way that provides different information for different users. It adds an additional, digital layer over the physical layer, and thus can change "the perception of the linguistic landscape" (Gorter 2013: 204). AR language education examples range from simply providing additional information in language centers, self-access centers, or classrooms by posting QR codes to more involved projects, such as location-based games (Holden and Sykes 2011).

Regarding designing physical spaces, AR technologies present new possibilities in customizing spaces for individual users and adding additional information through a digital layer. For example, they can provide further details or information in different languages through text, sound, videos, or interactive features. AR can streamline certain processes, such as reserving spaces, checking out items, or collecting data. Another feature is increased wayfinding by providing mapping and information data. And it can certainly be included in more formal curricula and language courses.

Virtual Reality

VR allows users to create or experience "immersive 3D virtual worlds that encompass a user's entire field of vision using a dedicated headset" (Bonner and Reinders 2018: 34). Such technologies also include haptic feedback and immersive sound to mimic actual physical experiences. There has been a lot of interest recently about how VR technologies, which are becoming more mainstream, less expensive, lighter, and less tethered, can be used in language education (e.g., Ijiri 2022; Novash 2022; Tytarenko 2022).

For the purposes of physical spaces, VR is interesting because it further blurs the line between the physical and the virtual. As is the case with AR, once common and clear, distinctions between the two spheres are disappearing. Of course, VR can be used anywhere. Within designed language learning environments, there are a few implications and considerations. Language centers can provide VR spaces for language classes as well as individual use. This might include additional displays and computers that can record what happens in the virtual space. Empty space that allows for safe usage of VR headsets for multiple users is also important when incorporating VR. Flexibility, as discussed in Chapter 4, is beneficial in this case. Another aspect to consider is providing alternatives to VR, which poses accessibility issues and can cause adverse effects in some users. We are still at the beginning to investigate different possibilities for VR and language education. One advantage of VR is the ability to blend out extralinguistic means of communication and allow for asymmetrical use of VR headsets (Kronenberg and Poole 2022), while the ability to generate immersive experiences can be beneficial in different types of language learning scenarios.

In the science fiction novel "Ready Player One," the protagonist and most people live a large part of their lives in an immersive and sophisticated VR world. They also go to school in these virtual worlds. But interestingly, these schools are merely mimicking their physical counterparts:

> The school bell rang and a warning flashed in the corner of my display, informing me that I had forty minutes until the start of the first period. I began to walk my avatar down the hall, using a series of subtle hand motions to control its movements and actions. I could also use the voice commands to move around,

if my hands were otherwise occupied. I strolled in the direction of my World History classroom, smiling and waving to the familiar faces I passed. I was going to miss the place when I graduated in a few months.

(Cline 2011: 29)

Instead of completely rethinking what might be possible, traditional space-time structures are merely perpetuated in this new realm:

> There are hundreds of school campuses here on Lulus, spread out evenly across the planet's surface. The schools were all identical, because the same construction code was copied and pasted into a different location whenever a new school was needed. And since the buildings were just pieces of software, their design wasn't limited by monetary constraints, or even the laws of physics. So every school was a grand place of learning, with polished marble hallways, cathedral-like classrooms, zero-g gymnasiums, and virtual libraries containing every (school-board-approved) book ever written.

(Cline 2011: 31–2)

As we investigate VR further in the coming years, we should think beyond such a limiting vision, both for the design of the virtual worlds, but also for how we design our physical spaces within which such new worlds might be experienced.

Other Extended Reality Spaces

While AR and VR are commonly thought of when XR is discussed, there are other spaces that utilize some of the same concepts of hybridity. The layering of physical and virtual spaces can be achieved through other means, including physical space design. An interesting example is immersive rooms, which consist of only screens. Donnally Spasova (2019) describes a third-semester Russian class visiting different places in Russia in a round 360 specialty classroom. In a way, the room provides a collective VR experience for groups that still allows for students to see and interact with each other in the physical space. Another shared XR space for language is the planetarium. A pilot project by the Center for Language Teaching Advancement and the Abram's Planetarium at Michigan State University investigates L2 planetarium shows (Cornell 2023). Another interesting experiment in blurring physical and virtual spaces for language learning includes telepresence robots (Liao and Lu 2018). These robots can be steered by someone who is remote, but who can not only interact with those in a physical location, but also navigate the physical space and have a presence in a different location other than the navigator's body, while also being able to see, be seen, speak, and listen.

Figure 5 Round, experimental 360 classroom.

There are currently new XR technologies developed, including AR projectors or "Parallel Reality" displays, which allow public displays to show different information to different viewers. This requires facial recognition but is already a reality at Detroit's Metro Airport (Kramer 2022). This technology further changes our physical spaces as now each user sees and experiences something different. This kind of convergence, of course, is not new. In some ways, movie theaters are precursors of shared XR spaces. Nowadays we have movie theaters that have not only 3D capabilities, but 4D, 5D, 6D, 7D, 8D, and even 9D. While the distinctions and details, which might not be necessarily interesting for educational purposes, are less important, the ability to mix simulated spaces with physical sensations is a powerful experience for humans and allows us to experiment with further blending the two worlds. The convergence of spaces will further erase the distinction that we still currently have. Architects and space designers are already increasingly mindful of digital and virtual experiences and possibilities, while programmers, digital designers, and experience architecture professionals and creatives are also thinking about not only the virtual aspects but also physical ones:

> Augmented reality, Internet of Things, robotics, and artificial intelligence are transforming our living spaces—houses, offices, public places, and so on—in

digitally enriched environments that blur the distinction between the "real" and the "simulated." In these hybrid phygital ecosystems, objects, tools, and even bodies can be turned into "programmable interfaces," creating totally novel ways of experiencing space. For this reason, providing paradigmatic examples of phygital spaces is not easy: the possible ways in which the physical and digital worlds can be mixed are simply unlimited.

(Gaggioli 2017)

There are possibilities for interaction in physical spaces that we currently associate with digital spaces: "As devices allow for more efficiency and collaboration, we may come to expect the same synergy from the physical places we occupy. Our needs may demand more participatory interfaces in place of traditional public spaces. These areas may become 'wiki-spaces,' interactive environments where occupants are not just observers but active participants" (del Signore 2020).

Conclusion

New types of mixed and XR spaces continue to erase boundaries between physical and virtual domains. It is likely that we will see rapid technological innovations in this area which will likely also have an impact on language education. It is not the goal of this book to speculate what these unlimited space possibilities might be. But we should be aware that the distinctions between physical spaces are increasingly intertwined with digital and virtual spaces and be mindful how they can be leveraged in language education.

Imagining Physical Language Learning Spaces in a Post-Covid-19 World: The New Normal of Ubiquitous Hybrid Learning Spaces

When Covid-19 forced many instructors into emergency remote education and shut down physical campuses, many experienced for the first time what it means to not be able to come physically together for an extended amount of time. It highlighted that campus and physical spaces and places were more than simply the default and habits: they were missed. So much that university students recreated their brick-and-mortar campuses in detail in digital spaces, for example, in the game Minecraft (Anderson 2020). While digital spaces provided alternative and safe spaces, the forced experiment also showed that remote emergency language teaching does not equal true, carefully designed online language teaching. Language educators shared how thankful yet frustrated they were when their physical interactions were taken away.

Rather than arguing whether online spaces or physical spaces are different, an important takeaway is that each has its advantages, disadvantages, affordances, and challenges. It forced all educators to ask questions that until then mostly only learning spaces experts, specialists, and researchers had been confronted with: What is the importance of being physically close together? What kind of environment do we prefer if we have the choice? How can we be more mindful of the attributes and affordances of each? And how can we overcome the false dichotomy of either/or: either physical, face-to-face learning, or virtual learning? In short: How can we normalize hybrid spaces and develop more sophisticated, nuanced, and intentional understandings of them?

Can We Predict the Future of Physical Language Learning Spaces?

It is difficult to predict what and how our physical spaces will develop, not just in education but across different sectors. This includes the unwritten future of remote work, the need for physical offices, and how they are designed. In education, the use of online courses, new pedagogies and technologies, and more flexible offerings were not created by the situation the pandemic brought about. Rather, it made them more visible and accelerated or decelerated certain trends already happening across higher education. In their white paper, Felix et al. (2020) discuss accelerating trends; for example, increased utilization of time, reductions in large lecture halls, increasing classroom space per seat to lower density and provide higher flexibility, online/on-campus convergence, increased student mental health issues, and increased remote work. They propose that decelerating trends appear to be a decline in campus expansions—a decline in shared, multipurpose, and open workspaces; decreased occupancy; and decreased utilization of space.

Building resilience and adaptability into new spaces is important as we navigate shifting patterns and expectations, many of which are external to the institutions. An appropriate design response can positively distinguish institutions and programs that are able to adapt to new paradigms in many ways, including their physical spaces. Resilient physical spaces are intertwined with resilient approaches to teaching:

> We define resilient teaching as the ability to facilitate learning experiences that are designed to be adaptable to fluctuating conditions and disruptions. This teaching ability can be seen as an outcome of a design approach that attends

to the relationship between learning goals and activities, and the environments they are situated in. Resilient teaching approaches take into account how a dynamic learning context may require new forms of interactions between teachers, students, content, and tools. Additionally, they necessitate the capacity to rethink the design of learning experiences based on a nuanced understanding of context.

(Quintana and DeVaney 2020)

Just redesigning spaces is not sufficient without reimagining pedagogy at the same time. An example for language learning spaces are physical spaces for testing, a common point of contention in language center design: without addressing how we assess our students, how often, and why, we cannot start to reimagine a language computer lab that is mainly used for testing purposes. Addressing our goals, beliefs, and values around language learning is crucial before replacing furniture or removing walls.

Normalizing Hybridity

As discussed above, there is a wide spectrum of hybrid learning spaces, and they are not only ubiquitous but also normalizing. Skill and Young (2002: 24) wrote over two decades ago: "past patterns suggest that the likely future will be neither solely online learning nor solely instructor-led classroom learning." Around the same time, Van Lier (2003: 61) concluded that "computers do not need to be isolated and concentrated in labs in which students work individually on drills or programs of various kinds. Rather, the technology can enhance and enrich classrooms themselves." For today's generation, Selingo (2018: 25) suggests designing a "mix of learning environments and activities, both face-to-face and online."

There are increasingly sophisticated approaches to investigate and understand the complexity that the plurality of spaces affords. For example, sociomaterial and sociocultural approaches provide frameworks to analyze and understand how we can better use hybrid spaces to foster language education, and how we can better design such spaces at our institutions. Spatial understanding of learning contexts, which also includes spaces such as workplaces, international space, and the home (Brooks et al. 2012), is an increasingly important concept for students, educators, and current and future leaders.

It is difficult to predict all possibilities and future conventions around hybrid spaces. Perhaps a way forward is to think about them less rigidly, less polarized, and less sharply divided. Rather than regarding physical and virtual space design as separate and incongruous domains, we should regard them as intertwined, interdependent entities. We might rather conceive them as essential components in a new language learning space ecosystem, constantly shifting and adapting: "today's learning contexts are a hybrid of overlapping physical and virtual spaces which flow into and out of each other, tied together by new technologies. In an ideal scenario (and growing numbers of real-world scenarios) physical and virtual learning spaces reinforce each other's plasticity" (Pegrum et al. 2014: 338). What we can do in the face of uncertainty is to be more intentional and more nuanced in our approach to spaces. For that, we need to develop a new literacy of learning spaces that can support language learning's many, complex aspects. This new literacy should include finding common connectors between spaces and understanding the dual design of interior design and interface design.

Spaces of Choice

The plurality of spaces allows learners and other stakeholders to make meaningful choices. In the higher education landscape, it is important to consider the different options available and provide those that best match learning goals, effectiveness, efficiency, values, and learner preferences. In a way, physical spaces now face competition from not only other physical spaces, but increasingly from virtual and hybrid spaces. One solution for language education is to create conditions that make such spaces places that students *want* to be in: "Atmosphere determines where we voluntarily choose to spend our time, how long we remain in a given location, and thus, the degree to which a particular environment can be considered immersive" (Montgomery 2020: 342–3). This means actively listening to not only their views, but also their wishes, ideas, and dreams. Our physical spaces, if we want them to remain relevant and vibrant for language learning, cannot be an afterthought but require deliberate and intentional design and curation: "Although many educators have become increasingly (perhaps even aggressively) vocal over the environmental learning conditions of the virtual world ... most have remained almost complacent about the conditions of the physical learning environments where they ply their craft on a near-daily basis and where the vast majority of learners gather ... " (Skill and Young 2002: 23).

Paradigm Shifts

While many of our language pedagogies, curricula, and technologies have become more sophisticated, our physical spaces have not changed and adapted as quickly. Davidson (2017: 6) laments that "we're still going to school the way we did in 1993, which is to say, pretty much as we did in 1983." Of course, changing the built environment is more difficult and costlier than changing non-physical spaces. But physical educational spaces and the resulting built pedagogy reinforce old paradigms and prevent us to fully embrace new ones. Grosvenor and Burke (2008: 10–11) discuss how our limitations in imagination prevent us from considering completely different educational space systems:

> Whatever the type of school, a group of people comes together to design a structure based upon ideas about what the teacher or learner should be doing when they interact. It is these ideas that create classrooms, situate corridors and locate specialist rooms, common spaces and surrounding areas in particular ways. Apart from the usual limitations that result from planning regulations and local requirements, and in a much more fundamental way, the group's collective experience acts as a limitation on its capacity to imagine a different educational future.

Whenever there is a possibility to reimagine a language space, we must consider what might be possible in the future. One example of new paradigms is strategic course-sharing, which is currently researched at the Center for Language Teaching Advancement (CeLTA) at Michigan State University and the Title VI-Funded Center for Less Commonly Taught Languages (NLRC) that it houses. Sharing language courses that other institutions do not offer could support more language program diversity, make programs more sustainable and resilient, and can create inter-institutional synergies and opportunities. The blurring of institutional boundaries requires a rethinking of traditional classrooms, language centers, offices, and campuses. What would spaces look like that would optimally support more common course sharing?

Because we cannot predict the future, we should design frameworks that allow current and future stakeholders create and recreate spaces as they need them. For that we must not be afraid to experiment, build prototypes, and assess what works and what doesn't. The hybrid learning atelier ("das hybride Lernatelier") at the Bauhaus-Universität Weimar, Germany, is an example of an experimental hybrid space that can be constantly changed to continuously and iteratively test new solutions and their effects on education. Several language centers (Kronenberg and Schwienhorst 2021) have similarly embarked on such iterative prototyping and testing.

Conclusion: The Future of Physical Language Learning Spaces

Designing physical language learning spaces presents a greater challenge in practice than in theory due to the intricate and unpredictable nature of the many factors involved: "Physical, brick-and-mortar learning spaces have a lifespan that easily outlasts the definitions and learning theories of which they are an embodiment. In this sense, they contribute to the 'inertia' ... associated with the face-to-face lecture by actively constraining the kinds of learning that they make possible via the limited affordances that characterise them" (Thomas 2010: 502–3). Monahan (2005: 33) discusses how built learning spaces have profound effects for a long time:

> Whether older spaces enforce discipline or encourage autonomy, they continue to constrain and inflect any new designs or pedagogical changes; spaces and practices co-construct one another in iterative development patterns, and rooms continue to teach older lessons even when individuals, curricula, or technologies move on. Still, realizing that technological change is contingent, embodied, and politically situated can open up education to the future potentialities harbored in material forms.

Being mindful of their cost, longevity, and rigidity, does it still make sense to invest in physical spaces for language learning instead of more nimble, cheaper, and more adaptable virtual and digital spaces?

We should not underestimate, or dismiss, physical spaces in this increasingly digital world. In fact, I would argue that they are becoming more valuable. During the first class after the pandemic, my students were ecstatic to be back in person, to see each other, to socialize, and to be in one physical place instead of many digital spaces at once. Despite the many hurdles to get to that place, we all together experienced that we are more than mind, more than our digital interfaces. We were made very aware that learning and experiences are embodied, that cognition is embodied and situated, that we learn together, and that we are social animals. The attraction of the physical world did not go away. Rather, there is a new appreciation for the embodied learning *in addition to* realizing the value of virtual spaces. To leverage it fully, we cannot simply keep building generic, sub-optimal learning spaces. Instead, we need to pay closer attention to the affordances that different modalities provide and be more aware of the advantages physical spaces provide in addition to those of virtual ones. Rather than replacing face-to-face language learning, digital and physical learning spaces co-exist. As a new normalization of hybridity is setting in, we need to rethink how we design and use our physical language learning spaces and weave the plurality of spaces at our disposal. Physical space design can support and enable the crossing of boundaries of physical and virtual worlds. There has been a disconnect between the development of physical and virtual spaces. Many innovations in recent years were in digital realms, not physical ones:

> The physical environments of universities and colleges are increasingly coming under scrutiny. This is for several reasons. The development of innovative types of learning—more interactive, informal, and social—is challenging a conventional lecture theatre, seminar room and specialist lab arrangement. New technologies are interacting with physical space to suggest different kinds of blended and hybrid relationships. And institutions are looking to use their estates' resources more effectively.
>
> (Boys 2015: 95)

Finding common connectors, fostering integration, and overcoming the physical/virtual dichotomy are important steps toward developing a more holistic path forward. This requires a new literacy in space design, both physical and digital, for language educators. Being able to navigate new hybrid spaces and to understand modality affordances and constraints will be an important skill to have for future language educators and professionals. This mastery in blending goes beyond just physical and virtual spaces, but includes social spaces, conceptual spaces, international spaces, and imaginary spaces.

Physical spaces provide more than functionality—they are also physical manifestations and embodiments of values, goals, and communities. In her discussion of the city, Kern (2020: 11) recalls how materiality and the imaginary are powerfully intertwined: "I think I learned then that a city—its dangers, thrills, culture, attraction, and more—resides in the imagination as well as in its material form. The imagined city is shaped by experience, media, art, rumor, and our own desires and fears." This matters not only for campus tours for prospective students and their families, but it is also important for all stakeholders. Physical spaces are more than mere architectural containers, they are reflections and manifestations and send powerful messages about values, expectations, acceptable and accepted behaviors, belonging, forms of communication, identity, and communities. The *how*, *what*, and *where* of physical spaces matter: "By making clear that the educational space is valuable, the administration is able to demand the due respect for it from learners" (Freire and Freire 1997: 97). For example, a highly structured language center with rows of computers for testing sends a different message than a student-run, collaboratively decorated language cafe with mismatched furniture. Such spaces produce different attitudes toward language education, levels of anxiety, and belonging. Fenwick (2015: 91) posits that "[E]ducators as well as students can look more closely at what material elements most influence their learning and teaching processes, how materials limit or enhance possibilities for learning, why particular educational or learning practices become stabilised and powerful and when these black boxes create problems."

The processes of *how* we design and curate language learning space, and with whom, matter. Including all stakeholders and giving them real agency and a voice can produce better solutions than if the spaces are only designed by specialists. The design should consider the post-occupancy phase, be human centered, localized, and situated. Language learning spaces are there to structure the resources for learning for a particular community, not a generic one. Van Merriënboer et al. (2017: 266) discuss how sometimes starting from scratch can be easier than redesigning existing spaces:

> Whilst it seems plausible that the participatory approach described here could be adapted to the interior re-design of classrooms, it seems that the changes would be major and that further research would be necessary to render it suitable for that purpose, given the challenges of legacy environments. Perhaps the problems here are not so different from those concerning innovation in education: designing new programmes is much easier than re-designing existing ones. This seems like a worthwhile endeavour, not only because there are more existing schools than new ones, but also because, in time, the newness wears off, pedagogies evolve, and buildings become inhabited by different cohorts of teachers and learners.

Space design is an iterative, never-ending process. Spaces are not finished products but are assemblages that are always in flux. They are also complex and not only architectural entities. Rather, they are enmeshed in a web of factors to consider: buildings, processes, hierarchies, histories, legacies, cultures, curricula, groups of people, and individuals. Language learning is not a universal truth but a complex web of beliefs, values, goals, experiences, expectations, and policies. It overlaps and is sometimes equated with other terms, such as teaching or credentialing. Seemingly simple design decisions must consider a number of much more complex factors that cannot be generalized.

Localizing, individualizing, and humanizing spaces involves considering identities, connectedness, belonging, and wellbeing. These human factors are not always taken into account when conceptualizing discipline-specific learning spaces, and yet they are of importance to individuals but can also provide fertile conditions for learning. In short, we should think less about learning spaces and more about *creating* learning places: "In addition to materials and meanings, places are marked by practice. People, in combination with various objects, are always doing things. To many observers this has been the most important defining feature of place—a kind of choreography of deeply engrained habits and semi-organized rhythms that makes a place distinctive. Places gather practices. They are lived" (Cresswell 2019: 181). Metrics to assess language learning outcomes shouldn't be the only indicator for effective learning spaces. Places are not created through design processes, rather they are transformed from spaces by various stakeholders, including students themselves (Murray and Lamb 2018a). Middleton (2018: 45) argues that "Placemaking is an idea usually associated with urban planning and sociology where it refers to the shaping of a public realm to maximise shared value. It is a community-centred approach to removing alienating silos and negotiating beyond the narrow focus of professions, disciplines, and agendas that affect space and inhibit a sense of place." Instead, we can see them as assemblages (Cresswell 2019), constantly adapting and defying categorization and generalization. Rather than accepting default, generic learning spaces, it is worth placing an emphasis on intentionality in our design and conceptualization of physical language learning spaces. This means being aware of how our physical spaces have become normalized, and how we should question the validity and relevance of our built environment. Overcoming normalization is difficult but worthwhile work to do in order to truly innovate.

It is this book's purpose to create a basis for more research and an increased awareness about physical language learning spaces. Murray and Lamb (2018c: 260) point:

> to the need for theoretical and research approaches that do not only consider learners' identities, spaces and places but view them as mutually constitutive. Learners with their cognitive, affective and physical systems form and are

formed by the learning environment. Because learners and the environments they constitute are constantly changing, being shaped and reshaped through their ongoing interaction, the field of language education needs theoretical and research approaches that take embodied experience, space and time into account.

Sociomaterialism provides a promising framework that looks beyond architectural design or overly theoretical analysis of the matter. Sociomaterial approaches can support research through "resources to systematically consider both the patterns as well as the unpredictability that makes educational activity possible. They promote methods by which to recognise and trace the multifarious struggles, negotiations and accommodations whose effects constitute the 'things' in education: students, teachers, learning activities and spaces, knowledge representations such as texts, pedagogy, curriculum content, and so forth" (Fenwick 2015: 84). We should investigate the details that are often overlooked or deemed unimportant, like architectural features or materialities, and integrate theory and praxis. Guerrettaz (2021: 60) discusses how "[P]edagogical ergonomics" can be useful for understanding physical language learning spaces as it grounds "itself in teaching practice in a particular sociocultural, political, and physical space." Furthermore, even though it "bears some similarity to the notion of affordance from ecological frameworks and sociocultural theory (SCT), pedagogical ergonomics focuses on what actually happens rather than on hypothetical opportunities for learning."

To find out which language learning spaces are effective, we must first create them. This can be done incrementally and iteratively and does not have to be an all-or-nothing approach. Small changes, the introduction of an element of unexpectedness, or changes in atmosphere can trigger reframing processes that challenge what is expected, what is acceptable, what is the norm. Only when physical changes take place can we truly begin to understand how they affect language learning.

References

Ackermann, E. (2004), "Constructing Knowledge and Transforming the World," in M. Tokoro and L. Steels (eds.), *A Learning Zone of One's Own: Sharing Representations and Flow in Collaborative Learning Environments*, 17–35, Amsterdam: IOS Press.

ACTFL World-Readiness Standards for Learning Languages. Available online: https://www.actfl.org/sites/default/files/publications/standards/World-ReadinessStandardsforLearningLanguages.pdf (accessed October 6, 2022).

Alzubaidi, E., J. M. Aldridge, and M. S. Khine (2016), "Learning English as a Second Language at the University Level in Jordan: Motivation, Self-Regulation and Learning Environment Perceptions," *Learning Environments Research*, 19 (1): 133–52.

Anderson, P. (2020), "Campus Is Closed, So College Students Are Rebuilding Their Schools in Minecraft," *The Verge*, March 31, 2020. Available online: https://www.theverge.com/2020/3/31/21200972/college-students-graduation-minecraft-coronavirus-school-closures (accessed January 3, 2023).

Aronin, L. (2018), "Theoretical Underpinnings of the Material Culture of Multilingualism," in L. Aronin, M. Hornsby and G. Kiliańska-Przybyło (eds.), *The Material Culture of Multilingualism*, Educational Linguistics, 21–45, Cham: Springer International Publishing.

Aronin, L. and M. Ó Laoire (2013), "The Material Culture of Multilingualism: Moving beyond the Linguistic Landscape," *International Journal of Multilingualism*, 10 (3): 225–35.

Baggerman, A. (2012), "Pandora's Box: Classrooms and Equipment in the Memory of Autobiographers," in S. Braster, I. Grosvenor, and M. del M. Del Pozo Andrés (eds.), *The Black Box of Schooling a Cultural History of the Classroom*, 159–82, Brussels: P.I.E. Peter Lang.

Bard, N. (2018), "Language Tutoring Services and the Language Center," in E. Lavolette and E. F. Simon (eds.), *Language Center Handbook*, 173–88, Auburn, Alabama: International Association for Language Learning Technology.

Baumeister, R. F. and M. R. Leary (1995), "The Need to Belong: Desire for Interpersonal Attachments as a Fundamental Human Motivation," *Psychological Bulletin*, 117: 497–529.

Bax, S. (2003), "CALL-Past, Present, and Future," *System*, 31 (1): 13–28.

Bax, S. (2011), "Normalisation Revisited," *International Journal of Computer-Assisted Language Learning and Teaching*, 1 (2): 1–15.

Bayne, S. (2004), "Smoothness and Striation in Digital Learning Spaces," *E-Learning and Digital Media*, 1 (2): 302–16.

Beatty, B. J. (2019), *Hybrid-Flexible Course Design* (1st edition). Provo: EdTech Books. Available online: https://edtechbooks.org/hyflex (accessed January 9, 2023).

Bendele, U. (1984), *Krieg, Kopf und Körper: Lernen für das Leben - Erziehung zum Tod*, Frankfurt am Main: Ullstein.

Benson, P. (2021), *Language Learning Environments: Spatial Perspectives on SLA*, Bristol, UK: Multilingual Matters.

Bijker, W. E. (1997), *Of Bicycles, Bakelites, and Bulbs: Toward a Theory of Sociotechnical Change*, Cambridge, MA: MIT Press.

Bijker, W. E., T. P. Hughes and T. J. Pinch, eds. (1987), *The Social Construction of Technological Systems: New Directions in the Sociology and History of Technology*, Cambridge, MA: MIT Press.

Bisson, M.-J., W. J. B. van Heuven, K. Conklin, and R. J. Tunney (2013), "Incidental Acquisition of Foreign Language Vocabulary through Brief Multi-Modal Exposure," *PLOS ONE*, 8 (4): e60912.

Blake, R. J. (2008), *Brave New Digital Classroom: Technology and Foreign Language Learning*, Washington, DC: Georgetown University Press.

Bonner, E. and H. Reinders (2018), "Augmented and Virtual Reality in the Language Classroom: Practical Ideas," *Teaching English with Technology*, 18 (3): 33–53.

Bown, J. (2020), "Conclusions," in J. Bown, D. P. Dewey, and W. Baker-Smemoe (eds.), *Language Learning in Foreign Language Houses*, 11–25, Auburn: International Association for Language Learning Technology.

Bown, J., D. P. Dewey, and W. Baker Smemoe (2020), "Introduction," in J. Bown, D. P. Dewey and W. Baker-Smemoe (eds.), *Language Learning in Foreign Language Houses*, 11–25, Auburn: International Association for Language Learning Technology.

Boys, J. (2011), *Towards Creative Learning Spaces: Re-thinking the Architecture of Post-Compulsory Education*, New York: Routledge.

Boys, J. (2015), *Building Better Universities: Strategies, Spaces, Technologies*, New York: Routledge.

Brabazon, T. (2007), *The University of Google: Education in the (Post) Information Age*, Hampshire, England: Ashgate.

Brand, S. (1994), *How Buildings Learn: And Fail to Learn*, New York: Viking.

Brooks, R., A. Fuller, and J. Waters (2012), "Afterword: From Changing Spaces of Education to Changing Spaces of Learning," in R. Brooks, A. Fuller, and J. Waters (eds.), *Changing Spaces of Education: New Perspectives on the Nature of Learning*, 261–2, New York: Routledge.

Brown, S. (2016), "'Heat Maps' Give Michigan State a New View of Campus Climate: Visualizations of Survey Responses Show Where Students Feel They Belong, or Don't," *Chronicle of Higher Education*, October 23. Available online: https://www.chronicle.com/article/heat-maps-give-michigan-state-a-new-view-of-campus-climate/ (accessed February 24, 2023).

Brown, S. and C. Vaughan (2014), *Play: How It Shapes the Brain, Opens the Imagination, and Invigorates the Soul*, New York: Avery.

Burbules, N. C. and T. A. Callister (2000), *Watch IT: The Risks and Promises of Information Technologies for Education*, Boulder: Westview Press.

Burke, C. (2005), "Light: Metaphor and Materiality in the History of Schooling," in M. Lawn and I. Grosvenor (eds.), *Materialities of Schooling: Design, Technology, Objects, Routines*, 125–43, Oxford: Symposium Books.

Burr, V. (1996), *An Introduction to Social Constructionism*, London; New York: Routledge.

Burr, V. (2003), *Social Constructionism*, London: Routledge.

Carbone, E. (2001), "Arranging the Classroom with an Eye (and Ear) to Students with ADHD," *TEACHING Exceptional Children*, 34 (2): 72–82.

Casciani, D. and F. Musante (2016), "What Does Light Do? Reflecting on the Active Social Effects of Lighting Design and Technology", in S. Crabu, P. Giardullo, F. Miele, and M. Turrini (eds.), *Sociotechnical Environments*, 693–710, Milano: STS Italia Publishing.

Caulfield, J. (2011), *How to Design and Teach a Hybrid Course: Achieving Student-Centered Learning through Blended Classroom, Online and Experiential Activities*, Sterling: Stylus Pub.

Cerbin, S. L. and W. J. Chew (2017), "Teaching and Learning: Lost in a Buzzword Wasteland," *Inside Higher Ed*, December 5. Available online: https://www.insidehighered.com/views/2017/12/05/need-theory-learning-opinion (accessed February 2, 2023).

Chou, P. T.-M. (2010), "Attention Drainage Effect: How Background Music Effects Concentration in Taiwanese College Students," *Journal of the Scholarship of Teaching and Learning*, 10 (1): 36–46.

Cheryan, S., S. A. Ziegler, V. C. Plaut, and A. N. Meltzoff (2014), "Designing Classrooms to Maximize Student Achievement," *Policy Insights from the Behavioral and Brain Sciences*, 1 (1): 4–12.

Choi, H.-H., J. J. G. van Merriënboer, and F. Paas (2014), "Effects of the Physical Environment on Cognitive Load and Learning: Towards a New Model of Cognitive Load," *Educational Psychology Review*, 26 (2): 225–44.

Clifford, J. and D. S. Reisinger (2019), *Community-Based Language Learning: A Framework for Educators*, Washington, DC: Georgetown University Press. https://doi.org/10.2307/j.ctv7cjw41

Cline, E. (2011), *Ready Player One*, New York: Crown Publishers.

Collenberg-González, C. (2020), "The Deutsche Sommerschule Am Pazifik: A Model and Asset to Small German Programs," in M. Etzler and G. Maier (eds.), *Outreach Strategies and Innovative Teaching Approaches for German Programs*, London: Routledge.

Conacher, J. E. and H. Kelly-Holmes (2007), "Thinking beyond Technology: Towards a Broader Understanding of New Language-Learning Environments," in J. E. Conacher and H. Kelly-Holmes (eds.), *New Learning Environments for Language Learning: Moving beyond the Classroom?*, 19–31, Frankfurt am Main: Peter Lang.

Cornell, C. (2020), "Accessibility Essentials in Online Language Teaching," *FLTMAG*, June 8, 2020. Available online: https://fltmag.com/accessibility-essentials-in-online-language-teaching/ (accessed October 15, 2022).

Cornell, C. (2023), "CeLTA + Planetarium Partnership." Available online: https://celta.msu.edu/projects/planetarium-languages-partnership/ (accessed January 15, 2023).

Cornfield, R. R. (1966), *Foreign Language Instruction: Dimensions and Horizons*, New York: Appleton-Century-Crofts.

Costello, C. Y. (2000), "Schooled in the Classroom," in E. Margolis (ed), *The Hidden Curriculum in Higher Education*, 43–60, London: Routledge.

Cowley, S. J. (2012), "Cognitive Dynamics: Language as Values Realizing Activity," in A. Kravchenko (ed), *Cognitive Dynamics in Linguistic Interactions*, 15–46, Newcastle: Cambridge Scholars.

Cox, A. M. (2018), "Space and Embodiment in Informal Learning," *Higher Education*, 75 (6): 1077–90.

Cranz, G. (1998), *The Chair: Rethinking Culture, Body, and Design*, New York: W. W. Norton.

Cresswell, T. (2014), *Place: An Introduction*, Hoboken: John Wiley & Sons.

Cresswell, T. (2019), *Maxwell Street: Writing and Thinking Place*, Chicago: University of Chicago Press.

Crook, C. and G. Mitchell (2012), "Ambience in Social Learning: Student Engagement with New Designs for Learning Spaces," *Cambridge Journal of Education*, 42 (2): 121–39.

Dakin, J. (1973), *The Language Laboratory and Language Learning*, London: Longman.

Davidson, C. N. (2017), *The New Education: How to Revolutionize the University to Prepare Students for a World in Flux*, New York: Basic Books.

Degrave, P. (2019), "Music in the Foreign Language Classroom: How and Why?," *Journal of Language Teaching and Research*, 10 (3): 412–20.

del Signore, M. (2020), "Collaboration and Digital Spaces," *Academic Minute*, February 18. Available online: https://academicminute.org/2020/02/marcella-del-signore-new-york-institute-of-technology-collaboration-and-digital-spaces/ (accessed February 3, 2023).

Determan, J., M. A. Akers, T. Albright, B. Browning, C. Martin-Dunlop, P. Archibald, and V. Caruolo (2019), "The Impact of Biophilic Learning Spaces on Student Success." Available online: https://cgdarch.com/wp-content/uploads/2019/12/The-Impact-of-Biophilic-Learning-Spaces-on-Student-Success.pdf (accessed January 5, 2023).

Dewey, D. P. (2004), "A Comparison of Reading Development by Learners of Japanese in Intensive Domestic Immersion and Study Abroad Contexts," *Studies in Second Language Acquisition*, 26 (2): 303–27.

Dewey, J. (1991), *The School and Society and the Child and the Curriculum*, Chicago: University of Chicago Press.

Dittoe, W. (2006), "Seriously Cool Places: The Future of Learning-Centered Built Environments," in D. G. Oblinger (ed), *Learning Spaces*, 3.1–3.11. Educause.

Available online: www.educause.edu/research-and-publications/books/learning-spaces (accessed January 5, 2015).

Dober, R. P. (1992), *Campus Design*, New York: John Wiley & Sons.

Dockrell, J. E. and B. M. Shield (2006), "Acoustical Barriers in Classrooms: The Impact of Noise on Performance in the Classroom," *British Educational Research Journal*, 32 (3): 509–25.

Donnally Spasova, S. (2019), "Your Classroom in 360: Ideas for Using Enhanced Reality in Your Class," *FLTMAG*, June 13. Available online: https://fltmag.com/your-classroom-in-360 (accessed October 20, 2022).

Doorley, S. and S. Witthoft (2012), *Make Space: How to Set the Stage for Creative Collaboration*, Hoboken: John Wiley & Sons.

Dovey, K. (2010), *Becoming Places: Urbanism/Architecture/Identity/Power*, London: Routledge.

Ducate, L., L. Lomicka, and G. Lord (2012), "Hybrid Learning Spaces: Re-Envisioning Language Learning," in F. Rubio and J. Thoms (eds.), *AAUSC 2012 Volume – Issues in Language Program Direction: Hybrid Language Teaching and Learning: Exploring Theoretical, Pedagogical and Curricular Issues*, 67–91, Boston: Heinle.

Dwyer, A. and J. Dale (2020), "The Language House as Global Programming: Pomona College's Oldenborg Center," in J. Bown, W. Baker Smemoe, and D. P. Dewey (eds.), *Language Learning in Foreign Language Houses*, 117–40, Auburn: International Association for Language Learning Technology.

Edgell, R. A. and P. Kimmich (2015), "A New View on Innovation and Language: Design Culture, Discursive Practices, and Metaphors," *Journal of Creativity and Business Innovation*, 1: 107–28.

Edwards, R. and R. Usher (2008), *Globalisation and Pedagogy: Space, Place and Identity*, 2nd edition, London: Routledge.

Eickhoff, H. (1993), *Himmelsthron und Schaukelstuhl: die Geschichte des Sitzens*, München: Hanser.

Engman, M. M. and M. Hermes (2021), "Land as Interlocutor: A Study of Ojibwe Learner Language in Interaction on and with Naturally Occurring 'Materials,'" *The Modern Language Journal*, 105 (S1): 86–105.

Ericson, J. E. (2020), "A Case Study in Integrated Learning: Building a Japanese Garden," in D. Jennifer Brown, P. Dewey, and W. Baker-Smemoe (eds.), *Language Learning in Foreign Language Houses*, 141–65, Auburn: International Association for Language Learning Technology.

Felix, E. (2021), "The Pandemic May Have Permanently Altered Campuses. Here's How," *Chronicle of Higher Education*, March 15. Available online: https://www.chronicle.com/article/the-pandemic-may-have-permanently-altered-campuses-heres-how (accessed January 3, 2023).

Felix, U. (2007), "Multiplying modalities: Opening Up the Fourth Dimension to the Online Learner," in J. E. Conacher and H. Kelly-Holmes (eds.), *New Learning

Environments for Language Learning: Moving beyond the Classroom?, 33–42, Frankfurt am Main: Peter Lang.

Felix, E., A. Smith Hanby, A. Griff, and A. Wirth Lorenzo (2020), "How College and Universities Can Emerge from the COVID Crisis Stronger Than Before," April 27. Available online: https://www.brightspotstrategy.com/whitepaper/higher-ed-after-covid-19/ (accessed November 11, 2022).

Fenwick, T. (2015), "Sociomateriality and Learning: A Critical Approach," *The SAGE Handbook of Learning*, 83–93, 55 City Road: SAGE Publications Ltd.

Fenwick, T., R. Edwards, and P. Sawchuk (2011), *Emerging Approaches to Educational Research: Tracing the Sociomaterial*, London: Routledge.

Ferster, B. (2014), *Teaching Machines: Learning from the Intersection of Education and Technology*, Baltimore: Johns Hopkins University Press.

Fiell, C. and P. Fiell (2000), *1000 Chairs*, Köln: Taschen.

Fisher, R., A. Harris, and C. Jarvis (2008), *Education in Popular Culture: Telling Tales on Teachers and Learners*, New York: Routledge.

Fitzpatrick, K. (2019), *Generous Thinking: A Radical Approach to Saving the University*, Baltimore, MD: JHU Press.

Flack, J. and M. Mitchell (2020), "Complex Systems Science Allows Us to See New Paths Forward," *Aeon Essays*. Available online: https://aeon.co/essays/complex-systems-science-allows-us-to-see-new-paths-forward (accessed January 2, 2023).

Folkins, J. W., J. C. Friberg, and P. A. Cesarini (2015), "University Classroom Design Principles to Facilitate Learning: The Instructor as Advocate," *Planning for Higher Education*, 43 (2): 45–62.

Forty, A. (2000), *Words and Buildings: A Vocabulary of Modern Architecture*, New York: Thames & Hudson.

Foucault, M. (1977), *Discipline and Punish: The Birth of the Prison*, New York: Pantheon Books.

Freire, P. and A. M. A. Freire (1997), *Pedagogy of the Heart*, New York: Continuum.

Frey, N., D. Fisher, and D. Smith (2020), "Trauma-Informed Design in the Classroom," *Educational Leadership*, 78 (2).

Fritzsche, S., L. Giupponi, E. Heidrich Uebel, F. A. Kronenberg, C. P. Long, and K. Van Gorp (2022), "Languages as Drivers of Institutional Diversity: The Case of Less Commonly Taught Languages," *Language Educator*, 17 (1): 45–7.

Gaggioli, A. (2017), "Phygital Spaces: When Atoms Meet Bits," *Cyberpsychology, Behavior, and Social Networking*, 20 (12): 774.

Garrett, N. and P. Liddell (2004), "The New Language Centers and the Role of Technology: New Mandates, New Horizons," in S. Fotos and C. Browne (eds.), *New Perspectives on CALL for Second Language Classrooms*, 27–40, Mahwah, NJ: L. Erlbaum Associates.

Gee, J. P. (2004), *Situated Language and Learning: A Critique of Traditional Schooling*, New York: Routledge.

Giupponi, L., E. Heidrich Uebel, and K. Van Gorp (2018), "Strategies for Language Centers to Support Online Language Education," in E. Lavolette and A. Kraemer (eds.), *Language Center Handbook 2021*, 61–90, Auburn: International Association for Language Learning Technology.

Godlewska, A. (2013), "Dislocation Pedagogy," *The Professional Geographer*, 65 (3): 384–9.

Godwin-Jones, R. (2019), "Riding the Digital Wilds: Learner Autonomy and Informal Language Learning," *Language Learning & Technology*, 23 (1): 8–25.

Goleman, D. (2007), *Social Intelligence: The New Science of Human Relationships*, New York: Bantam.

Goodall, S. (1997), "The Schoolroom," in K. Kulpa (ed), *Short Takes: Brief Personal Narratives and Other Works by American Teen Writers*, 86–7, Taipei: Bookman Booksen.

Gopalan, M. and S. T. Brady (2020), "College Students' Sense of Belonging: A National Perspective," *Educational Researcher*, 49 (2): 134–7.

Gorter, D. (2013), "Linguistic Landscapes in a Multilingual World," *Annual Review of Applied Linguistics*, 33: 190–212.

Graetz, K. A. (2006), "The Psychology of Learning Environments," *EDUCAUSE Review*, 41 (6): 60–75.

Grinnell (N.d.), "*Marcus Family Global Kitchen*." Available online: https://www.grinnell.edu/academics/global/institute/global-kitchen (accessed February 11, 2023).

Grosvenor, I. and C. Burke (2008), *School*, London: Reaktion Books.

Grosvenor, I., M. Lawn, and K. Rousmaniere, eds. (1999), *Silences & Images: The Social History of the Classroom*, New York: P. Lang.

Guerrettaz, A. M. (2021), "Materials-in-Action: Pedagogical Ergonomics of a French-as-a-Foreign-Language Classroom," *The Modern Language Journal*, 105 (S1): 39–64.

Guerrettaz, A. M. and B. Johnston (2013), "Materials in the Classroom Ecology," *The Modern Language Journal*, 97 (3): 779–96.

Gulson, K. N. and C. Symes (2007), "Knowing One's Place: Educational Theory, Policy, and the Spatial Turn," in K. N. Gulson and C. Symes (eds.), *Spatial Theories of Education: Policy and Geography Matters*, 1–16, New York: Routledge.

Hagen, L. K. (2017), "Kaputnik: Lessons from the Life and Death of the Language Lab," in F. A. Kronenberg (ed), *From Language Lab to Language Center and beyond: The Past, Present, and Future of the Language Center*, 13–27, Auburn: International Association for Language Learning Technology.

Hamilton, D. (2013), *Towards a Theory of Schooling (Routledge Revivals)*, Hoboken: Taylor and Francis.

Hapgood, F. (1993), *Up the Infinite Corridor: MIT and the Technological Imagination*, Reading: Addison-Wesley.

Harmer, J. (2007), *How to Teach English*, London: Pearson Education.

Harrison, A. and L. Hutton (2014), *Design for the Changing Educational Landscape: Space, Place and the Future of Learning*, London: Routledge.

Hart-Davidson, B. (2020), "Imagining a Resilient Pedagogy," *CAL News*, April 6. Available online: https://cal.msu.edu/news/imagining-a-resilient-pedagogy/ (accessed December 12, 2021).

Henshaw, F. G. and M. D. Hawkins (2022), *Common Ground: Second Language Acquisition Theory Goes to the Classroom*, Indianapolis: Focus.

Higgins, C. (2017), "Space, Place, and Language," in S. Canagarajah (ed), *The Routledge Handbook of Migration and Language*, 102–16, London: Taylor & Francis.

Hobbs, M. and K. Dofs (2018), "Spaced out or Zoned in? An Exploratory Study of Spaces in Two New Zealand Tertiary Learning Insitutions," in G. Murray and T. Lamb (eds.), *Space, Place and Autonomy in Language Learning*, 201–18, London; New York: Routledge.

Hocking, E. (1964), "Language Laboratory and Language Learning. Monograph No. 2," *AV Communication Review*, 13 (2): 238.

Holden, C. L. and J. M. Sykes (2011), "Leveraging Mobile Games for Place-Based Language Learning," *International Journal of Game-Based Learning (IJGBL)*, 1 (2): 1–18.

Huebener, T. (1959), *How to Teach Foreign Languages Effectively*, New York: New York University Press.

Huppertz, N. (2004), *Handbuch Waldkindergarten Konzeption - Methodik - Erfahrungen*, Oberried: PAIS Verlag.

Hutchinson, J. C. (1967), "Planning for Language Laboratory Facilities," in J. Michel (ed), *Foreign Language Teaching: An Anthology*, 355–70, New York: Macmillan.

Hutchison, D. and D. W. Orr (2004), *A Natural History of Place in Education*, New York: Teachers College Press.

Ijiri, A. (2022), "Reimagining Language Lessons for Immersive Learning in Virtual Reality," *FLTMAG*, March 2. Available online: https://fltmag.com/reimagining-language-lessons-for-immersive-learning-in-virtual-reality/ (accessed January 17, 2023).

Imamura, Y. (2018), "Adopting and Adapting to New Language Policies in a Self-Access Centre in Japan," *Relay Journal*, 1 (1): 197–208.

Jones, K. (2021), "Outdoor Classrooms a Breath of Fresh Air for Some Students, Professors," *The Student Life*, September 16. Available online: https://tsl.news/outdoor-classrooms/ (accessed February 1, 2023).

Journal of Learning Spaces (n.d.). Available online: http://libjournal.uncg.edu/jls/about/editorialPolicies#focusAndScope (accessed February 21, 2023).

Kann, A. (2022), "Local and Global Perspectives on Language Cafes—a 10-Year Perspective from Start-Up to Post-Covid," Cercles Conference, September 17, Porto, Portugal.

Karacan, C. G. and E. Mollamehmetoğlu (2022), "Augmented Reality in Language Education: dARe to Know," *FLTMAG*, October 20. Available online: https://fltmag.

com/augmented-reality-in-language-education-dare-to-know (accessed January 8, 2023).

Kern, L. (2020), *Feminist City: Claiming Space in a Man-Made World*, London: Verso.

Kohls, C. (2019), "Hybrid Learning Spaces for Design Thinking," *Open Education Studies*, 1 (1): 228–44.

Kollar, I., F. Pilz, and F. Fischer (2014), "Why It Is Hard to Make Use of New Learning Spaces: A Script Perspective," *Technology, Pedagogy and Education*, 23 (1): 7–18.

Koutamanis, A. and Y. Majewski-Steijns (2012), "An Architectural View of the Classroom," in S. Braster, I. Grosvenor, and M. Del Pozo Andrés (eds.), *The Black Box of Schooling a Cultural History of the Classroom*, 203–22, Brussels: Peter Lang.

Kramer, S. (2022), "Delta Air Lines Wows with Parallel Reality," *Forbes*, October 19. Available online: https://www.forbes.com/sites/scottkramer/2022/10/19/delta-airlines-wows-with-parallel-reality (accessed February 18, 2023).

Kramsch, C. J. (1993), *Context and Culture in Language Teaching*, Oxford: Oxford University Press.

Kroll, L. (1984), "Anarchitecture," in C. R. Hatch (ed), *The Scope of Social Architecture*, 166–81, New York: Van Nostrand Reinhold.

Kronenberg, F. A. (2014), "Language Center Design and Management in the Post-Language Laboratory Era," *IALLT Journal*, 44 (1): 1–16.

Kronenberg, F. A. (2016), "Curated Language Learning Spaces: Design Principles of Physical 21st Century Language Centers," *IALLT Journal*, 46 (1): 63–91.

Kronenberg, F. A. and F. Poole (2022), "From Buzzword to the Classroom—Exploring VR Gaming for Language Learning," *FLTMAG*, November 3. Available online: https://fltmag.com/from-buzzword-to-the-classroom-exploring-vr-gaming-for-language-learning (accessed December 5, 2022).

Kronenberg, F. A. and K. Schwienhorst (2021), "Building for Sustainable Change: Co-Designing Language Centers in Germany and the United States," in E. Lavolette and A. Kraemer (eds.), *Language Center Handbook 2021*, 217–42, Auburn: International Association for Language Learning Technology.

Kuhlthau, C. and C. Cole (2012), "Third Space as an Information System and Services Intervention Methodology for Engaging the User's Deepest Levels of Information Need," *Proceedings of the American Society for Information Science and Technology*, 49 (1): 1–6.

Laiduc, G., S. Herrmann, and R. Covarrubias (2021), "Relatable Role Models: An Online Intervention Highlighting First-Generation Faculty Benefits First-Generation Students," *Journal of First-Generation Student Success*, 1 (3): 159–86.

Lankshear, C., M. Peters, and M. Knobel (1996), "Critical Pedagogy and Cyberspace," in H. A. Giroux (ed), *Counternarratives: Cultural Studies and Critical Pedagogies in Postmodern Spaces*, 149–88, New York: Routledge.

Laurillard, D. (2002), *Rethinking University Teaching: A Conversational Framework for the Effective Use of Learning Technologies*, 2nd edition, London: Routledge.

Lave, J. and E. Wenger (1991), *Situated Learning: Legitimate Peripheral Participation*, Cambridge, UK: Cambridge University Press.

Lavolette, E. and A. Kraemer (2017), "The Language Center Evaluation Toolkit: Context, Development, and Usage," in F. A. Kronenberg (ed), *From Language Lab to Language Center and beyond: The Past, Present, and Future of the Language Center*, 147–60, Auburn: International Association for Language Learning Technology.

Lavolette, E. and A. Kraemer, eds. (2021), *Language Center Handbook 2021*, Auburn: International Association for Language Learning Technology.

Lavolette, E. and E. F. Simon, eds. (2018), *Language Center Handbook*, Auburn: International Association for Language Learning Technology.

Lawn, M. (1999), "Designing Teaching: The Classroom as a Technology," in I. Grosvenor, M. Lawn, and K. Rousmaniere (eds.), *Silences & Images: The Social History of the Classroom*, 65–82, New York: P. Lang.

Learning Space Rating System (n.d.), Educause. Available online: https://www.educause.edu/eli/initiatives/learning-space-rating-system (accessed February 15, 2013).

Ledgerwood, M. (2017), "Foreword, or Musings on over Fifty Years of Using Technology for Language Learning," in F. A. Kronenberg (ed), *From Language Lab to Language Center and beyond: The Past, Present, and Future of the Language Center*, 6–12, Auburn: International Association for Language Learning Technology.

Lee, N. and S. Tan (2013), "Traversing the Design-Language Divide in the Design and Evaluation of Physical Learning Environments: A Trial of Visual Methods in Focus Groups," *Journal of Learning Spaces*, 2 (1): 1–7.

Lefebvre, H. (1991), *The Production of Space*, Oxford, UK: Blackwell.

Leonardi, P. M. (2012), 'Materiality, Sociomateriality, and Socio-Technical Systems: What Do These Terms Mean? How Are They Related? Do We Need Them?', in P. M. Leonardi, B. A. Nardi, and J. Kallinikos (eds.), *Materiality and Organizing: Social Interaction in a Technological World*, 25–48, Oxford: Oxford University Press.

Levy, M. and G. Stockwell (2006), *CALL Dimensions: Options and Issues in Computer-Assisted Language Learning*, London: Routledge.

Liao, J. and X. Lu (2018), "Exploring the Affordances of Telepresence Robots in Foreign Language Learning," *Language, Learning & Technology*, 22 (3): 20–32.

Liu, F., S. Sulpizio, S. Kornpetpanee, and R. Job (2017), "It Takes Biking to Learn: Physical Activity Improves Learning a Second Language," *PLOS ONE*, 12 (5): 1–15.

Loewen, S. and M. Sato (2017), "Instructed Second Language Acquisition (ISLA): An Overview," in S. Loewen and M. Sato (eds.), *The Routledge Handbook of Instructed Second Language Acquisition*, Routledge Handbooks in Applied Linguistics, 1–12, New York: Routledge.

Looney, D. and N. Lusin (2019), "Enrollments in Languages Other than English in United States Institutions of Higher Education, Summer 2016 and Fall 2016: Final Report," *Modern Language Association*. Available online: https://www.mla.org/content/download/110154/2406932/2016-Enrollments-Final-Report.pdf (accessed November 8, 2022).

Löw, M. (2016), *The Sociology of Space: Materiality, Social Structures, and Action*, trans. D. Goodwin, New York: Palgrave Macmillan.

Lundström, A., J. Savolainen, and E. Kostiainen (2016), "Case Study: Developing Campus Spaces through Co-Creation," *Architectural Engineering and Design Management*, 12 (6): 409–26.

MacPhee, L. (2009), "Learning Spaces: A Tutorial," *EDUCAUSE Review Online*, March 26. Available online: https://er.educause.edu/articles/2009/3/learning-spaces-a-tutorial (accessed February 5, 2023).

Markus, T. A. and D. Cameron (2002), *The Words between the Spaces: Buildings and Language*, London: Routledge.

Massey, D. B. (1994), *Space, Place, and Gender*, Minneapolis, MN: University of Minnesota Press.

Massey, D. B. (1997), "A Global Sense of Place," in T. Barnes and D. Gregory (eds.), *Reading Human Geography: The Poetics and Politics of Inquiry*, 315–23, London: Arnold.

Massey, D. B. (2001), "Talking of Space-Time," *Transactions of the Institute of British Geographers*, 26 (2): 257–61.

Mathews, B. and L. A. Soistmann (2016), *Encoding Space: Shaping Learning Environments That Unlock Human Potential*, Chicago: ACRL.

McFadden, B. (2021), "Realia for Radical Teaching," *Language Magazine*, August 25. Available online: https://www.languagemagazine.com/2021/08/25/realia-for-radical-teaching/ (accessed February 1, 2023).

McGregor, J. (2003), "Making Spaces: Teacher Workplace Topologies," *Pedagogy, Culture and Society*, 11 (3): 353–77.

Mehrabian, A. (1981), *Silent Messages: Implicit Communication of Emotions and Attitudes*, Belmont: Wadsworth.

Merrill, J. (2020), "Student Perceptions of a Total Immersion Environment," in D. Jennifer Brown, P. Dewey, and W. Baker-Smemoe (eds.), *Language Learning in Foreign Language Houses*, 169–203, Auburn: International Association for Language Learning Technology.

Michelson, W. (1970), *Man and His Urban Environment: A Sociological Approach*, Reading: Addison-Wesley.

Middleton, A. (2018), *Reimagining Spaces for Learning in Higher Education*, London: Palgrave Macmillan.

Miles, M. (1997), *Art, Space and the City: Public Art and Urban Futures*, London: Routledge.

Milgrom, R. (2008), "Lucien Kroll: Design, Difference, Everyday Life," in *Space, Difference, Everyday Life: Reading Henri Lefebvre*, 264–81, New York: Routledge.

Miller, R. E. (1998), *As If Learning Mattered: Reforming Higher Education*, Ithaca: Cornell University Press.

Mills, N. (2013), "Situated Learning through Social Networking Communities: The Development of Joint Enterprise, Mutual Engagement, and a Shared Repertoire," *CALICO Journal*, 28 (2): 345–68.

Monahan, T. (2002), "Flexible Space & Built Pedagogy: Emerging IT Embodiments," *Inventio*, 4 (1). Available online: http://publicsurveillance.com/papers/built_pedagogy.pdf (accessed February 15, 2023).

Monahan, T. (2005), *Globalization, Technological Change, and Public Education*. London: Routledge.

Montgomery, C. (2020), "Community by Design: Crafting Space for Living, Learning, & Language Development," in D. Jennifer Brown, P. Dewey, and W. Baker-Smemoe (eds.), *Language Learning in Foreign Language Houses*, 335–68, Auburn: International Association for Language Learning Technology.

Moreno Martínez, P. L. (2005), "History of School Desk Developments in Terms of Hygiene and Pedagogy in Spain (1838–1936)," in M. Lawn and I. Grosvenor (eds.), *Materialities of Schooling: Design, Technology, Objects, Routines*, 71–95, Oxford: Symposium Books.

Murray, G. and N. Fujishima (2016a), "Exploring a Social Space for Language Learning," in G. Murray and N. Fujishima (eds.), *Social Spaces for Language Learning: Stories from the L-Café*, 1–12, London: Palgrave Macmillan.

Murray, G. and N. Fujishima (2016b), "Understanding a Social Space for Language Learning," in G. Murray and N. Fujishima (eds.), *Social Spaces for Language Learning: Stories from the L-Café*, 124–46, London: Palgrave Macmillan.

Murray, G. and T. Lamb (2018a), *Space, Place and Autonomy in Language Learning*, London; New York: Routledge.

Murray, G. and T. Lamb (2018b), "Space, Place and Autonomy: An Introduction," in G. Murray and T. Lamb (eds.), *Space, Place and Autonomy in Language Learning*, 1–6, London; New York: Routledge.

Murray, G. and T. Lamb (2018c), "Space, Place, Autonomy, and the Road Not Yet Taken," in G. Murray and T. Lamb (eds.), *Space, Place and Autonomy in Language Learning*, 249–62, London; New York: Routledge.

Mynard, J., M. Burke, D. Hooper, B. Kushida, P. Lyon, R. Sampson, P. Taw, and B. Kushida (2020), *Dynamics of a Social Language Learning Community: Beliefs, Membership and Identity*, Bristol: Multilingual Matters.

Nair, P. and R. Fielding (2005), *The Language of School Design: Design Patterns for 21st Century Schools*, Minneapolis: DesignShare.

Nespor, J. (1994), *Knowledge in Motion: Space, Time, and Curriculum in Undergraduate Physics and Management*, London: Falmer Press.

NFLRC (n.d.), "Project-Based Language Learning". Available online: https://nflrc.hawaii.edu/projects/view/2014a/ (accessed February 3, 2023).

Novash, M. (2022), "Why VR?," *FLTMAG*, October 13. Available online: https://fltmag.com/why-vr/ (accessed January 20, 2023).

NSSE (2020), "Annual Results 2020—Engagement Insights: Survey Findings on the Quality of Undergraduate Education." Available online: https://nsse.indiana.edu/research/annual-results/2020/index.html (accessed February 24, 2023).

Oblinger, D. (2006), *Learning Spaces*, Boulder: EDUCAUSE.

Oldenburg, R. (1999), *The Great Good Place: Cafés, Coffee Shops, Bookstores, Bars, Hair Salons, and Other Hangouts at the Heart of a Community*. New York: Marlowe.

Olsen, E. (2020), "Mid-doors: The Zone between Inside and Outside That Could Change Building Design," *Fast Company*, November 17. Available online: https://www.fastcompany.com/90575944/mid-doors-the-zone-between-inside-and-outside-that-could-change-building-design (accessed January 2, 2023).

OWP/P Architects, VS Furniture, and Bruce Mau Design (2010), *The Third Teacher: 79 Ways You Can Use Design to Transform Teaching & Learning*, New York: Abrams.

Papert, S. (1980), *Mindstorms: Children, Computers, and Powerful Ideas*, New York: Basic Books.

Parker, P. (2018), *The Art of Gathering: How We Meet and Why It Matters*, New York: Riverhead Books.

Parsons, C. S. (2017), "Reforming the Environment: The Influence of the Roundtable Classroom Design on Interactive Learning," *Journal of Learning Spaces*, 6 (3): 23–33.

Paul, A. M. (2021), *The Extended Mind: The Power of Thinking Outside the Brain*, Boston: Houghton Mifflin Harcourt.

Pegrum, M., N. Hockly, and G. Dudeney (2014), *Digital Literacies*, London: Routledge.

Peker, E. and A. Ataöv (2020), "Exploring the Ways in Which Campus Open Space Design Influences Students' Learning Experiences," *Landscape Research*, 45 (3): 310–26.

Pettit, M. (2022), "The Effect of Physical Environment and Classroom Routines in a World Language Classroom," October 21, MIWLA Conference, Lansing, MI.

Pomona (2021), "Taking Academia Outdoors," *Pomona College News*, September 13, 2021. Available online: https://www.pomona.edu/news/2021/09/13-taking-academia-outdoors (accessed January 5, 2023).

Pouler, P. J. (1994), "Disciplinary Society and the Myth of Aesthetic Justice," in B. C. Scheer and W. F. E. Preiser (eds.), *Design Review: Challenging Urban Aesthetic Control*, 175–86, Boston, MA: Springer US.

Quintana, R. and J. DeVaney (2020), "Laying the Foundation for a Resilient Teaching Community," *Inside Higher Ed*, May 27. Available online: https://www.insidehighered.com/blogs/learning-innovation/laying-foundation-resilient-teaching-community (accessed October 9, 2022).

Rajaee Pitehnoee, M., A. Arabmofrad, and A. Modaberi (2020), "'English as a Foreign Language Elementary Learners' Perceptions of Classroom Physical Environment with Regard to Structural vs. Symbolic Features," *Journal of Research in Childhood Education*, 34 (4): 496–505.

Ramli, N. H., S. Ahmad, and M. H. Masri (2013), "'Improving the Classroom Physical Environment: Classroom Users' Perception," *Procedia - Social and Behavioral Sciences*, 101: 221–9.

Rankin, A. (2018), "Rethinking the Traditional Classroom: Is Deskless or Flexible Seating Right for You?," October 19, MIWLA Conference, Lansing, MI.

Rapoport, A. (1990), *The Meaning of the Built Environment: A Nonverbal Communication Approach*, Tucson: University of Arizona Press.

Reinders, H. and C. White (2016), "20 Years of Autonomy and Technology: How Far Have We Come and Where to Next?," *Language Learning & Technology*, 20 (2): 143–54.

Robert, J. (2022), "Modality Preferences," *Educause 2022 Students and Technology Report*, October 3. Available online: https://www.educause.edu/ecar/research-publications/2022/students-and-technology-report-rebalancing-the-student-experience/modality-preferences (accessed October 10, 2022).

Roby, W. B. (2004), "Technology in the Service of Foreign Language Learning: The Case of the Language Laboratory," 2nd edition, in *Handbook of Research on Educational Communications and Technology*, 523–41, Mahwah: Lawrence Erlbaum.

Rogers, E. M. (2003), *Diffusion of Innovations*, 5th edition, New York: Free Press.

Rybczynski, W. (2017), *Now I Sit Me Down: From Klismos to Plastic Chair: A Natural History*, New York: Farrar, Straus and Giroux.

Saettler, L. P. (2005). *The Evolution of American Educational Technology*, Mahwah: Lawrence Erlbaum.

Salaberry, M. R. (2001), "The Use of Technology for Second Language Learning and Teaching: A Retrospective," *The Modern Language Journal*, 85 (1): 39–56.

Salen, K. and E. Zimmerman (2003), *Rules of Play: Game Design Fundamentals*, Cambridge, MA: MIT Press.

Samuels, J., K. Gaugler, and F. A. Kronenberg (2018), "The Road to the Lost City of 'C': From Simulation to Reality," *Language Educator*, 13 (4): 44–7.

Sanders, E. B.-N. and P. J. Stappers (2008), "Co-Creation and the New Landscapes of Design," *CoDesign*, 4 (1): 5–18.

Sarup, M. (1982), *Education, State and Crisis: A Marxist Perspective*, London: Routledge.

Savin-Baden, M. and Society for Research into Higher Education (2008), *Learning Spaces Creating Opportunities for Knowledge Creation in Academic Life*, New York: McGraw Hill/Society for Research into Higher Education & Open University Press.

Schenker, T. and A. Kraemer (2018), "The Role of the Language Center in Community Outreach: Developing Language Enrichment Programs for Children," in E. Lavolette and E. F. Simon (eds.), *Language Center Handbook*, 71–88, Auburn: International Association for Language Learning Technology.

Schratzenstaller, A. (2010), "The Classroom of the Past," in K. Mäkitalo-Siegl, J. Zottmann, F. Kaplan, and F. Fisher (eds.), *Classroom of the Future: Orchestrating Collaborative Spaces*, 15–39, Rotterdam: Sense Publishers.

Schumacher, J. (2018), *The Shakespeare Requirement*, 1st edition, New York: Doubleday.

Schwarz, R. (2017), *Waldkindergarten*, Berlin: Cornelsen.

Sebastian, P., S. Gopalakrishnan, and H. H. Hendricks (2018), "Language Laboratories and Centers: Looking to History and Anticipating the Future," in E. Lavolette and A. Kraemer (eds.), *Language Center Handbook 2021*, 3–30, Auburn: International Association for Language Learning Technology.

Selingo, J. J. (2018), *The New Generation of Students: How Colleges Can Recruit, Teach, and Serve Gen Z*, Washington, DC: Chronicle of Higher Education.

Simon, E., A. Kraemer, F. A. Kronenberg, B. Lavolette, and A. Sartiaux (2017), "Language Center Evaluation Toolkit," *International Association for Language Learning Technology*. Available online: https://v.gd/toolkit (accessed October 10, 2022).

Simons, G. and D. S. Baldwin (2021), "A Critical Review of the Definition of 'Wellbeing' for Doctors and Their Patients in a Post Covid-19 Era," *International Journal of Social Psychiatry*, 67 (8): 984–91.

Skill, T. D. and B. A. Young (2002), "Embracing the Hybrid Model: Working at the Intersections of Virtual and Physical Learning Spaces," *TL New Directions for Teaching and Learning*, 2002 (92): 23–32.

Stang, R. (2016), *Lernwelten im Wandel: Entwicklungen und Anforderungen bei der Gestaltung zukünftiger Lernumgebungen*, Berlin: De Gruyter.

Stapleton, H. (2022), "Using the Language Resource Center to Build Community on the Language Learning Journey," *FLTMAG*, June 1. Available online: https://fltmag.com/language-resource-center-to-build-community/ (accessed August 1, 2022).

Sterling, S. (forthcoming), "Research Ethics and Community Engaged Scholarship," in De Costa et al. (eds.), *Ethical Issues in Applied Linguistics Research*, John Benjamins.

Strange, C. C. and J. H. Banning (2001), *Educating by Design: Creating Campus Learning Environments That Work*, San Francisco: Jossey-Bass.

Sun, M. (2017), "Fostering a Language Center-Based Research Community," in F. A. Kronenberg (ed), *From Language Lab to Language Center and beyond: The Past, Present, and Future of the Language Center*, 99–109, Auburn: International Association for Language Learning Technology.

Sutherland, J. and R. Sutherland (2010), "Spaces for Learning," in K. Mäkitalo-Siegl, J. Zottmann, F. Kaplan, and F. Fisher (eds.), *Classroom of the Future: Orchestrating Collaborative Spaces*, Technology-Enhanced Learning, 40–60, Rotterdam: Sense Publishers.

Taylor, A. P. and K. Enggass (2009), *Linking Architecture and Education: Sustainable Design for Learning Environments*, Albuquerque: University of New Mexico Press.

Taylor, T. L. (2002), "Living Digitally: Embodiment in Virtual Worlds," in R. Schroeder (ed), *The Social Life of Avatars: Presence and Interaction in Shared Virtual Environments*, 40–62, New York, NY: Springer.

"The Enactment Effect: A Systematic Review and Meta-Analysis of Behavioral, Neuroimaging, and Patient Studies (Updated October 31, 2022)" (2022), *Medical Imaging Law Weekly*, November 15, 6573. Available online: https://link-gale-com.proxy1.cl.msu.edu/apps/doc/A726387638/ITOF?u=msu_main&sid=ebsco&xid=ad64e125 (accessed February 24, 2023).

Thomas, H. (2010), "Learning Spaces, Learning Environments and the Dis'Placement' of Learning," *British Journal of Educational Technology*, 41 (3): 502–11.

Thornburg, D. D. (1996), *Campfires in Cyberspace*, San Carlos, CA: Starsong Publications.

Thornton, K., C. Taylor, A. D. Tweed, and H. Yamashita (2018), "JASAL and the Self-Access Learning Center Movement in Japan," in E. Lavolette and A. Kraemer (eds.), *Language Center Handbook 2021*, 31–59, Auburn: International Association for Language Learning Technology.

Tohidi, H. and M. M. Jabbari (2012), "The Effects of Motivation in Education," *Procedia - Social and Behavioral Sciences*, World Conference on Learning, Teaching & Administration - 2011, 31: 820–4.

Toohey, K., D. Dagenais, A. Fodor, L. Hof, O. Nunez, A. Singh, and L. Schulze (2015), "'That Sounds So Cooool': Entanglements of Children, Digital Tools, and Literacy Practices," *TESOL Quarterly*, 49: 461–85.

Tversky, B. (2019), *Mind in Motion*, New York: Basic Books.

Tyack, D. and L. Cuban (1995), *Tinkering toward Utopia: A Century of Public School Reform*, Cambridge, MA: Harvard University Press.

Tytarenko, O. (2022), "Immersive VR in the Development of Speaking Skills," *FLTMAG*, October 28. Available online: https://fltmag.com/immersive-vr-in-the-development-of-speaking-skills/ (accessed January 6, 2023).

Uebel, E. H., F. A. Kronenberg, and S. Sterling, eds. (2023), *Language Program Vitality in the United States: From Surviving to Thriving in Higher Education*, Cham: Springer.

United Kingdom (1943), "UK Parliament." Available online: https://www.parliament.uk/about/living-heritage/building/palace/architecture/palacestructure/churchill/ (accessed January 31, 2023).

Van Lier, L. (1996), *Interaction in the Language Curriculum: Awareness, Autonomy, and Authenticity*, London: Longman.

Van Lier, L. (2003), "A Tale of Two Computer Classrooms: The Ecology of Project-Based Language Learning," in J. Leather and J. Van Dam (eds.), *Ecology of Language Acquisition*, 49–63, Dordrecht: Kluwer Academic Publishers.

Van Lier, L. (2004), *The Ecology and Semiotics of Language Learning: A Sociocultural Perspective*, Norwell: Kluwer Academic Publishers.

van Merriënboer, J. J. G., S. McKenney, D. Cullinan, and J. Heuer (2017), "Aligning Pedagogy with Physical Learning Spaces," *European Journal of Education*, 52 (3): 253–67.

Wannarka, R. and K. Ruhl (2008), "Seating Arrangements That Promote Positive Academic and Behavioural Outcomes: A Review of Empirical Research," *Support for Learning*, 23 (2): 89–93.

Warner, C. and B. Dupuy (2018), "Moving toward Multiliteracies in Foreign Language Teaching: Past and Present Perspectives ... and beyond," *Foreign Language Annals*, 51 (1): 116–28.

Waters, A. (2009), "Advances in Materials Design," in M. H. Long and C. J. Doughty (eds.), *The Handbook of Language Teaching*, 311–26, Chichester: Wiley-Blackwell.

Weick, K. E. (1976), "Educational Organizations as Loosely Coupled Systems," *Administrative Science Quarterly*, 21 (1): 1–19.

Wenger, E., R. A. McDermott, and W. Snyder (2002), *Cultivating Communities of Practice: A Guide to Managing Knowledge*, Boston: Harvard Business School Press.

Whiteside, A. L. (2014), "Conclusion: Advancing Active Learning Spaces," *Active Learning Spaces: New Directions for Teaching and Learning* (137): 95–8.

Whitham, R., S. Moreton, S. Bowen, C. Speed, and A. Durrant (2019), "Understanding, Capturing, and Assessing Value in Collaborative Design Research," *CoDesign*, 15 (1): 1–7.

Williams, J. E. (1965), *Stoner*, New York: Viking Press.

Wilson, J. R. (2000), "Fundamentals of Ergonomics in Theory and Practice," *Special Issue: Fundamental Reviews in Applied Ergonomics*, 31 (6): 557–61.

Woolner, P. (2010), *The Design of Learning Spaces*, London: Continuum.

Wright, H. M. and R. Gardner-Medwin (1938), *The Design of Nursery and Elementary Schools*, London: Architectural Press.

Yaden, B. and C. Evans (2017), "Envisioning New Spaces—the Human Element," in F. A. Kronenberg (ed), *From Language Lab to Language Center and beyond: The Past, Present, and Future of the Language Center*, 83–98, Auburn: International Association for Language Learning Technology.

Yang, Z., B. Becerik-Gerber, and L. Mino (2013), "A Study on Student Perceptions of Higher Education Classrooms: Impact of Classroom Attributes on Student Satisfaction and Performance," *Building and Environment*, 70: 171–88.

Zamenopoulos, T. and K. Alexiou (2018), *Co-Design as Collaborative Research*, Bristol: University of Bristol/ AHRC Connected Communities Programme.

Zheng, D., Y. Liu, A. Lambert, A. Lu, J. Tomei, and D. Holden (2018), "An Ecological Community Becoming: Language Learning as First-Order Experiencing with Place and Mobile Technologies," *Linguistics and Education*, Studying the visual and material dimensions of education and learning, 44: 45–57.

Zheng, D., K. Newgarden, and M. Young (2012), "Multi-Modal Analysis of Language Learning in World of Warcraft Play: Languaging as Values-Realizing," *Re-CALL*, 24: 339–60.

Index

Please note that entries marked with an *f* refer to figures.

Abrams Planetarium Partnership 94
access/accessibility 43, 147–8, 161
acoustics/sound in classrooms 42–3, 58, 100, 124. *See also* light/electrical lighting in classrooms
active learning spaces 19, 23, 38, 128, 142
adaptability 72, 119, 127, 165
adaptation 73, 103, 105–8, 128, 139, 142–4
affect/affective 41, 52–5, 64
    emotions, J. Boys on 53
    negative 52
affordances 1–2, 7, 16, 21–2, 26, 30, 49, 52, 59–60, 64, 80–1, 91–2, 94, 96, 130, 134, 143–4, 150, 155–6, 165, 169–70, 173
agora-like spaces 79, 84
airplane lighting systems 124
alternative language learning spaces 89–97
    biophilic design 93–4
    nonlanguage learning campus spaces 94
    off-campus community spaces 95
    outdoor spaces 91–3
    programmable space 90–1
    studios 90
ambient attributes 51, 123–6, 137–8, 141
American Council on the Teaching of Foreign Languages (ACTFL) 42, 57
Arbeitskreis der Sprachenzentren (AKS) 71
Aronin, L. 2, 18
Asian Languages House at Colorado College 93
assessment 15, 46, 54, 66, 144, 146
audio-lingual method 23, 26, 69, 137
augmented reality (AR) 159–61. *See also* virtual reality (VR)
authenticity 52, 56, 93, 157
autonomy/autonomous 4, 13, 19, 33, 54–5, 62–3, 71, 73, 77, 86, 103, 169

Bax, S. 57
    on normalization 23, 38
    sole agent fallacy 39
belonging 14, 55, 64, 78, 86, 88, 90, 148–51, 155, 171
Benson, P. 3, 13, 17, 20, 49–50, 89
    language/nonlinguistic resources for learners 47
    views of language learning environment 15
Bijker, W. E., defining technologies 21, 39
biophilic design 93–4
Bonner, E. 94, 160
Boys, J. 3, 10, 97, 117, 123, 144
    on affective emotions 53
Bruce Mau Design 99, 142
built environment 9, 42, 45, 100, 117, 127, 135, 145, 149–50, 168, 172
built pedagogy 5, 7, 29, 39, 42, 45–6, 55, 69, 109, 129
    Monahan on 29–30
    Oblinger on 30

Campus Maintenance Office 103
careful space design 52
Center at Rhodes College 113
Center for Language Teaching Advancement (CeLTA) 94, 144, 162, 168
chair-sitting culture 131–2
Churchill, Winston, Commons Chamber's rectangular design 29
classrooms 2, 5, 7–8, 10, 15–16, 30–3, 65–6, 74, 88
    acoustics/sound in 42–3, 58
    classroom ecology 63
    in Germany 8, 20, 32
    innovations 24–8, 43
    intentional design of 1–2, 4–6, 9, 21–2, 29, 35–6, 39, 44
    light/electrical lighting in 43–4, 58, 86

materials 5, 16–17, 22, 37, 43, 48–52
   as normalized technologies 21–3
   student-teacher position in 53–4
   traditional 25, 31, 60
classroomscape 11, 30, 96
classroom style 106–8
co-design process 120–1, 143–4
cognition/cognitive 2, 42–3, 48–9, 53, 55, 72–3, 170
   cognitive load 43, 50, 54
   distributed 35
   embodied 35
   extended 2, 34–6, 155
   situated 34
collaborative spaces 71, 79, 121–2, 129
communication/communicative approaches 4, 23, 26, 41, 49, 56, 64, 77, 79–80
   bodies for 53
   communication channels 27–8, 80
   extralinguistic elements of 49, 161
   interpersonal 44, 57–8
   interpretive 42–3, 57–8
   presentational 42, 44, 57–8
community 12, 29, 42, 44–5, 67, 73, 87, 95, 99, 143, 149–51
community-based language learning (CBLL) 61–2
community-based learning (CBL) 4, 45, 61
computer laboratories 3, 69, 102, 105, 112, 115, 120–1, 128, 136, 139, 166.
   See also language laboratory/lab
conceptual learning spaces 4, 7, 10–13, 38
convertibility 127
co-presence 74
course management system 21, 39
Covid-19 pandemic 1–2, 12, 47, 70, 74, 77, 91–2, 151, 155
Cox, A. M. 34, 47, 73, 79
Cranz, G. 58, 130
credentialing 39, 46, 113, 172
culturally concentrated knowledge 146
curated spaces 66, 74, 78
curriculum 23, 33–4, 39, 77, 100, 114
cyberspace 157, 159–60

Davidson, C. N. 65, 88, 167
decorations 125
dedicated learning spaces 12, 41, 51, 70, 114, 119

DEI (diversity, equity, and inclusion) 119, 145
design and administration of learning space 99
   adaptation 105–8
   design phase 102
   finances 104–5
   inertia 103
   loosely coupled systems 103–4
   postoccupancy phase (*see* postoccupancy process)
   predesign phase 101–2
design attributes 74, 80, 90, 100, 122–38
   ambient attributes 51, 123–6, 137–8, 141
   fixed and closed spaces 129
   furniture 129–36
      arrangements 134–6
      chairs 132–3
      ergonomics 131–2
      other furniture 134
      symbolic and cultural functions 129–31
      tables 133–4
   spatial attributes 123, 126–9, 137, 141, 153
   technological attributes 123, 136–8, 141
design phase 101–2
deskless language teaching 49, 134
Deutsche Sommerschule am Pacific 79
Dewey, J. 31, 37
digital-only spaces 1, 158
digital spaces 1, 155–7, 159, 164, 169
digital technologies 138, 155
dining halls 35, 67, 77–8, 94
dislocation pedagogy 94
displacement 94
distributed cognition 35
diversity 145–7
Doorley, S. 74, 79, 81, 87, 89
drop-in spaces 74

ecosystem 3, 12, 14, 65, 70, 81, 87–9, 93, 132–4, 167
educational institutions, design of 29, 31, 36, 100, 111
educational technology 21–2
effective learning space 3–4, 12, 18, 118, 172
Eickhoff, H. 130–2
electrical lighting 19, 43

electronic book (eBook) 156
elementary EFL learners 110
embodied cognition 35
emotions/emotional 53, 55–7, 74, 94, 149–50, 152
emplacement 149
Enggass, K. 55, 116, 122, 136
Engman, M. M. 17, 48, 61, 114
environmentally facilitated approach 80
ergonomics 5, 36, 131–2, 173
Ericson, J. E. 75
European Framework for Languages 45
evolutionary design 142–4
experiential learning 5, 38, 44, 61
experimental spaces 23, 92, 168
extended cognition 2, 34–6, 155
extended reality (XR) 159–64
    augmented reality 160–1
    other XR spaces 162–4
    virtual reality 161–2
extralinguistic elements of communication 49, 161

face-to-face interactions 69, 112, 137, 152, 156, 169–70
Fenwick, T. 17, 49, 57, 73, 171
finances 104–5, 139
First Place 75. *See also* Second Place; Third Place
flexibility 14, 19, 28, 41, 64, 72, 77, 108, 111, 113, 119, 123, 126–9, 133, 142, 147, 161, 165
flipped classroom approach 28
flooring materials 43, 82, 124
floor-sitting culture 131
fluidity 49, 62, 86, 127, 135, 150
food spaces, language learning 76–8, 80, 91
foreign language (FL) education 42, 53, 63, 65, 96
foreign language housing (FLH) 75
formal learning space 3, 8, 13, 16, 23, 38, 49, 57–8, 63, 66–7, 73, 75, 77, 79, 91, 118, 133, 136, 140. *See also* informal learning space
Forty, A. 8, 126
Foucault, M. 30–2
furniture 5, 17, 19, 22, 24, 30, 32–3, 37, 43, 47, 49, 55–6, 58, 85–7, 100–1, 108, 129–36, 152

    arrangements 59, 134–6
    chairs 129–33
    desk design 133
    ergonomics 131–2
    non-educational furniture 133
    other furniture 134
    symbolic and cultural functions 129–31
    tables 133–4

gap design 140
gathering spaces 74, 77, 81, 84
generic learning space 3, 9–11, 14, 18, 20, 41, 117, 172
Germany 82, 168
    classrooms in 8, 20, 32
    language centers in 70–1
gestures 35–6, 47–9, 59, 75, 77
glass elements 125
Global Kitchen at Grinnell College 78
Guerrettaz, A. M. 2, 15, 30, 35, 50, 52, 63, 96, 173
    polysemiotic action formation 50

hallways 1, 44, 82–6, 88, 90, 129
    active 84
    passive 84
    student sitting on the floor with laptop 85f
Hermes, M. 17, 48, 61, 114
heterogeneous assemblages 17
higher education, learning spaces 1, 3–4, 14, 18–19, 29, 67, 86, 113, 133, 146, 148, 151, 167
hybrid spaces/hybridity 1, 28, 38, 136, 155–9
    post-Covid-19 164–8
        future prediction 165–6
        normalizing hybridity 166–7, 170
        paradigm shifts 167–8
        spaces of choice 167

identities 10, 56–7, 67, 88, 150
immersion (immersive language learning spaces) 61, 67, 76, 78–80, 160, 162
inclusive design process 120–1, 145–7
Indiana State University 91
Indigenous languages 46, 93, 110, 150
inertia 23, 65, 100, 103–4, 169

Infinite Corridor at the Massachusetts Institute for Technology 82
informal learning space 3, 8, 11, 13, 49, 56–8, 63, 66, 73, 75, 91, 118. *See also* formal learning space
initial design 5, 43–4, 100–1, 119, 147
innovation diffusion theory (IDT) 25, 27–8
innovations 24–8, 43, 78, 113, 140, 144, 164, 170
  in language education 60–3
institutional spaces for learning 3–4, 11, 65, 95, 100, 109
instructed language learning 18, 20, 46, 65–6
instructed second language acquisition (ISLA) 20, 65. *See also* second language acquisition (SLA)
intentional design 1–2, 4–6, 9, 21–2, 29, 35–6, 39, 44, 95, 99, 108, 146
interdisciplinary/interdisciplinarity 4, 7, 23, 36, 38, 44, 88, 94, 111
interlocutor communication 14, 49, 53, 57–60
International Association for Language Learning Technology (IALLT) 71, 144
interpersonal communication 44, 57–8
interpretive communication 42–3, 57–8
interstitial space 88
invisible language learning spaces 23, 30, 33, 38, 67, 80–9
  ecosystems 3, 12, 14, 65, 70, 81, 87–9, 93, 132–4, 167
  hallways (*see* hallways)
  offices 1, 86–7
  storage spaces 87
  thresholds 81–2

Japan
  Japanese garden 93
  language centers in 71
Japan Association for Self-Access Learning (JASAL) 71
Jilk, Bruce A., montage of gaps 140

K-12 institutions 18–19, 51, 70, 78, 86
Kern, L. 8, 127, 145, 148, 170
kitchen learning space 78

knowledge acquisition 57
Kramsch, C. J., "position of subordination," language learners 53

L1 51, 56
L2 26, 35, 42, 49, 52–3, 56, 59–60, 65, 71, 75, 77, 82, 92, 124–5, 155, 162
Lamb, T. 3, 54, 159, 172
language cafes 58, 67, 77, 171
Language Center Evaluation toolkit 144
language centers 1, 5, 19, 52, 55, 58, 65, 67–73, 78, 90, 96, 134, 148, 161
  values-based approach 112–13
  video viewing room at 106*f*
language classroom 8, 15–16, 30, 35, 38, 43, 50–1
  normalization of 18–28
  notes posted by maintenance staff 106–7*f*
language corridors 67, 75
language education/learning 1–3, 5, 7, 14–15, 17–18, 22–3, 26, 28, 35, 37, 39–41, 86, 89, 93, 96, 100, 115, 119, 136, 146, 171–2
  areal and individual perspectives, Benson's 15
  foreign 42
  goals and standards 42–6
    communication 42–4
    communities 44–5
    connections 44
    language teaching methods 45–6
  interlocutor communication 14, 49, 53
  nonlanguage learning campus spaces 94
  out-of-class research 3
  physicality of learner 47–52
    affect, motivation, and wellbeing 52–4
    extended mind 49–50
    identity 56–7
    materials and scaffolding 50–2
    motivation 54–6
    stress and anxiety 54
  practices and innovation in 60–3
    community-based language learning 61–2
    immersive spaces 61

individual learners 62–3
project-based language learning 26, 28, 38, 45, 61
technology-enhanced language learning/teaching 62
language houses 1, 61, 67, 75
language laboratory/lab 20, 26–7, 55, 62, 65, 68–72, 127, 137, 166
  compatibility 26
  complexity 26–7
  innovation 24–6
  lab sessions 69
  observability 27–8
  relative advantage 25
  trialability 27
language programs 4, 103, 114, 128, 168
languages for specific purposes (LSP) courses 46
language teaching methods 4–5, 14, 17–18, 23, 26, 38, 42, 45–7, 60
  deskless 49, 134
Lawn, M. 16–17, 21, 23, 28, 30, 37
learning space design 3–6, 10, 13, 20, 29–33, 43
learning spaces 7–8, 10–12, 15, 27, 31, 37, 39
  cultural reinforcements 24–5
  defined by *Journal of Learning Spaces* 11
  and language learning goals and standards 42–6
libraries 3, 13, 41, 74, 90, 162
light/electrical lighting in classrooms 43–4, 58, 86, 100, 124. *See also* acoustics/sound in classrooms
liminal spaces 81–2, 84, 97
linguistic landscape 53, 59, 89, 125, 160. *See also* nonlinguistic
loosely coupled systems 103–4
Löw, M. 8–10, 34, 67, 159
LSC rating system 144

magnet place 74
Martínez, Moreno 37, 133
materiality/materialities 10, 16, 20, 34–6, 39–40, 48–9, 51–2, 56–7, 67, 109, 137, 170. *See also* sociomaterialism/sociomateriality

Michelson, W., intersystems congruence 30
Michigan State University (MSU)
  Abram's Planetarium at 162
  CeLTA 94, 144, 162, 168
  rock example 141–2
  values of 109–10
Middlebury Language Schools 79
Middleton, A. 150, 159, 172
  emplacement 149
  interstitial space 88
migrant workers, outdoor classroom for 91
mission, educational 5, 31–2, 37, 69, 71, 99, 109, 114
mixed reality. *See* extended reality (XR)
modifiability 127, 135
Monahan, T. 127, 169
  on built pedagogy 29
montage of gaps 140
Montgomery, C. 76, 133
motivation 54–6, 155
multimedia language classrooms 137–8
Murray, G. 3, 54, 159, 172

National Survey of Student Engagement (NSSE) 148
natural spaces 14, 93–4
non-classroom spaces 65, 143
non-design professionals 115
nonlinguistic 47, 56, 59. *See also* linguistic landscape
non-normalized technologies 23
normalization 7, 23–5, 28, 141, 155–6, 170, 172
  classrooms as normalized technologies 21–3
  defined by Bax 23, 38
  of hybridity 166–7, 170
  of language classroom 18–28

Oblinger, D., on built pedagogy 30
off-campus community spaces 95
offices 1, 86–8
Oldenborg Center at Pomona College 76–7
one-room schools 130
open learning spaces 58, 124
outdoor spaces 91–4

ownership 55–6, 81, 86, 108, 112, 116, 120, 127–8
OWP/P Architects 99, 142

participatory design process 118, 120–1, 136, 142–4
pedagogical ergonomics 5, 36
pedagogical technology 23
place(s) 7, 9–10, 13, 17, 34, 67–8, 117, 146, 149
postoccupancy process 102–3, 105, 119, 123, 138–45, 147, 171
  assessing learning spaces 144
  iterative and participatory design 142–4
  spaces of possibility 141–2
power 100–1
predesign phase 101–2
presentational communication 42, 44, 57–8
priming process 34
printed book 156
procedural attributes 139
programmable space 90–1
project-based language learning (PBLL) 26, 28, 38, 45, 61
project-based learning (PBL) 61
properties of learning spaces 20, 29–30, 36, 41–6, 63, 74–5
psychomotor domain 1, 52

"Ready Player One" novel 161
reciprocal adaptation process 108
"Redesigning Learning Spaces," Horizon Report (2017) 3
redesign/redesigning old spaces 4, 6, 18, 46, 99–101, 113, 122, 134, 143, 166, 171
Reggio Emilia approach, environment as third teacher 37
Reinders, H. 94, 160
remote emergency teaching 2, 164
residential learning spaces 5, 46, 61, 67, 75–7, 91
resilient teaching 165–6
RV-based language learning space 91

Savin-Baden, M. 12, 157–8
scalability 18, 127
scripts 143–4

seating arrangements 59
second language acquisition (SLA) 3, 20, 42, 56, 90. *See also* instructed second language acquisition (ISLA)
second language learning 56, 61–2, 66, 114
Second Place 75. *See also* First Place; Third Place
sedentary learning 48
segmentation 32, 45–6
self-access centers (SACs) 3, 35, 71, 119, 160
self-contained classrooms 19
self-service spaces 74
Selingo, J. J. 86, 128, 151–2, 160, 166
"The Shakespeare Requirement" novel 104
Silent Way 48
situated cognition 34
smooth space 8
social interactions 39, 59, 74, 76, 80, 134, 150
social learning spaces 1, 8, 13, 24, 41, 44, 55, 63, 67, 70–80, 91, 94, 112, 119, 152, 170
  characteristics of 73–5
  designing 79–80
  immersive language learning spaces 78–9
  language learning food spaces 76–8
  residential language learning spaces 5, 46, 61, 67, 75–6
social system 28
sociofugal spaces 74, 84
sociomaterialism/sociomateriality 5, 15–18, 20, 38–40, 47, 80, 111, 119, 137, 139–40, 166, 173. *See also* materiality/materialities
sociopetal spaces 74, 150
space(s) 7–10, 29–30, 53, 56, 58, 63, 96, 99–100, 109, 117, 138, 146, 149
space of possibility 70, 113, 141–2
space-time 8, 11, 73, 162
Spanish Language Department 103
spatial attributes 91, 123, 126–9, 137, 141, 153
spatiality 8
specialized learning space 11, 19, 96, 112
specific language spaces 20, 55
Språkstudion at Stockholm University, Language Café at 77

stakeholders 2, 20, 27, 34, 39, 55, 57, 96, 99–100, 102–3, 108, 113–14, 116, 119–22, 126, 128, 137, 141–3, 147–8, 152, 158, 168, 171–2
stand-alone devices 62
standardization 33, 103, 131
"Stoner" novel 100–1
storage spaces 34, 87, 89, 134
striated space 8
studios 69, 90
sub-optimal learning spaces 101, 170
Suggestopedia 48
support spaces 44, 53, 71–2
sustainability 113, 121–2
symbolic learning space 18, 38, 51, 110–12, 129–31, 148

target language 20, 41, 50–1, 58, 62, 65, 86
task-based language teaching 26
Taylor, A. P. 55, 159
teacher proofing 33
teaching boxes, traditional 38, 65
technology 5, 7, 19–21, 33, 38–9, 68–9, 73, 92, 119, 128, 132, 160–1
    Bijker's definition of 21, 39
    classrooms as normalized technologies 21–3
    educational technology 21–2
    non-normalized 23
    pedagogical technology 23
    social technologies 62
    technological attributes 123, 136–8, 141
    technology-enhanced language learning/teaching 62
    technology-focused space 113
    technology-heavy active learning 23
theoretical learning spaces 13
Third Place 75, 84, 146. *See also* First Place; Second Place
Thornburg, David D. 11–12, 83
360 specialty classroom 162–3
thresholds 1, 67, 77, 81–3, 87, 89, 91, 125, 146–8
tinkering 143
total physical response (TPR) 37, 48
transitions 81–2, 84, 86, 97
transitory spaces. *See* hallways
transparency 82, 86, 124, 150
Tversky, B. 59, 75

the United States 4, 13, 42, 45, 52, 67, 69, 72, 78, 82, 86, 93, 104, 137
universal design for learning (UDL) 147
U-shaped (horseshoe) arrangements 59

value- and mission-driven design 108–22
    administrative staff 119–20
    cleaning staff 118–19
    collaborative language learning space design 121–2
    design processes 115
    examples
        language center 112–13
        space of possibility 113
        testing room 113
    faculty 116–17
    media technicians and IT staff 119
    mission and goals 114
    participatory and inclusive design processes 120–1
    stakeholders 116
    structural features 110–11
    students 118
    symbolic features 110–12
    values 109–10
Van Lier, L. 17, 20, 69, 166
versatility 127
virtual learning spaces 6, 12–13, 21, 25, 28, 38, 58–9, 62, 69, 92, 157–8, 163–4, 170
virtual reality (VR) 161–2. *See also* augmented reality (AR)
vision 5, 28, 33, 60, 70, 113–14, 122, 145, 161–2
visual ambiance features 125
VS Furniture 99, 142

Watering Hole metaphor 83–4
wellbeing 54, 78, 145, 151–2
Witthoft, S. 74, 79, 81, 87, 89
World-Readiness Standards for Language Learning, ACTFL 42
World Wide Web 62
writable surfaces 86, 125, 141

zero spaces. *See* invisible language learning spaces

www.ingramcontent.com/pod-product-compliance
Lightning Source LLC
Chambersburg PA
CBHW052118300426
44116CB00010B/1711